I0446992

© 2012

JAMES FOSTER ROBINSON

Dedicated to all the ghosts in California

Thanks to my wife Betty for her encouragement and to Michele Tyler. The cover picture is from a Halloween pumpkin she carved.

Contents

INTRODUCTION

California, the Golden State, is the third largest state by land area in the USA. It has close to 38,000,000 living souls and an unknown number of ghosts. I created this guide for those who are interested in ghosts, whether they believe in them or not. This guide is NOT an in-depth investigation of haunted places but an introduction to the many ghosts of California. As such, I have not elaborated on each ghostly appearance, but gave you just enough detail to pique your morbid curiosity.

The ghosts told about here are from legends, tales and reported sightings from citizens of California and others. I have not been able to ascertain whether or not they are true, nor will I try. I will leave that to the "professional" ghost hunters and the experts. I present them here solely for interest's sake and morbid curiosity.

I have not arranged the stories by region as there is no consensus as to what regions there are in California. There are numerous lists but little or no information as to what counties belong in what region. Therefore, I have arranged the ghost stories by counties and then communities alphabetically.

Lock your doors and turn on all your lights but one to read by. Sit down in a comfortable chair, and start reading. If you hear strange sounds, pay no attention. Keep on reading. If you see something out of the corner of you eye, ignore it. Just keep on reading. You might be ok... maybe... Just Maybe!!!

One final note If you are the owner of any property mentioned in this book and do not wish to have any story about your property printed in future editions of this book, please contact me by email at jimrobinson@hotmail.com. As I am both the author and publisher and publish the book online through createspace.com and amazon.com, I can made changes as necessary.

As publisher and author all mistakes in this book are, of course, mine.

James Foster Robinson

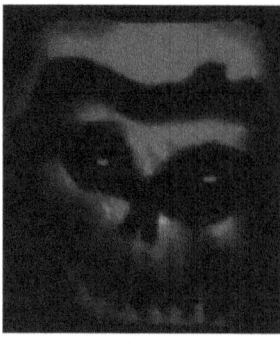

COUNTIES

CHAPTER A
Alameda County

Alameda County, the seventh most populous in California in 2010, covers most of the East Bay area of the San Francisco Bay region.

ALAMEDA

Alameda, a city on the island of Alameda in the San Francisco Bay area next to Oakland in Alameda County, has at least four haunts. An old abandoned Insane Asylum near the intersection of Marina Village Parkway and Mariner Square Drive is said to be haunted by patients long passed away. If by chance you get permission to go inside, you may hear a loud scream as soon as you pass through the main door. Be careful, it may be that someone or something is right behind you. Then you may hear screaming coming from some room deep in the gloomy building. Does it give you the chills? It does me. Outside, stand in the front and look for the fifth window on the second story on the right. Watch carefully. The blinds will open and close by themselves! Run!

They say that the Kaufman Auditorium in Alameda may be haunted. People have reported nearing strange noises and have seen an obviously female ghost wandering around back stage. The USS Hornet nicknamed named The Grey Ghost and moored at historic Alameda Point on San Francisco Bay in Alameda is haunted by the spirits of sailors killed on board. Tools disappear but turn up later after exhaustive searches. Unseen hands open and close doors. Things fall off shelves or move across the floor all by themselves. Or are ghostly hands pushing them? Heads, also known as toilets, flush by themselves. Visitors and caretakers have seen phantom sailors rushing about as if carrying out orders. Some people have even been pushed or grabbed by the spirits. A long past-away student still attends Washington Elementary School in Alameda. The ghost of a thirteen year old boy has been spotted in the halls late at night. Workers, alone at night, have experienced cold chills and have heard strange scratching noises and unexplained knocking. Maybe the ghostly student was looking for his next class?

BERKELEY

The city of Berkeley sits on the east shore of San Francisco Bay in Alameda County in northern California. If you stay at the Claremont Spa and Resort in Berkeley, you just might make the acquaintance of Mrs. Thornberg who lived in the English-style castle that was there until 1901. You can not miss her. Dressed in victorian style clothing, she wanders the gardens and verandas. No, she is not a history re-enactor but a ghost! You may also see the ghost of a young girl who, they say, died there some years ago. Drop by the University of California, Berkeley Campus, and and take a look at Room 219 in the Spirit Tower. The spirit of a former professor named Henry Stephens lived there during his tenure until he passed away at the age of sixty. Several visitors since then have met his ghost while staying in that room.

CASTRO VALLEY

Castro Valley in Alameda County, named after a rancher and ex-Mexican Army soldier, is said to be the fifth most populous unincorporated area in California, and the twenty-third in the United States as of 2000. The Cabot Theater in castro valley has an unseen patron whose ghostly laughs have been heard by employees. The workers have also seen shadows moving up and down the aisles late at night. Maybe the spirits are waiting for a showing of "Casper, The Friendly Ghost".

Once upon a time, actually in the early 1980's, a preschool was located near the end of Redwood Road in Castro Valley - or, so the story goes. A demented man apparently using a knife killed all the children there. Only a rusting swing set and the decaying basement of the tragic building remains. Visitors to the site say it is haunted. The swings moved by themselves and one can hear the long dead children playing. Have you been there and heard the kids?

DUBLIN

Dublin, a suburban city of the East San Francisco Bay region of Alameda County, had been previously known as Amador and Dougherty's Station. The Microdental Laboratories has an unseen presence that, apparently, tries to keep getting into the building. Someone unseen pushes on the front door as if someone or something wanted in. That door can only be unlocked by a button at the reception desk. But the door keeps unlocking by itself. Maybe the ghost is just trying to be helpful.

Late on the night of December 11th. 1998, a police officer was shot and killed during a robbery at the newly opened Outback Steakhouse. Staff and patrons have reported experiencing several cold spots since that night. Does the spirit of the slain officer still linger trying to do his duty?

FREMONT

The city of Fremont in Alameda County, named after "the Great Pathfinder", John Charles Fremont, is the fourth largest city by population in the San Francisco Bay area.

The Bay Street Salon, once a slaughter house and a fire station, is apparently haunted. Staff, while alone, have been bugged by some unusual happenings. They would find the bathroom door locked when it had previously been unlocked. They had to get a key to unlock it and always found no one - alive, at least - there. Then there is the matter of the self flushing toilet that was not an auto flush. It would flush all by itself when no one was on it.

Ghostly figures dressed in Victorian style clothing have been spotted roaming around Lord Bradley's Bed and Breakfast Inn in Fremont. Visitors have heard heavy footsteps made by unseen persons as well as other strange noises late at night. Do some long gone patrons still linger at their favorite bed and Breakfast?

Morris Canyon Road at Fremont is haunted. Those in the know advise you to not drive down that canyon road at night. If you have the courage or, should I say, stupidly, you may hear unexplained knocking noises. If you by chance made it halfway down that scary road, you may hear the laughter of a small boy. Only he is not alive. Years ago, his parents found him hanging from the rafters in the basement of a cottage at the end of the road. When the police arrived, they found no body. But they did find a great deal of blood on the shore of the creek. If you made it pass the eerie knocking and the scary laughter to the banks of that terrible creek, you just might see blood on the creek bank. Is it worth it? No. There is no trespassing on the site. If you are determined to go, you may not only have to deal with ghosts, you may have to deal with the cops!

The Mission San Jose in Fremont, built in the late 1700'd, has had a bit of bad luck over the years. The original mission was destroyed and then the old church was level by the 1906 earthquake. The mission was rebuilt in the 1800's and the church in the late 1900's. Many think the mission is haunted. The graves in the floor of the church and in front of the alter give some people ideas. People have reported a strange mist and cold spots inside the mission, while others have experienced mysterious mists and uncanny feelings by the fountain in the courtyard outside. If you venture into the graveyard next to the church, you might be frightened by unexplained crying and strange whisperings. Then there are cold spots near those graves in the church floor. Wait! That is not all - several native-looking specters have been spotted coming from an old tavern across the street, crossing the street, entering the mission grounds and then disappearing into thin air!

Stories are told about a haunting on the Niles Canyon Road at Fremont near Highway 84/680 between Pleasanton and Sunol. They say that a young lady named Lowery, riding in a horse drawn carriage, was thrown near this spot when a horseless carriage spooked the horses. She was run over and killed by a second horseless carriage. Legend has it that a ghostly woman in white, accompanied by strange lights, has been seen near the cemetery. Some people dispute this. They have done extensive research in newspapers from that era and found no evidence that a woman called Lowery was ever killed in an accident in the canyon. There is no cemetery on the road. But the stories persist. The Niles Canyon Ghost, as she is called, hitches a ride to one of the bridges, where she gets out and disappears. Has anyone given the Niles Canyon Ghost a ride?

The Ohlone Burial Grounds down the road from Mission San Jose has been the site of orbs being photographed. Are these orbs ghosts or something else?

The women's bathroom in Building 3 at Ohlone College in Fremont has a haunted mirror. When you look into it, they say you can see a woman wearing a blue dress from the 1960's looking back at you.

Recently, the Washington High School in Fremont was rebuilt. However, the old Senior Hall was left as it was. Students in the Senior's Hall at night have heard footsteps in the hallway when no one was there. Does a former student or staff member still hang around the school?

HAYWARD

The city of Hayward can be found in the East Bay area of Alameda County. A number of ghosts can also be found here. A female specter wearing, of all things, a Little Bo Peep costume, and accompanied by a male companion, are not shy about appearing at around 10:00 PM near Robinson Hall at Cal State University. Now, she would be a ghost I would like to meet. Little Bo Peep!

A ghost named George must have in life loved the movies so much that he haunted the upstairs and Theatre 4 and 5 of the General Cinema Southland across from the mall in Hayward. As of March, 2008, the theatres have been torn down and replaced with three restaurants. I wonder if George misses his movies or maybe he is now having a ghostly meal in one of the restaurants.

There is a place near Hayward called Hayward Plunge and, apparently, has quite the stories attached to it, complete with mass murder and ghosts! They say that, in the 1960's, a swim coach at the memorial park pool somehow tricked a number of local kids into a nearby woods one night and killed them all. Their bodies were found in a creek. Now the spot is haunted by the ghosts of these murdered children, who plead and cry for your help if you go into the park late at night. You will hear their phantom footsteps and their laughter. Watch out for cold spots and mysterious mini-mudslides, said to be caused by the ghosts of the murdered children. Just the thought of those unfortunate souls is enough to send chills up you back! Well, at least mine!

Many people feel that cemeteries are perfect places for haunting. In the case of Lone Tree Cemetery at Hayward, this well may be the case. Visitors to the graveyard have heard whispers and mysterious thumps when walking through the main part of the cemetery. Strange faces have been spotted peeking out of the bushes. Flashes of light and the chiming of unseen bells had been reported. People have seen movements out of the corner of their eye, glimpsed shadows in the distance and have even seen orbs with their naked eye. These orbs have also been captured on camera. When the video on the camera was played back, strange noises were heard. Flowers and such placed on tombstone have unexplainably disappeared. This cemetery sounds like a good one to stay out of at night.

An employee, who was killed by a dropped engine block, still hangs around Vic Hubbards in Hayward. He does not seem to be too upset being a ghost as he usually can be found in the warehouse behind the shop clowning around on the risers.

LIVERMORE

The city of Livermore in Alameda County used to be called Livermores, Livermore Ranch and Notthingham. Years ago, a groundskeeper at the Sanitarium, a tuberculosis hospital in Livermore, went mad and shot all the children. Now, apparently, you can still hear their screams. This story might be just a urban legend.

NEWARK

Newark, a city in Alameda County lies to the east of the southern end of San Francisco Bay and is surround by Fremont. The Newark Mall in Newark in Alameda County has at least two ghosts. The one in the TILT Arcade seems to like to play arcade games. Late at night it keeps turning the games on after they had been turned off . Doors to the Arcade often will not unlock and seem to be stuck. One worker heard what sounded like a little girl screaming when he was alone one night. The phantom of a little girl has been seen disappearing through the emergency exit without opening it. Maybe she is the one than many feel is watching them when they are alone in the Arcade.

The Anchor Blue in Newpark Mall in Newark had a ghost who hung around the stockroom and who apparently did not like one female employee. When she was alone in the stockroom, the ghost pushed things over. Employees in the office would hear crashing noises from the stockroom but saw no one in there when they checked the security cameras. The phantom liked to play a little. It would set off a sensor on one of the jeans on the jean wall. Employees would disable it. Then another sensor would go off on the wall. Now there is a ghost with a problem - a fixation on jeans and a girl! Sounds like a frustrated male spook.

OAKLAND

Oakland, the county seat of Alameda County, is a major west coast port located on San Francisco Bay. It is also home to a number of ghosts. If you go into the Holmes Book Company building, you may have to dodge books thrown by a male ghost. No one knows why he is not a book lover.

Mills College in Oakland has a number of ghostly residents. A young woman continues to wait long after passing away on the steps of Orchard-Meadow Hall. Who is she waiting for? Another ghost to show up? A phantom carriage has been seen a number of times on an old road that runs behind Ethal Moore Hall and Mary Morse Hall.   someone who may have loved the stage is often seen and heard walking across the stage in the campus theatre in Lisser Hall. Some say it is Louis Lisser, a music teacher for whom the hall was named. Other feel it is Susan Mills who was waked many years ago in the original building at that spot.

Oakland Hills lies along the eastern edge of Oakland. Jouquin Miller Park, in Oakland Hills, is haunted by a ghost at night. A woman crossing a street in the park one foggy night was hit by a truck and killed. They say she still continues walking in the park in spectral form. Local legend has it that park authorities had a hut and a model house built for her to live it.

The Oakland S.P.C.A has a pet cemetery. Some people have wondered who the lady was that they saw gardening there. Why? Because the gardener is a man. And he reportedly did not have to do any work inside as the grounds inside cemetery is weed free. The woman doing the gardening is apparently a ghost!

Patterson Pass is one of the most dangerous roads in Alameda County, with the most dangerous part between Livermore and I-5. It is also said to be haunted. A number of years ago, a bus load of kids broke down at Marker 157 and everyone got out to try and push it. The bus rolled backwards and crushed everyone. Local legend says that if you stop you car at Maker 157, put it in neutral, the long dead students will push you car. They even say that you can hear their footsteps on the gravel and see their finger prints on your car.

PLEASANTON

Pleasanton, a city in Alameda County, also called Alisal and Pleasonton at one time, has at least two resident ghosts. The building where the Gay 90's Pizza is located was built back in the 1800's. A female spirit dressed in blue walks around the second floor. She is blamed for the words "Boo! Boo!" found on the inside of the restroom mirror. The mirror has been replaced several times but the words keep reappearing. She has violently shoved people from behind and moved things around.

The bar area of the restaurant at the Pleasanton Hotel seems to be the hangout for whatever or whoever is haunting the building. The vintage light fixtures swing back and forth all by themselves for a short time before stopping abruptly. They also dim off and on with no explanation. If you are prancing about the dance floor, watch out for a cold spot on the north edge of the area. It may cause you to lose your rhythm! Ladies, when you are in a stall in the ladies room, do not be surprised if you hear a knocking on the stall door. There will be no one there! And that is not all. You may be shocked to see, when you look into the ladies room mirror, a man with a decorated festive hat staring back at you. Do not worry, just turn to see if he is behind you and he should disappear. Maybe! Local legend has it that there are sealed tunnels that used to connect with the local police station. Also, the hotel was once a very active "house of ill repute".

SAN LORENZO

San Lorenzo in Alameda County has been known in the past as Lorenzo and Squattersville and San Lorenzo Village. So far, I have found only one ghost story there. The staff of San Lorenzo High School have seen the phantom of a little girl walking up and down the halls of D Hall and sometimes wandering into the classrooms. She was apparently killed in a tractor accident on her father's farm where D Hall is now located.

VASCO ROAD

They say that a section of Vasco Road in Alameda County is haunted. If you stop your car in the right spot and get out of it, you can hear invisible people running around and breathing hard. Right! You have to find the right spot first.

Alpine County

I could not find any ghost stories for this County. If you know of any, please email me at jamesfosterrobinson@live.com or jimrobinson@hotmail.com.

Amador County
SUTTER CREEK
Sutter Creek Inn in Sutter Creek on State Route 49 in the heart of Northern California's

Sierra Foothill gold country and wine country in Amador County is still home to a long past away California Senator and his wife. The wife roams the hallway while the late Senator paces the upstairs of the main house.

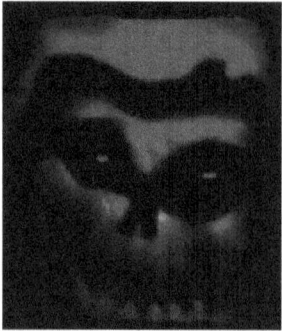

CHAPTER B
Butte County

BANGOR

The old fire station in the community of Bangor in Butte County had to be exorcized before they could tear it down and rebuilt it. It seems there was a nasty ghost or even a poltergeist that kept the firemen from getting a good night's sleep. A shadow was often seen darting around corners. What ever it was kept pulling parts off the fire engine, opening and closing doors and pinning the sleeping firemen down, giving everyone some anxious moments. The old building was supposed to be replaced in 2011. Lets hope that nasty ghost did not show up in the new building.

CHEROKEE

If you visit the Cherokee Cemetery in the community of Cherokee in Butte County at night, you might hear a noise like stomping. This might be related to the story of the town's sweetheart being murdered in the 1800's and that her killer was burned to death in the house across the street. Maybe he is angry because he did not get a fair trial, just frontier justice. The cemetery also has the grave of a young boy who passed away the same day as his father. Local legend says that if you place flowers on his grave, he will show his appreciation by appearing before you that evening and thanking you.

CHICO

Chico is the biggest city in Butte County for population. Laxson Auditorium at the California State University campus in Chico has a customer who seems to enjoy performances long after she is dead. Performers on stage see an older woman sitting in the same balcony seat every time. When someone went to that seat, no one was there!

MAGALIA

Magalia, a community in Butte County, used to be known as Butte Mills, Dogtown, and Mountain View. The restaurant, Magalia Depot, used to be a train station. Over the years ghosts have been seen in the building. Banging by unknown persons and voices in the vents have been heard. A floating head has been seen hanging around over the top of a freezer in the lower bakery. Water faucets turn on by themselves. Toilets flush when no one is using them. Lights flick on when no one has touched the electrical switches. According to local lore, there are three ghosts, a small child, a conductor and a woman in a house coat. The woman is apparently the only one seen. The other two are heard and/or sensed. I wonder who the floating head belongs to?

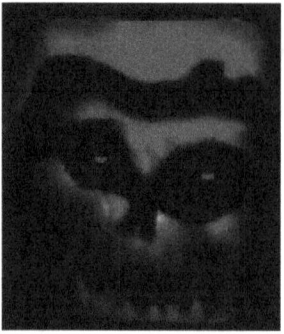

CHAPTER C
Calaveras County
DORRINGTON

The spirit of the original owner of the Dorrington Hotel in Dorrington, a community in Calaveras County, Rebecca Dorrington Gardner, is often seen walking through the hotel dinning room. She even trips the motion detector. Rebecca is still looking after her hotel. She apparently warned the owner of a dangerous gas leak in the kitchen. One year, however, she disapproved of fake Christmas trees in the rooms by knocking them all over every night. Rebecca has company in the form of several others ghosts.

MOKELUMNE HILL

Mokelumne Hill in Calavares County is another community which had other names. It used to be called Big Bar, Mok Hill, and The Hill. The owner of the Hotel Leger in 1880, George Leger, was shot to death in a gambling argument. He still hangs around the hotel. Visitors and staff can smell fresh cigar smoke in his old upstairs room.

MURPHYS

The small community of Murphys in Calavares County has been known by many names - Murphy's, Murphy's Camp, Murphy's Diggins, Murphys New Diggings, and Queen of the Sierra. You can feel something is different when you walk into Murphys Historical Hotel, 4 Main Street in Murphys. Apparently a bookkeeper, who was shot and thrown over a balcony, now roams the second floor. People have reported the feeling of being watched and an unseen presence.

Colusa County

I could not find any ghost stories for this county. If you know of any, please email me at jamesfosterrobinson@live.com or jimrobinson@hotmail.com.

Contra Costa County
ANTIOCH

Antioch, a city in Contra Costa County, is another community that used to be called by other names such as East Antioch, Smith's Landing, and Marsh's Landing. The White Witch haunts the Black Diamond Mines at Antioch. There are two women thought to be this ghost. First is a nanny called Mary, who was accused of witchcraft in the 1800's, when all the children she looked after died of illness. After she was executed for her alleged crimes, she haunted the mines as an all white ghostly figure. The other lady, thought to be the White Witch, was known as Sarah Norton, a midwife. On her way to deliver a baby, she was crushed by a carriage when it overturned. She was buried in the Rosehill Cemetery at Antioch when previous attempts to bury her in a cemetery at Somersville was prevented by fierce storms. Sarah can often be seen floating among the cemetery tombstones. She has also been seen around Somersville, and the Marsh Creek Road.

The Empire Mine Road in Antioch has been called the Gates of Hell. Where the golf course is now at the end of the road, there used to be an old Insane Asylum. Many people died there and some were not happy about it. Before the building was demolished, screams of the long dead could be heard. Things were thrown at people by unseen hands which also pushed people. I wonder if the golfers on the course noticed any unusual activity. Maybe they had already been to the 19th hole and fortified their spirits! There is supposedly an old railway tunnel at the end of Empire Mine Road where you can heard the voices of the dead coming from the end of the tunnel. It may be torn down now. They also say there is an old slaughter house at the first bend in the road. The ghost of an old man patrols the grounds to make sure nothing is wrong and to protect people. If you go on the grounds, you might feel that someone is watching you and you might hear footsteps and the clanking of chains. It is advisable to not even try to check this road out as, apparently, the whole area is posted NO TRESPASSING! The voices you hear just might be the police reading you your rights.

BAY POINT

Formerly known as West Pittsburg, Bay Point is a suburb just west of the city of Pittsburg in eastern Contra Costa County. In 1978, a boy named Ryan hung himself from a basketball hoop at Riverview Middle School when it was Pacifica High. He has been, a number of times since then, been seen still hanging from that basket ball hoop.

BRENTWOOD

Antioch Gravity Hill is near the city of Brentwood in Contra Costa County. This hill is said to be haunted by some helpful ghosts. A school bus, returning home from a field trip in the 1950's, skidded into a wash and all the children on the bus drowned. Locals say that if you park at that same spot, put your car in neutral, the ghosts of the dead kids will push it up the hill to save you from harm.

Brady Hall at Mount Saint Mary's may be haunted by a ghost who does not like the poem "Living Hand" when it is read in English class. It opens and then slams the classroom door shut! The door is designed to only be opened by turning the handle. Carondelet Dormitory at Mount Saint Mary's has it share of specters. Doors open by themselves and ghostly nuns have been spotted walking around the building.

BYRON

The Hot Springs Hotel is located in the community of Bryon about five miles from Brentwood in Contra Costa County. The remains of the old Orange Hotel exits nearby and is thought to be haunted. The ghosts of an old man dressed in white rags and a young boy who runs through the halls are two phantoms that have been seen. There may be more as dark shadows appear and disappear at random. If you listen carefully you can hear dragging noises at the main entrance.

CLAYTON

The city of Clayton, formerly known as Claytonville and Clayton's, is in Contra Costa County. The Pioneer In has seen a lot of trouble over the years. The second floor collapsed and was rebuilt. Then it burnt down. It also has a ghost that likes to touch people on the hands and shoulders.

The Clayton Club used to be called the Eagle Saloon. The original building was moved from San Francisco to Clayton back in the 1860's. It too has its resident ghost. This unseen presence likes to move things like glasses around and turn the lights off and on. Patrons and staff have also felt many cold spots, which are supposed to be caused by ghosts using the energy in that area to manifest.

The Keller Mansion was built on an old Indian graveyard in the early 1920's. Bones are still found when people dig around in the old basement. Beware! Many feel that the ghosts of Native Americans who like to move things around, may not like you disturbing the bones.

The La Croquett Restaurant in Clayton has a history dating back to 1857. Many years ago, a young girl was shot in a shootout and died after being brought into the restaurant. A blood stain still remains on the floor where they laid her. Her ghost can still be seen from time to time playing in the street where she was shot.

Morgan Territory Road near Clayton was an old logging road running from Santa Cruz to Eastern Contra Costa County. There is a legend that Joaquin Murrieta known as the California Bandit El Dorado had buried his ill gotten gains under an old oak tree somewhere along the Morgan Territory Road. Many have seen a ghost standing by an old oak tree on the road. Some feel that it is the ghost Murrieta guarding his buried loot. Many have tried to find and many have failed.

CONCORD

The largest city in Contra Costa County is Concord and it has at least three haunted sites if not more. Theater 12 in the Brendan Theaters 14 Complex has a female ghost patron complete with invisible kids that laugh and talk during a movie even when no children are present. The band plays on in B Hall at Clayton Valley High School in Concord even after all the students in the band were killed in a bus accident on I-5. On the night of the first day of school every year, they say you can hear their ghostly music. The phantom of a teenage male who hung himself from the roof over a balcony on the second floor of the English building at Mount Diable High School in Concord many years ago can still be seen, noose and all. Students and staff have reported cold spots and ghostly voices and noises at that spot at night.

CROCKETT

There is an old road that runs between Crockett and Rodeo in Contra Costa County where you just might see an apparition as you drive along it late at in the summer. Watch for a woman dressed all in white who runs out into the middle of the road and tries to flag you down. But she is not there when you look in your rear view mirror, assuming you did not stop. Has any one stopped for her and what happened? The story goes that her car broke down and she was killed by a car when she tried to wave it down.

LAFAYETTE

The Lafayette Park Hotel in Lafayette, a city in Contra Costa County, is home to the apparition of a young girl who jumps on the beds and cries out for her Mother. There are cold spots around the building and doors slam all by themselves. The vending machines dispense drinks by themselves and pictures fall off the walls. If you don't mind the crying, jumping on the bed, doors slamming and pictures falling, you may get a free pop!

PITTSBURG

So many places in California had a variety of names over the years. Pittsburg in eastern Contra Costa is no different, having been known as Black Diamond and New of the Pacific. The old and abandoned Riverside Elementary site has at least three spectral residents, a woman with long, brown hair, a young girl with long, blonde hair and a man standing about five feet ten inches tall. You know that the man is around when you hear a faint deep voice coming out of thin air. Lights are seen in the building late at night. The alarm to the site often can not be set or reset at night even though there appears to be nothing wrong with it. Doors open and close by themselves. Footsteps, voices and other unexplained sounds have been heard. Things just seem to move or fall over by themselves. Are all three ghosts acting up or something else?

The Pittsburg High School has at least two phantoms in the building. They say that a male student shot and killed by a gunman can still be heard screaming for his life and running, followed by gunshots. A young girl supposedly hung herself in the dark room at the high school. Now you can feel cold chills up your back and neck caused by her ghostly presence.

RICHMOND

Richmond, a city in western Contra Costa County, is located in the East Bay area of the San Francisco Bay Area. The specter of a woman is often seen looking for something in the Point Isabel Regional Shoreline Park. She fades away when someone approaches her. If you walk in the third floor halls of Salesian High School after school hours, you might sense a ghostly presence. Students have and they are sure it is a ghost. Get permission from the school authorities before trying to go there after hours or you might make the acquaintance of another presence - the police!

CHAPTER D
Del Norte County
CRESCENT CITY

The county seat and only incorporated city in Del Norte County, Crescent City has two phantom residents. The new IC Ward in the Sutter Coast Hospital in Crescent City is felt to be haunted by many people. When the unit was closed down due to lack of patients, workers would hear a buzzer go off in a room. When they checked the room, the buzzer would stop and start in another room. The buzzers can only be turned off at the nurses desk. Was the buzzer pusher a long dead patient from the old IC Unit trying to get someone's attention in the new ward?

When the new owners of the Tsunami Lanes in Crescent City several years ago started remodeling, they heard footsteps on the wooden walkway behind the pin-setters. When they investigated, there was no one there. Does a former pin-setter. long passed away, still trying to set the pins?

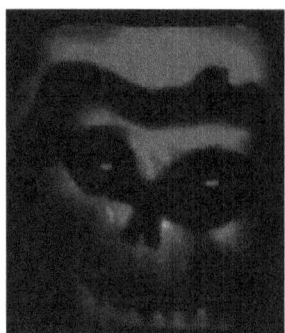

CHAPTER E
El Dorado County
CAMERON PARK

Bass Lake Road at Cameron Park in El Dorado County has two spooks. There is a bench by the reservoir where you can see either the ghost of a girl dressed in a white gown or an old man smiling back at you. The man is happy. It is his special bench as it is, apparently, dedicated to him.

COLOMA

The community of Colomo, once known as Colluma and Culloma, was once a town serving gold miners in the 1800's. Customers in the Bell's General Store can still hear the old bell that used to ring when people entered the store. The bell was removed many years ago. The Marshall Monument was dedicated to James marshall who found the first two nuggets at Sutter's Mill in 1848. Even though he was a partner of Sutter, Marshal died with out anything to his name. His shadowy form follows visitors to his monument.

The Pioneer Cemetery in Coloma can be found across from the Vineyard House on a hill on the left after you drive up Highway 19 to Cold Springs Road and turn left on it. The Schieffer family plot is guarded by the specter of a woman with hair parted in the middle and put up in a bun as well as wearing a long, flowing, Burgundy dress. You can see her from the road as she waves to you and other passersby to come in and visit with her at the grave site. I wonder how many have accepted her invitation.

The Sierra Nevada House in Coloma has a mischievous ghostly guest called Christopher. He is blamed many harmless pranks such as turning off teakettles, hiding the knives and forks and moving pots and pans around the building. However, there is bad spirit called Mark who haunts Room 4, where he apparently shot his girlfriend.

The Vineyard House in Coloma is haunted by its original owners. A number of tragedies occurred there as well as some executions. Several children died as well as the male owner who died after going crazy from syphilis. In addition to the owners haunting the place, there are three men dressed in victorian clothing, drunk and singing, seen ascending the stairs. Once, something unseen slid a glass down the bar in the basement to the bartender who was cleaning other glasses. Others have heard the rustling of unseen skirts and felt a cold spot near the kitchen. The phantom of a young boy often appears to dinners asking for help mashing his carrots and peas. The Vinyard House has been featured on the popular TV shows "That's Incredible!" and "Ripley's Believe It Or Not".

The Wah Lee Store and Museum in Coloma has an unusual audio display. The chatter of customers long gone and the sound of a meat cleaver on a butcher's block is said to be still heard in the general store.

EL DORADO

El Dorado, Spanish for the Golden, was formerly known as Eldorado, Mud Spring, and Mud Spring. This small community in El Dorado County has a hunted cemetery. If you visit the El Dorado Cemetery after dark, with permission of course, you might be fortunate to see with your own eyes orbs and ectoplasm floating around. You may also hear the voice of a small, invisible child. An elderly man has been spotted in a driver's rear view mirror leaning on the back of his car and looking in. The driver took off and later found a set of hand prints dragged across his car's trunk. Was it a real person leaning on the trunk or a ghost! Many feel that it was a ghost!

GEORGETOWN

They say that the American River Inn in Georgetown, a small community once known as Growlersburg in El Dorado County, is haunted by an old miner long since passed away. Maybe he was the growler that the place was once named after and is upset by the change in name. Another long passed away miner, definitely not a growler, was captured by a digital camera. Standing outside the historical Fire Department building, he smilingly pointed at a map on the side of the Fire hall. In the back ground, living volunteer fire fighters were practicing ladder drills. A woman, in despair from losing her lover back in the old mining days, killed herself by jumping from the upstairs balcony of the Georgetown Hotel. Her ghost is still seen in the upstairs rooms.

PLACERVILLE

Placerville, the county seat of El Dorado County, used to be known as Old Dry Diggings, Dry Diggings, and Hangtown. The Carey House Hotel is said to be very haunted with at least four ghosts and Room 212 is apparently the most haunted. A man named Arnold Wiedman lived with his wife and baby in Room 212 where he died because of influenza in the late 1800's. He is said to still be there. Visitors to the room have also experienced cold spots there as well as in other areas. The hotel's most famous ghost is Stan Levine. He was stabbed to death on the staircase by an irate husband who did not like his advances towards his wife. He is still there and still likes attractive women, pinching them on their behinds. He also whistles and moves things around.

The ghost of a bearded man in a top hat hangs around the mezzanine of the Chamber of Commerce building in Placerville. He apparently looks a lot like the town's official hangman shown in a old photo taken when Placerville was called Hangtown. Back then, most of the hanging were done on the site where the present Chamber of Commerce is now located at 542 Main Street.

The Empire Theater, now closed down, had a gaggle of ghosts that walked up and down the aisles and hung out in the bathrooms. Theater goers and staff experienced cold spots in many places. You should know by now what that means. Ghosts are thought to tap into the energy in an area to make a manifestation. The Hangman's Tree Cafe sits where an old oak tree was that was used to hung convicted criminals years ago. The ghosts of hanged outlaws and claim jumpers are said to bother employees and customers in the cafe. Maybe the living were sitting at a table a dead man wanted. People driving by claimed to have seen the phantoms as plain as night at this little restaurant at 305 Main Street in Placerville.

The Soda Works, a coffee shop and saloon, at the end of Main Street has a problem. The owner, who apparently past away, seems to want to stick around the shop. He opens and closes doors, turns bathroom taps on and hangs around the upstairs bar.

POLLOCK PINES

Ghost Mountain Ranch outside of Pollock Pines in El Dorado County has the site of many reports of unusual phenomena. A picture of a full body apparition was taken by a visitor in Cabin 13 on the Ghost Mountain Ranch. Some think it is the ghost of a murdered miner. Balls of light have been seen darting about the area. Ethereal music has been heard in the ranch office. A phantom named "Old mountain Man" (probably because the ghost looks like a mountain man) walks about the camping area. At the various buildings, doors open and shut by themselves and the sound of invisible women laughing as well as other strange noises can be heard. Someone or something tugs at people's shirts in the saloon. Patrons have also seen a light figure dash across the bar room. Who or what ever is there in the saloon likes Cheryl Crowe's "Leaving Las Vegas" as it often played when the Stereo/CD Player turns on by itself. The unseen person may wear a green shirt as an startled employee saw a specter wearing one. Doors have slammed open and shut during electrical storms and once on New Year's Eve when there was no wind blowing. Yes there is a lot of ghostly activity at the Ghost Mountain Ranch.

SHINGLE SPRINGS

Shingle Springs in El Dorado is another place that has been known by other names in the past - Shingle Spring and Shingle. A strange mist sometimes hovers over La Casa Drive even in good weather. No explanation has been found for the phenomenon. The ghostly form of a mountain lion has been seen entering into the erie mist and the ghost of a native American exit from the other side. Early in the morning or late at night, what sounds like drumming by native Americans who once lived in the area can be heard.

CHAPTER F
Fresno County
CENTERVILLE

Channel Road in the Centerville area near Sanger in Humbolt County is also called Snake Road because of its twisty curves. The specter of a woman is often seen in the section by the King River. She is apparently searching for her two daughters who drowned with her when their car went into the river.

DEL RAY

Del Ray, a community in Fresno County, was once known as Clifton. The Del Ray Cemetery is haunted. A tomb lights up at night all by itself. Something or someone moans and cold spots abound. Researchers using a EMF detector had it go off like there was no tomorrow. Yes, I would say that the Del Ray Cemetery is haunted.

DUNLAP

Dunlap Cemetery in the community of Dunlop in Fresno County has seen some strange thinns happen. When visitors walk through the middle of the cemetery towards the entrance, they often hear footsteps behind them. When they look, no one is there. Some unmarked graves have cold spots near them. Three tall ghostly figures are occasionally glimpsed standing by several big oak trees on the property. Some people have recorded the voice of an elderly man telling them to leave him alone. They have also recorded a strange voice chanting something intelligible. Sounds like these spectral residents do not like visitors.

FRESNO

The city of Fresno is the county seat for Fresno County and is home to some interesting ghosts. Several years ago, a garbage can with the dismembered body of a prostitute was found near a railway crossing on Peach Avenue. Shortly there after people began seeing a woman standing near the crossing. She seemed to be watching the cars go by, perhaps in the hope of seeing her killer. Many have reported feeling an erie sensation at the time of her sighting.

The Adorable Poodle Salon has experienced some poltergeist activity. Heavy potted plants have been found to have been moved during night when the store was locked and shuttered. One worker kept feeling someone kissing her but no one was there. When she complained to the owner that a ghost would not stop kissing her, whatever it was stopped kissing her. Lights going on and off by themselves, doors opening and closing by themselves, cold spots showing up even in warm weather and the scary feeling of being watched when no other living people was in the building strongly suggests that either a poltergeist or a ghost was present in the Adorable Poodle Salon.

If you visit the Muex House, a museum on the corner of Tulare and R streets in downtown Fresno, do not mention ghosts in front of the staff. They believe the place is not haunted or at least do not want to talk about it. Others feel that it is home to several spirits. Reports have it that in the morning the staff find door knobs missing off some of the doors inside even though the place was locked tight all night. Well, maybe not tight enough to stop ghosts. The laughter of invisible children have been heard upstairs in the building. People in the house after hours have reported hearing strange noises like knocking. Objects have gone missing only to turn later up in another spot. The fuzzy shape of a human has been seen in a window by people passing by. You visit the place and you decide if it is haunted. Just don't mention ghosts to the staff.

The Sand Lady of Pindale has been seen at night on Pindale Avenue in Fresno and, for no apparent reason, throws sand in the eyes of people walking by her. If you are walking on Pindale Avenue some night and you spot an old Spanish lady carrying a small tote bag, be careful. Protect your eyes! It just might be the Sand Lady of Pindale!

St. John Hall in Fresno has a ghostly presence, a nun, who appears at times in the basement of the hall.

A more than one hundred year old building in Fresno, now the site of the Vendo Company, was once the Pinedale Military Base, a lumber yard and an interment camp for Japanese during World War II. The place is haunted. Someone unseen grabs at your ankles in the mezzanine. The spirit of a Japanese woman has often been seen sitting on a bench near the cooling tower. Whispering and the sounds of choking have also been heard on the property. They say that a Vendo employee who hung himself in an upstairs bathrooms still hangs out there.

Roosevelt High School in Fresno has at least two apparitions. One is a boy who killed himself in the boy's washroom in the East Hall. People have heard strange noises in the washroom such as coughing when no one was in it. Many have experienced a cold sensation when they go there. Locked and used for storing things, it was reopened in the fall of 2007. The other was a boy named Lester who died during a presentation in the auditorium. His ghost has been seen on stage and an unseen presence has been felt back stage. Last but not least, there is the phantom of a long deceased janitor occasionally seen standing at the back of the auditorium.

The Fresno Metropolitan Museum is haunted. After the museum is closed at night, the night watchmen have heard a child giggling in the upstairs galleries and the sound of running footsteps. They found no one when they searched the premise. Is there a long passed away child who loved the Met so much that he or she still hangs out there.

An unspecified apartment in the very old Summer Set Apartments at 2103 North Angus Street in Fresno was the site of some unusual happenings. Late every night, one tennant in the apartment could hear someone in the kitchen next to his bedroom going though the dishes. The mysterious noise would last only a few minutes before it would stop. After his next door neighbor moved out, he started hearing the sound of running water coming from the empty apartment. Then one night he heard a noise like someone was trying to open the locked drawer on a stand beside the bed. When he looked he saw a white figure down on one knee with a hand on the drawer handle. Sure sounds like the place is haunted.

A Tyler Street house in Fresno is notorious for poltergeist phenomena. Since the mid 1980's, many occupants have left the house because of the terrifying events. Red eyes stare out of darkened bedrooms and closets. Objects just don't stay on countertops. They fly off them! Badly battered bodies of dead cats keep turning up in an upstairs closet in the house even if the residents did not own any pets!

HERNDON

The community of Herndon, once known as Sycamore, is nine miles northwest of downtown Fresno in Fresno County. The Ibrona, as Mexicans call her, haunts the banks of the San Juaquin River and, in particular, the overpass at Herndon on Highway 99. She died of sadness after her two kids drown while swimming in the river. Her bright white spirit now walks on top of the water looking for her lost children and calling for them with the voice of the wind.

KERMAN

The small town of Kerman, formerly known as Collis, lies at the intersection of State Route 180 and State Route 145 in Fresno County. The historical Kerney Mansion, build one hundred years ago, is located near some haunted railway tracks. Beware of the Kerney Witch dressed in all white who will follow you if you cross the railway tracks at night. Do not look into her eyes! If you do, local legend says you will die!

Go to Kerney Park and wait until 1:30 AM and you might have the eerie pleasure of hearing children laughing. Of course, there are no children present, unless you brought yours.

KINGSBURG

It is interesting that so many communities in California had different names. Kingsburg, a city in Fresno County, had at least five different names before getting its present one. It has been known as Kings River Switch, Drapersville, Kingsburgh and Wheatville. There was an old church on the north side of Bangor Street that, before it was torn down, was known for its spectral occurrences. Though there is no power to the building, lights could be seen burning in it at night. The church doors seemed to lock and unlock all by themselves. What looked like people have appeared in the windows at night even though the same windows were boarded up during the day. Other windows that were nailed shut, opened and closed by themselves. Something or someone would ring the bell in the bell tower even though the bell had been removed many years before. There there were the strange phantoms that seemed to hang around the place. An old man would lean against the wall on the porch before turning and walking through the closed doors. Human like creatures with tails and wings often stood on the roof top. Spectral children played in the front yard and orbs of light sported around the building. Those foolish people who tried to enter that cursed ground were chased off the property by things with no faces or legs below the knees. Yes, that old church was definitely a place to steer clear of. Right?

REEDLEY

The old Opera House in Reedly has a spectral guest named Jessica. This lady likes to move things around, open and close doors and turn the lights off and on as well as patting people on the head. There may be other ghostly denizens as people alone in the building have heard voices coming from other parts of the building. And do not forget the cold spots. No good haunting should be without them.

SANGER

The city of Sanger in Fresno County has at least two ghost stories of interest. In the mid 1900's, a young orphan boy, who had stolen something to eat, was chased by the owner of the food and, even though the kid begged for his life, he was shot to death in a housing development on Acadia Street. Residents of the house at 87 Acadia that was built after the incident claimed that the dead boy was seen in their hallway begging for his life.

SELMA

They say that the Block Buster Video store in Sanger is haunted. Employees tell of hearing people talking in the office when it was definitely empty. They have also heard the office door slam shut by itself, and heard keys rattling. Shadows have flitted about the building and many have experienced a strong feeling of being watched when no one was around. Was it a ghost of a disgruntled costumer or something that escaped from one of the horror movies for rent?

CHAPTER G
Glenn County
WILLOWS

The community of Willows is the county seat of Glenn County. A canal in Willows is said to be haunted by the ghost of the people who have drown in it. If you walk along its banks at night, it will feel like someone is behind you. They say that it is the ghosts of the drown following you. When you look back, however, they will, thank goodness, be gone.

CHAPTER H
Humboldt County

ARCATA

The Humbolt Brewery in Arcata, a city on the Arcata Bay in Humboldt County, is haunted by the original owner. He mainly hangs out in the pub but has been known to make his presence known in the rest of thee building as well as several other establishments nearby. Like many other ghosts, he likes to move furniture, dishes and other objects in the presence of both employees and patrons.

EUREKA

Eureka is the county seat of Humbolt County and its leading city. The auditorium in the Eureka High School has two restless ghosts hanging around there. A man fell from a balcony in the 1920's during construction and was decapitated. Maybe he is still trying to find his head. A young female student, so despondent after losing the lead role in a school play, hung herself during the presentation of the play, in the lighting booth in full view of the girl won the part. The actress apparently did not notice the hanging girl and continued doing the show. The hung girl is also still hanging around the auditorium.

Fort Humboldt, a state historical park in Eureka, is still being watched over by a former Base Commander who passed away from malaria in 1859. His ghost moves large, heavy objects across the floor during the night Lights turn off and on by themselves and objects fall off shelves and walls as if pushed by unseen hands. The commander is often seen looking out of a window in the old hospital building. Maybe the fort is not up to his military standards and he is trying to do something about it.

FERNDALE

The Victorian village of Ferndale in Humbolt County is home to a spirit known as Bertha. She is often seen late at night in the Hart Theater. Sometimes she strolls in the form of a ghostly cat down the aisles during a performance. She also likes to answer the phone at night when no living person is in the building and also likes to lock bathroom doors from the inside.

SCOTIA

Formerly known as Forestville, the community of Scotia in Humboldt County has a number of hauntings. Frank is a friendly ghost who makes his home in the Scotia Inn. He will sometimes bounce a basketball back to you if you first bounce it to him. Voices, scrapping of feet and other other ghostly sounds can be heard in the Inn. Another story tells of a little girl who was bouncing a ball when it went over the balcony. She grabbed for it and fell to her death. Now she and her mother haunts the room she stayed in. Others tell of hearing a non-existent baby crying at times. Another story concerns a bride to be who killed herself when her fiance changed his mind. Now, in fury at the betrayal, she smashes mirrors and slams doors.

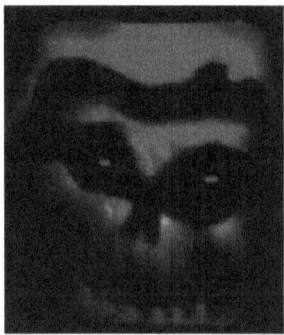

CHAPTER I, J
Imperial County
CALEXICO

Calexico High School in the city of Calexico has a female ghost that just won't leave school. A cheerleader, she was killed in a car accident after leaving a football game. Now she walks around the school late at night, or on the football field early in the morning. She may be responsible for doors slamming and lights turning off and flickering. Maybe she is looking for one last chance to do some cheerleading? Not much is known about the ghosts who have been spotted at the apparently burnt down El Charro. Are they spectral customers trying to get a meal?

EL CENTRO

The city of El Centro is the principal city of Imperial County. The Central Union High School has two areas that appear to be the abode of ghosts. Often you can hear the sound of a basketball being bounced and invisible fans cheering in the gym. Sounds like a ghostly game is still going on there. The school's library and its basement are also thought to be the abode of phantoms. At night, doors slam by themselves, loud foot steps are heard as well as the voices of invisible people talking in the back of the library. The basement is dark and damp with a maze of rooms. Used for detentions in the 1980's, it was known as the dungeon. Now you can hear laughter, crying and ghostly footsteps. Are some long ago students still serving their detentions?

Employees at the Crest Theater have heard disembodied voice talking to them at night. The sound system would come on by itself and blast out music. Then they have to contend with cold spots even when the heat is on. Are the ghosts trying to tell them that they want to see a ghost movie like "Casper the Ghost?

If you drive along Dogwood Road in El Centro after midnight and you see a girl walking along the road, it might be to better offer her a ride. If you don't, she may sit on the hood of your car and try hard to make you crash! If you give her a ride, she will sit quietly in the car and slowly disappear into thin air! That's right! She is a ghost and was apparently killed in a terrible accident on the vary road.

The old Post Office Pavilion is now home to the Imperial Valley Arts Council in the center of the city of El Centro between 5th and Brighton streets. During the early evenings scratching noises on the walls and loud bangs are heard in the basement. Then there is the taping noise like that made on an old typewriter. No one seems to know who or what is causing all these strange noises.

In the old Fox Theater in El Centro, a cold spot in the aisle 8 may chill you. They say a man had died there. Maybe he is hanging around waiting for his favorite movie to come on.

HEBER

Locals feel that the old Heber School House in Heber, Imperial County, may be haunted.

Strange noises like the stomping of feet and the banging of erasers can be heard at different times coming from the abandoned building. They say that a front window was broken in the shape of a woman before vandals broke all the windows out. Is it a previous school teacher still teaching a ghostly class?

IMPERIAL

The city of Imperial is four miles north of El Centro in Imperial County. If you go to the Imperial Historical Cemetery at night, make sure you get permission. You will have enough to deal with without the police asking you why you are there. You may encounter a monk like figure by the entrance and sometimes see hooded, shadow like figures. The air in this cemetery is colder than outside it and both hot and cold spots abound. Don't be surprised if you experience a sense of not being wanted there and that someone is watching you. Green blue to fire red lights float among the tombstones and a flame-like mist rises out of a grave and then sinks back into it.

IMPERIAL VALLEY

La Llorona, the Crying Lady, roams the Imperial Valley, Southern California's Imperial County. She was Malinche, the Indian wife of the Spanish conquistador Cortez, who killed her two children by him when he tried to take the children back to Spain without her. She hid their bodies in a nearby river. Now, the Crying Lady, a tall, slender specter in a white tattered dress, walks the waterways of the Imperial Valley looking for her lost children.

Inyo County

CERRO GORDO

The old mining of Cerro Gordo overlooks the Owens Valley on the east side of the Sierra mountains in the Inyo Range in Inyo County. Belshaw House in Cerro Gordo may be haunted as people have reported seeing shapes out of the corner of their eye and experienced strange happenings such as tv's and lights flickering. So far, no one has reported seeing a full body apparition. However, a building called the Bunkhouse does have a phantom in the shape of a glowing mass that appears in the last room on the left. Balls of light have been seen in the kitchen and photos taken of them.

DEATH VALLEY JUNCTION

This tiny community on Highway 127 in the Mojave Desert in Inyo County used to be known as Amargosa and Death Valley. The Amargosa Hotel and Opera House there is the home of several ghosts of residents from the time of borax mining. The place as been featured on some documents and ghostly phenomena such as mysterious mists and lights orbs have been filmed.

CHAPTER K
Kern County
ARVIN

The mortuary in the city of Arvin is haunted by the White Lady. No one seems to know who she is or why she is there but she has been seen many times. A white light has also been seen in the mortuary. Choir music is also heard even though the PA system was off.

BAKERSFIELD

The city of Bakersfield in the south end of the San Joaquin Valley in Kern County has been named in many movies and is also very haunted. The Bakersfield Californian Newspaper Building has at least three resident spirits. A former editor of the newspaper "California" still walks through the old building's hallways. A German Shepard dog, apparently so well trained, that, even after it passed away, it waits patiently for its master to return. Then there is an old security guard who is still doing his duty. His ghost is often seen in the lunch room.

The phantoms of a young couple sixteen to eighteen years old are often seen near the top of the bleachers in the gym at the Bakersfield High School. She wears a prom dress and he wears a football jacket with the letters BHS on the back. Student and staff has also claimed that they feel that they are being watched when they are alone and some have experienced a strange chill the gym area. The auditorium of the high school may also be haunted by a worker who fell from the rafters when they were building the auditorium. There used to be a hospital on the site where the Quad at Bakersfield High School is now. They say that body parts from operations were buried at that spot and maybe the ghosts of past patients are looking for their lost limbs. A woman was murdered some years ago and her body buried in an old foundry across from Central Park in Bakersfield. When the foundry floor was dug up, her bones complete with bullet holes were found. They say she, clothed in flowing robes, can be seen floating along the canal in the park at dawn. The ghosts reportedly at Club Paradise is not friendly. These apparitions have been accused of groping and grabbing customers, locking employees in the storeroom, pushing people in the bar room hallway and moving things around. Perhaps in the crowded bar these spirits are trying to get some attention.

If you go early in the morning to the East Bakersfield High School, you can sometimes hear the ghostly sound of someone hammering or of something falling. They say that it is a janitor who fell off his ladder and broke his neck while tying to fix some ceiling lights.

If you are standing near the statue in Garces Circle in Bakersfield and see the statute's hands move or hear what sounds like the statue murmuring a prayer, then there just might be a major auto accident at the circle immediately after. Many have claimed seeing the statue move or hear it muttering just before many of the car accidents that have occurred over the years in that spot. In the school theater in Westley Anderson Hall at Highland High School, an old man still likes to play tricks on people even though he passed away years ago. When people are working on stage, he turns the lights off. He does not do it during performances as he likes to sit in the audience and watch the show. I wonder if any patrons of the arts has even realized that there may have been a ghost sitting beside them. This theater loving spirit also whispers in people's ears and rummages through the costume room. He is not the only ghost there. The ghostly figure of a teenage girl wearing 50's style clothing has been spotted walking around the stage.

The Kern Realty Group Building in Bakersfield, built in 1911, has at least three ghostly residents. A young man fell to his death during the construction of the place. His ghost is still hammering away while the spirit of an elderly lady stands and watches him, possibly to make sure that his is doing it right. The third ghost is that of a very angry man thought to be a previous owner. No one knows why he is angry. Maybe he does not like the changes to the building and the area. He apparently opens and closes windows and doors, switches lights off and on and rattles doorknobs. Disembodied voices and mysterious footsteps have been heard on the staircase. The present owners have, people say, gotten used to the antics of their spectral friends.

The Melodrama Musical Theater, built in the early 1970's as a toy store, is in the area known as Oildale in the north end of Bakersfield. The place is haunted by a ghost known as Harry. This spirit brushes against people in the stairwell and has been seen crossing the stage during performances as well as breaking mirrors. Some eerie things have also occurred in the ladies dressing room. Shadows not made by living people have been seen there and the sequin dresses rattle all by themselves on the clothes rack. Is it Harry sneaking around for a peak?

The Norris School in Bakersfield built in 1882 is now a museum and may be haunted by a former teacher or student. The tapping of invisible chalk on the blackboard can be heard. Is it a student writing over and over again that he or she will not do again whatever they did way back then? Ghostly children have also been seen playing outside the building.

They say that when you entered the Padre Hotel, a landmark in Bakersfield, you could immediately feel the presences of spirits. In 2007, the building was apparently converted into offices and condos. I wonder if the present tennants feel the presences of ghosts?

Pioneer Village in Bakersfield has its share of phantoms. The Weill House there was once the site of a ghostly birthday party. Did the birthday kid receive ghostly presents? What would ghosts like for their birthday?

A number of years ago, a picture of a Grade 8 Graduation class taken through a window in a local school revealed what appeared to be the ghost of a man hanging from the top of the auditorium. Was he late for his graduation or was he just hanging around?

Years ago, a woman was killed in a car accident on the Lerdo Highway near Bakersfield. Now dressed in a 1930-40's flowing gown, she floats along from east to west on Lerdo Highway between State Route 43 and Freeway 99.

DELANO

If you are driving on Browning Road in Delano, a city in Kern County thirty one miles north-northwest of Bakersfield, watch out for phantom hitchhikers. I have no information on who they are and what they look like and the stories may be someone's attempt to stop people from picking up hitchhikers on that road. But then again, they may be for real - as ghosts, that is!

KEENE

The community of Keene, once known as Wells, can be found in the foothills of the Tehachapi Mountains. Keene Hospital, once a large TB hospital but now abandoned, lies off a dirt road in back of the small town. The voices and laughter of kids can still be heard in the old children's ward. Strange noises and voices can also be heard in the rest of the building. Please remember to get permission to enter this and any site you may want to investigate.

MCFARLAND

If you go late at night to the recreation park off Highway 395 in McFarland, once known as Lone Pine, in Kern County, you might see the ghost of a little girl, three to four years old and dressed in a pink jacket and white shirt, sliding down the slide. No one seems to known who she is and why she is still playing there. Maybe her spirit is reliving some good times.

RIDGECREST

The city of Ridgecrest in the Indian Wells Valley in northeastern Kern County was once known as Crumville. I do not know why they changed it from Crumville. I like that name. Any how, the Burroughs High School Lecture Center has at least two resident ghosts. An man working on the building of the auditorium fell to his death from a scaffolding and is still there trying to finish his work. The second phantom is a male actor who was accidentally shot to death during a scene in a play where the main character gets shot. Someone put a real bullet in the prop gun and the rest is tragic history. When a play with a sad scene is performed, the left curtains blows by its self during that scene. Lights turn on by themselves after being turned off. There is a certain seat on the left side that anyone who sits in it complains of it being cold.

TEHACHAPI

Tehachapi in the Tehachapi Mountains between Bakersfield and Mojave in Kern Count, has at least two haunted sites. An old children's hospital that is now used by the UFW is said to be haunted. They say blood can still be seen in the old hospital bathrooms and a feeling of death is felt. Disembodied voices are heard and the children swings out of doors move of their own accord. People passing by a locked door blocking off the back part of the building heard someone or something banging on the other side and saw the door knob turn. I do not know if anyone felt brave enough to see who or what was on the other side of the door! Janitors working around a small memorial late at night in Wells Elementary School have heard footsteps and felt like someone or something was watching them even though they were the only ones in the school.

Kings County
HANFORD

Hanford, the county seat of Kings County, is located in the south central San Joaquin Valley. The Bastile Bar used to be a jail where an unknown number of people died for various reasons. Now, it seems, the dead may be haunting the Bastile, scaring the cooks in the kitchen and, apparently causing the new stairs to the bathrooms appear old and fail at different times. A mausoleum in the Calvary Cemetery is very strange. It opens up every friday and disembodied voices are heard and spirits have been spotted wandering around mausoleum. One in particular, a lady in a white dress, has been circling the building since the early sixties.

When you first enter the Hanford Civic Auditorium, you might feel a very cold breeze even with all the windows closed. Go into the boys bathroom and you might heard some unseen people talking about legal issues. Latched windows unlatch and re-latch all by themselves. Go on Christmas Day and you might glimpse the ghostly form of a lawyer dressed in an old style brown suit and carrying a worn briefcase. Ghosts have been seen in the upper balcony as if they were watching a ghostly performance. The most well known phantom is that of a man with dark brown hair, brown eyes, and a black mustache, dressed in a white shirt and a black suit who applauds an unseen show. When it is apparently done, he stops applauding and disappears!

Not much is known about the old Hanford Sentinel Building except that people heard unexplained noises in the building and feel that it is haunted by at least one ghost.

Irwin Street Inn, a restaurant in Hanford, has at least three known ghostly presences, which are sometimes seen in the dinning room and on the second floor. There is also the usual slamming of windows, disturbing of bed sheets and , of course, the switching off and on of lights. There is a house at the intersection of Irwin Street and Bush Street in Hanford that may be haunted. Passersby had seen a spirit of an old man sitting in a chair inside the hallway. Empty stairs creaking, lights flickering, the sounds of laughter and booming are heard. They say that if you venture onto the second floor, be prepared for chilly winds and the sounds and visions of phantoms!

Workers in the Kings River Bank have reported seeing a ghost but little else is known about it. Now the old mental hospital on Irwin Street maybe be definitely haunted. Visitors to the old building claim that the spirit of the head nurse can be seen pacing the front porch. Try sitting on the front steps and you might get a scare. The head nurse supposedly comes out and talks to you for a few minutes before asking you to leave the property. Even though there is no electricity hooked up, people have seen a white light burning in a front window and a red light burning in a back porch window.

LEMOORE

The city of Lemore in Kings County was once known as La Tache and Lee Moore's. There is spirit of a woman who with a lantern walks the bush in the vicinity of Kings River at

Lemoore looking for two of her children drown in the river. She lost her life trying to save them. She now asks passersby to save them. They say that if you try to go into the river to save them, she will pull you under.

Lemoore High School at 101 E Bush Street is also haunted. Strange shadows have been seen in the Auditorium in the English building. The ghosts of two girls sitting in seats six and seven in the fifth row are often heard laughing while the specter of a man in a bolo hat sits in the balcony. The school theater also has some spirits hanging around. A teenage boy was working a spotlight for a play when he fell to his death. People say that you can still his screams as he fell. An old man, who died from a heart attack in the theater, can still be seen sitting in the last row. Maybe he is waiting for his favorite play to start again.

Each year on Halloween, the local drama club sponsors a haunted house in the Oddfellows Lodge. It seems that they have some ready made ghost helping out. These ghosts, spotted as shadows of people wearing clothes similar to the ones worn in the Victorian era, do not like the haunted house. A deep male voice has been heard telling visitors to leave them to alone. Visitors also experience hot and cold spots and a hall that seem unnaturally dark and foreboding. Some who stayed in there have heard voices call out their names and someone unseen pushed them with invisible hands. Strange red and green lights have been seen up on the roof. All of the phenomena reported is apparently not the doing of the club members but of something else. I bet it does make for a thrilling haunted house, though!

STRATFORD

Stratford is located 14 miles southwest of Hanford in Kings County. It has a haunted woods on Kings Avenue between 17th and 18th Avenue by a canal. Some time ago, a farmer, working the land, was killed when he fell off his tractor and under the disking machine. If you go into this haunted woods at night, be prepared to hear phantom footsteps behind you and the sound of breaking branches.

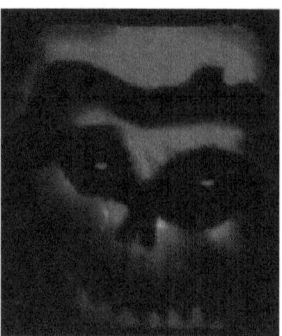

CHAPTER L
Lake County
CLEAR LAKE

A pioneer woman was killed by bandits when her husband was absent. The dastardly fiends then threw her body down a well that is supposedly still there. They say that at night her ghost carrying a lantern walks the shore of Clear Lake. Sometimes she serenades passersby by playing her fiddle.

Lassen County
RAVENSDALE

Ravensdale, a community in Lassen County, is seven miles southeast of Termo. The Secret Valley Inn, just off the main highway, has a ghostly guest. Years ago a woman was murdered in a bathtub in one of the rooms and today, she roams unseen around the building. But you know she is there by the sound of her invisible footsteps and her howling. The building also makes a lot of creaking noise which is apparently not attributed to its age or state of repair.

WESTWOOD

Marilyn Monroe's ghost has been seen near her tomb in Westwood Memorial Cemetery in Westwood, a community in Lassen County.

A home owned by Jean Harlow, the movie actress, sits in a quiet neighborhood in Westwood. When her husband, Paul Bern, shot himself, she blamed herself and took an overdose of sleeping pills but survived. Her parents forced her to leave that house in Weston and she died several years later in a new house that she built. They say that house in Weston is haunted by her. Dogs grow at something unseen in the upstairs bedrooms and people often hear someone whispering in their ear, "Please help me!". One night, new tenants felt a sensation like a heavy object hitting the bed. The kitchen lights go off and on by themselves and a mysterious shapeless light has been seen floating near the ceiling in the living room. Cold spots have been felt in the kitchen, the upstairs bedrooms and the downstairs area. There has been reported much more paranormal activity in the Harlow House.

Los Angeles County
AGOURA

Agoura is a community southeast of the city of Agoura Hills in Los Angeles County. Some years ago, a young man was hit and killed by a drunk driver in a white car on 101 Freeway near Las Virgines Road. The driver killed himself after he was tried and convicted. Now that fatal accident apparently happens over and over again. Others driver have reported having to swerve to miss a white car and crashing. The California Highway Patrol would investigate and find no evidence of the white car. It disappeared into thin air. If you drive that stretch of road, watch out for that white car!

AGOURA HILLS

Malibu Lake near Agoura Hills, a city in Los Angeles County, is home to the Lady of the Lake. This spirit is believed to be Margaret Hersh Robertson. Margaret would swim out to an island in the lake early every morning. After she passed away in 1993, the figure of a woman in a bathing cap, who looked like her, has been seen swimming just below the surface of the water.

ALHAMBRA

Alhambra, a community in the western San Gabriel Valley region of Los Angeles County, also has a number of spectral residents. Some years ago, a girl hung herself on the bridge at Alhambra High School. Now ghostly runners are heard and seen on the school track. A female ghost walks in and out of the kitchen in the Phoenix Inn in Alhambra and sits at tables and watches what you eat - or so they say. Ramona Convent Secondary School in Alhambra has a ghostly nun dressed in white that hangs out in the school library. Others have heard an invisible piano being played when no one else was in the building. Stories were told of swimmers legs being grabbed by something invisible in the water in the school pool. A student had apparently drowned in it and was maybe seeking help. The Scripps Kensington Library has a number of unusual phenomena. Staff have seen a ghostly form in the shape of a long sleeve shirt with no legs or head in the darken library. When the lights are switched on, the apparition disappears. It reappears several minutes after the lights are turned off. Once a heavy frying pan flew off its hook towards members of the startled staff. Many working there have experienced a number of frightening incidents.

A man and and old woman as well as a young boy haunt the Turner and Stevens Mortuary in Alhambra. Some witnesses of the scary activities believe the old woman is a mean spirit and is after the boy who is protected by the man. People passing mirrors opposite each other in the hallway have glimpsed either the man or the mean old woman in reflections for several seconds before they disappear. Books fly across the room as if flung by unseen hands just missing people. Footsteps by invisible presences are often heard and doors are slammed by unseen hands. Whistling can be heard after hours in the Ultrazone arena in Alhambra. Even though the fog machines are turned off, a fog will form in the building. Witnesses have reported that the lights near the back entrance change colors. No one knows why. It has got to be ghosts!

ALTADENA

Altadena is a small community in Los Angeles County. The Angeles National Forest, aka The Haunted Forest (Cobb Estate) at the top of Lake Avenue, has been the scene of strange unexplained screams and lights. Gravity Hill on Loma Alta Street in Altadena is supposedly haunted by three young kids who took a parent's car for a joy ride and were killed in an accident. Now if you park your car at the bottom of the hill, it is said that the dead kids will push it up the hill. People have also reported finding fingerprints on their cars after being pushed up the hill. I wonder if anyone took prints and checked them against the prints from the dead kids? Is Altadena's Zane Grey Mansion haunted? You judge. The building has a number of very cold spots near the pantry, kitchen, fireplaces and the library.

When certain people, unnamed of course, enter the kitchen, the clock there stops running. Then there are the mysterious footsteps by someone unseen that make their way across the pantry floor and into the dinning room. Hmm. Maybe it is Zane Grey.

ARCADIA

A certain place in Arcadia, a city in Los Angeles County, is said to be cursed, The lot at 5 W Live Oak Avenue has seen many failed business who usually started off well but soon failed. According to local lore, a certain brick wall all around the property is cursed and is responsible for the many failures. Who cursed it and why is not known but they say that the day the wall is removed is the day the curse will end. Apparently the wall is still standing. The Arboretum at 301 North Baldwin Avenue is haunted by the ghost of the 1930's actor Chief Buffalo Child Long Lance who committed suicide after his claim to be a Native American was exposed. His spirit has been seen in the house. If you happen to be in the entrance of Arcadia High School late some evening, you might hear the ghost of a janitor pushing his squeaky cleaning cart in the kitchen and indoor cafeteria. He must have loved his job so much that he is still there instead of going into the light.

One night in May of 1976, the Arcadia Poltergeist struck. All sizes of rocks started flying up off the ground striking buildings and people. Windows in buildings and cars were broken. The phenomena continued off and on for three months. Investigations of the strange events found no explanation. Eventually it was chalked up to the unexplained and forgotten by most people.

The Derby at 233E. Huntington Street in Arcadia was owned by the famous jockey "Iceman" before he was killed in a racing accident. Employees feel that the "Iceman" is still around keeping an eye on the place. They often hear footsteps ascending the stairs to his old apartment and his presence can be felt throughout the Derby. First Avenue Middle School used to have a pool until it was covered over after someone drown in it. They think that the person who drown may still be hanging around the premises. Phantom footsteps can be heard ever after the alarms are set. If the footsteps were made by someone of flesh and bones, they would have set the motion detector alarms off. They did not! Someone or something has banged loudly on the lockers and the doors of the girl's locker room. Water taps seem to turn off and on by themselves and toilets are flushed by unseen hands. Lockers locked one minute are found unlocked the next minute. Then there is the little boy bathed in a green glow who wanders through the darken halls at night. Is he the person who drowned in the now covered pool and is trying to find it to take another dip?

The Santa Anita Mall (Westfield Shopping Mall) in Arcadia and in particular the KB toy store is haunted by the spirit of a little boy wearing knickers like those from the early 1930's. Store employees have spotted him after hours in an aisle playing with toys. When they approached him, he disappeared before their eyes. The little ghost has also been spotted staring at the down escalator as if he had never seen one. When approached, the boy ran down the escalator without touching the steps and vanished when he got to the bottom. An elderly man in a yellow sweater is often seen entering the men's room at Taco Lita at Second and Durate but is never found in the bathroom. Apparently, he is a ghost with a bladder problem.

ARTESIA

They say that if you walk past a certain grave in a cemetery in the city of Artesia in southeast Los Angeles, you will see the ghost of a woman who died when her fiancee pushed her down the stair in the Red House during an argument. His ghost had better not show up there. She just might push him down some stairs.

AZUSA

A railway overpass bridge in the city of Azusa in Los Angeles County is home to the ghost of a transient and his faithful dog. They both have been seen walking the tracks at night.

BALDWWIND PARK

Baldwind Park is a city in the central San Gabriel Valley region of Los Angeles County. It is claimed that the ghost of the actor, Gary Cooper, can be heard walking and making thumping noises in the basketball gym and behind the stage early in the morning at Baldwind Park High School. I have not found out why they think it is Gary Cooper. Was he a student at the school? Do you know?

BELL GARDENS

Two schools in the city of Bell Gardens in Los Angeles County may be haunted. Someone unseen calls out people's names when those persons enter a a certain bathroom in the Suva Elementary School. The spirit of a little girl is often seen riding on the same swing all the time in the school's play ground. Once, a person riding on that very swing was thrown off by an unseen force and he smashed into a fence behind the swing. Was the little girl impatient for her turn at the swing? A janitor apparently killed himself on the third floor of Suva Intermediate School. He is still trying to do his job as his ghost has been seen roaming the halls of the school.

BELLFLOWER

Bellflower is a suburb of Los Angeles and a city in Los Angeles County. A story is told about a tragic event at Bell Flower High School. In the 1960's a student called Kaytlin got revenge on a boy who called her "Chicken Head". She gave him a soda laced with rat poison. After he died, she cut him up in pieces and hid the parts in a storage closet. His body was found months later by a cleaner. Now, in that room, blood stains appear and disappear on the floor and there is often the smell of rotting flesh. Some teachers have also reported finding body parts in the cabinets. These body parts quickly disappear only to reappear again. The theater at the high school is haunted by a female student who hung herself over the stage after being turned down for a part in a play and a devastating break up with her boy friend. Now, apparently in revenge, she makes a disconnected prop phone ring, causes spotlights to flicker when students are practicing a play, turns on an unplugged radio and keeps changing stations. All this is apparently because she did not get the part in the play. I wonder what she did to bug her ex-boyfriend? Maybe I don't. The ghostly form of a woman has been sighted in the stockrooms of the Kmart in Bell Flower. She always appears to be working but she is not a current living employee. No one seems to know who she is and why she appears there. If she likes to work that much, she can come and clean my house.

BEVERLY HILLS

Mention the name "Beverly Hills" and most people instantly think of the affluent city in the western part of Los Angeles County. It has at least three affluent haunted sites. The ghosts of John, Lionel and Ethyl Barrymore are said to be still in residence at the Barrymore Estate. The owners of the Doheny Mansion apparently find it hard to keep staff due to the ghostly activities there. Nightshift workers have reported hearing screams and strange sounds from certain parts of the mansion. Local legend has it that those certain parts of the mansion are locked off and no one is allowed in there. At the Pickford Mansion, there are at least two spirits in residence, one being Douglas Fairbanks. The other is thought to be, of course, Mary Picford.

BURBANK

Burbank is another well known city in Los Angeles County. Woodbury University, formerly a monastery, is haunted by a former nun, Mother Cabrini, who roams the campus. You can recognize her as her face is sculpted into the side of one of the buildings. Someone or something unseen often rings the bell in the bell tower late at night.

CALABASAS

Calabasas, yet another affluent city in Los Angeles County, has at least one haunt. The man who built and lived in the Leonis Adobe, an old ranch house from the 1800's, still hangs around there as its resident ghost.

CANOGA PARK

Canoga Park, once known as Owensmouth, is a district in the San Fernando Valley region of Los Angeles. There have numerous sightings of a man wearing all red standing at the drive through window at the Jack In the Box. He seems to disappear when they ask what he wants. Apparently, he may also be turning the milkshake machine on at odd times and moving furniture around after hours. Maybe the ghost wants ghostly milkshakes!

They say there is a ghost at Canoga High School in Canoga Park who likes to mess with the lights. I remember that at my high school the lights were always going off and on. Usually it was human pranksters. If anyone knows more about this ghost at Canoga Park High School, please email me at jimrobinson@hotmail.com.

The now empty (at least at the time of my research) Old Earth Island Manufacturing Facility, a small industrial business strip on Alabama Avenue, is haunted. There is a large warehouse, where late at night, unearthly screams of a woman can be heard. People have also seen the ghost that apparently did the screaming. This apparition seemingly lives in the attic area of a large walk in refrigerator. Every morning workers would find the door to this area unlocked. The place is now locked up and the owners may not like anyone trying to visit the ghost.

CARSON

The city of Carson in Los Angeles County is located thirteen miles south of downtown Los Angeles and fourteen miles from the LA International Airport. Some dark figures like shadows have been sighted walking around the Arco Refinery in Carson. Somehow, valves turn on by themselves. Speculation has it that the shadows may be the ghosts of previous workers killed in accidents in the early years of the plant. They may still be trying to do their jobs.

If you happen to drive by the area of Alameda and Wilmington/Del Amo Boulevard in Carson, you might encounter the ghost of a man dressed in clothes from the 1800's. Years ago, when a stage coach used to stop at the Dominquez Ranch at that spot, a man was apparently beaten to death there. His spirit has not yet gone to the light. As for the Dominquez House, now a museum, orbs of light have been spotted darting around late at night in the surrounding park.

Carson High School has a ghost who likes to run around the track at midnight. If you try to approach him, he will up and disappear. There is or was a mobile home at the northwest corner of Pacific Street and Banning Boulevard. A man was stabbed to death some time back and he now roams the area in spectral form between 10:00 PM and midnight.

CERRITOS

As you have probably figured out by now, many communities in California had different monikers until they settled on their present ones. Cerritoes in Los Angeles County used to be called Dairy Valley. The Cerritos High School has a small problem of mysterious banging noises in the girls locker room. If you are out by the track late at night, you might see a group of what looks like kids there. When you approach them, they disappear - not disperse but actually disappear into thin air.

CITY OF INDUSTRY

Puente Hills Mall, located in the City of Industry, a major regional shopping center in the San Gabriel Valley region of Los Angeles County is haunted. Employees at the Puente Hills Mall AMC Theater have seen little children running around the theater only to vanish in front of their startled eyes. The Broadway Department Store in the mall is apparently very haunted. Employees on the second floor have heard their names called by a disembodied voice. Music has been heard coming from a third floor locked stockroom. Employees working near the freight elevator have experienced feelings of chills and panic. Clothes have swung on clothes racks as if someone unseen was walking between them. In the Children's Department stockroom, the sound of breathing has been heard and cold breezes felt. A phantom person has been heard straightening the racks in the Lingerie Department before the store has opened. A pair of legs in black pants was spotted behind a bathrobe stand but disappeared when employees checked to see who was there. This is just a small sample of the activity that has occurred in the store before it was torn down in 1996 and replaced by the theater. Were some long gone store employees still trying to do their jobs? Are they still there in the theater wondering where the store went?

A woman committed suicide in the woman's restroom in the lower level in 2004. Now they say she may be haunting the mall itself. A dark image has been spotted in the mall's halls and in the mirror of the woman's restroom in the lower level. People working on the graveyard shift have reported hearing disembodied voices, strange noises in the ceiling like someone crawling in the air ducts and experienced cold spots.

CLAREMONT

Claremont is college town in eastern Los Angeles County about thirty miles east of downtown Los Angeles. The ghost of a small girl, five to six years old, dressed in native American clothing, sits by a garden pond, crying while watching the fish. Locals think she is a Cauhillian (pronounced Kaheeya) from a tribe who once lived in the area. She may be moaning the loss of her people's way of life. Visitors and staff to the garden have experienced sudden gusts of wind and cold spots and have heard disembodied sounds of crying.

The spirit of a former student of Claremont High School at Claremont may haunt the old gym. Students have heard what sounds like desperate whispering and screams coming from under the bleachers. A search of the area found no one and nothing that could have been the cause of the noise. Some students apparently have been pinned down by this ghost. They say that the name of the ghost is burnt into the gym floor, but no one, as far as I know, has said what that name was.

Several ghosts haunt Griswold's old school house in Claremont. Disembodied children's voices have been heard. Doors fly open by themselves. Visitors to the building feel like they are being watched by someone unseen. Then there is a white mist seen walking not floating around the building.

Walk down the east path of Thompson Creek trail in the late evening and you may be spooked by strange scratching noises and mysterious footsteps in the bushes on both sides of the trail. Shadowy figures may follow you or appear to be hiding in the bushes. People have reported clouds forming into the shape of skulls. The power lines overhead apparently crackle a lot and some feel these might have some to do with the strange activity on the east trail. There are reports of other strange activities in the Thompson Creek Woods. Visitors have reported seeing flying people who follow them until them leave the area. Boulders have been sighted levitating off the ground and people have claimed to have run into invisible walls blocking entrance to certain parts of the woods. Strange symbols that seem to bleed have been reported on trees and a cabin in the woods. If all that is told about Thompson Creek Woods in Claremont is true, that is one strange woods!

COMMERCE

Veterans Park in Commerce, a suburb of Los Angeles in Los Angeles County, is haunted by Martin, once a janitor at the park. Though passed away, he apparently still answers the telephone whether the park office is opened or closed. Martin is also apparently responsible for the usual ghostly antics of lights going off and on by themselves, doors opening and closing and even for the radio changing all by itself to a local Spanish station.

COVINA

You will find Covina, a small city in Los Angeles County, about twenty two miles east of downtown Los Angeles, in the Los Angeles-Long Beach metro area. Here they tell of the Legend of Zelda. She was a young girl of fifteen in the early 1900's who was kidnapped by a cult and sacrificed at the end of an underground tunnel. Now, anyone who tries to make it to the end of the tunnel will be caught by Zela and sacrificed. Is this true? I do not know. But, from what I have heard, noone has claimed that THEY made it to the end of the tunnel and returned.

Students and teachers at Covina High School has heard an odd moaning sound coming from the boys locker room. Late one night, a mysterious shadow shaped like a soccer player reportedly chased the whole soccer team out of the locker room. Maybe this phantom did not like the way they were playing.

DIAMOND BAR

Students at Diamond Bar High School in Diamond Bar, a city in eastern Los Angeles County, say that when you walk down the hall alone, you may feel a hand on your shoulder. When you turn to see who's there, there is no one. Then, do not be surprised that when you turn back to continue down the hall, there will be the startling sight of a girl with no eyes staring into your face. I have not found out yet what happens next. Does she continue to stare in your face? Does she just disappear? Locals say that she was a school cheerleader raped and killed by her boyfriend and some of his buddies. Maybe she is still trying to find her murderers and return the favor - killing them that is!

DOWNEY

The city of Downey sits in southeast Los Angeles County, thirteen miles southeast of downtown Los Angeles. Holydale, an abandoned Mental Hospital, may still be found behind the courthouse. Even though the electricity has been turned off, a light can be seen in the building. If you pass by a certain window, its curtain will close. Some people apparently entered the darken building one night and attempted to enter the basement. They were met with a barrage of books out of nowhere.

Strange things happen in the boys' locker room at West Middle School in Downy. When no one is in there, lockers can be heard slamming, showers turn on and off by themselves and toilets flush. Sounds like someone or something is glad to see all the boys go.

The Rio Hondo Hospital in Downy was torn down in 2005 and homes were apparently built on the site. When the hospital was up and running, many people experienced hot and cold spots, heard disembodied screams, saw doors open and close by themselves and sighted apparitions wandering the halls. I wonder if the people living in the houses built there are having any paranormal problems?

DUATE

Employers at the Spaghetti Factory in the city of Duate in Los Angeles County may have more to contend with then just customers. Rumor has it that a ghostly group of children can be heard playing games in the basement rest rooms. They are also blamed for dishes falling to the floor.

EAST LOS ANGELES

The city of East Los Angeles is also known as East L.A. or East Los. In Spanish, it is El Este de Los Angeles. Years ago, a ten year old boy was accidentally locked in the boys wash room for the night and was found in the morning strangled to death at the 4th Street Elementary School. Now his ghost has been seen playing on the monkey bars late at night. He has also been heard in both the boys and girls washrooms screaming for someone to open the doors and let him out.

The caretaker at Casa Del Mexicano in East L.A. thinks that there may be at least nine ghosts in the building. When he is up in his room at night, he hears knocking at the door, footsteps on the stairs but no one is there. Lights also turn on by themselves. During a Christmas play, the ghost of a Mexican man, wearing a squared shirt, jeans and boots was spotted sitting on top of one of the play's props. The usual cold spots have been experienced in that area of the stage. No one knows who he is and why he still hangs around.

People visiting the Evergreen Cemetery in East Los Angeles have heard disembodied voices and have seen unidentified things moving around among the tombstones. An apartment in a remodeled building across from Evergreen Cemetery has experienced some paranormal activity in the past. The TV, radio and water taps turned on by themselves and chairs moved across the floor. Sounds like someone jumping off a bed have been heard. A black shadow with red eyes has also been encountered. Of course, there are the usual cold spots where ghosts are active.

They say that if you are alone in one of the restrooms on the second floor of the Humphreys Elementary School in East L.A., you may have a terrifying experience. First you will hear a toilet in the left corner flush by itself. If you have the courage to check the toilet out, you will see blood coming out of the toilet. Suddenly the lights will go out and then come back on. If you look at the toilet again, it will be normal and you just might wonder if the whole thing had not happened. Maybe it did and maybe it didn't.

The Linda Vista Hospital, an old abandoned hospital on Chicago Street across from Hollenbeck Park in East Los Angeles, is still active in a paranormal way. Unauthorized visitors to the place at night have heard what sounds like a little girl laughing and playing in the building. Strange lights, screams, moaning sounds and cries have also been reported. Lights have also been seen turning on and off. A specter wearing a doctor jacket has been seen looking out a corner window on the top floor of the main building. Supposedly there are still cages in the building where they used to keep mentally ill patients and the ghost of one mentally ill patient has been seen walking around inside of one cage. Both warm and cold spots have been reported in the building.

EL MONTE

El Monte, a residential, industrial, and commercial city in Los Angeles County has a High School that is said to be haunted. Late one night some years ago in the early 1900's, a young man, for some unknown reason, hung himself in the El Monte High School auditorium. Since then there have been reports of unspecified strange happenings during the practice of plays. Oh yes, someone unseen plays the piano in the band room during the day.

There have been numerous sightings a phantom little girl in the attic of the gymnasium and that of a ghost of a man in the locker room room of the same building in Lambert Park.

If you hang around Mountain View High School in El Monte late at night, besides encountering the police, you just might see shadowy forms running around the track and playing football as well as a spectral figure hanging from the goal post.

ENCINO

Encino is Spanish for holm oak or evergreen. The community of Encino is a hilly area in the city of Los Angeles. The Bagel Nosh Restaurant was originally the L.A. Cabaret, a comedy club. It must have been very popular as it had two ghosts who frequented the place. One spirit was a pretty woman in clothes from the 1950's who sat happily in a corner booth. The other was a man who staked out the control room and the kitchen area. He did not seem troublesome but one night his presence was felt in the kitchen by the workers. Suddenly, they felt they were in danger and quickly exited the building. The workers felt that the ghost may have been warning them of some pending danger but nothing apparently happened. Maybe he was upset with what they were cooking?

The Los Encinos State Historic Park at 16756 Moorpark St, Encino has been investigated over the years for paranormal activity. Ghosts are said to haunt various structures in the park. Voices speaking in Spanish have been heard in the old Blacksmith shop. Icy spots have been encountered and a mist spotted in one corner. The spirits of a girl and a boy have been felt in the Eugene Carter House. The children were apparently murdered in the building in mysterious circumstance and may be waiting for someone to take their spirits to a safe haven.

GLENDORA

The ghost of a lady who was a former resident of the Bennett House in Glendora, Los Angeles County in the early 1910's, appeared at the first monthly tea of the members of the Daughters of the American Revolution after they had brought the house in 1982. It must have been an exciting tea!

One foggy morning in the mid 1990's, a very disturbed young man, after leaving a suicide note for his parents, shot himself on parking lot of Glendora High School across from where the boys locker room was located. Portable classrooms were erected later on that spot. A teacher in one of the portables saw in the corner of his eye a boy sitting at one of the desk. There was supposed to be no students in the room at this time. When he looked up, the boy had disappeared. Later, when the teacher returned from a break, the teacher in the classroom next door asked him what all the banging was in his classroom. The surprised teacher found out later that his portable sat on the exact spot wheer the boy had shot himself. Is the portable still there? Does the ghostly boy still show up for class?

They say that the Walmart in Glendora was built on an Indian burial ground. That might explain the mysterious events that have happened there. Workers in the garden center heard the door alarm go off at least ten times and shivered as cold gusts of wind swept through the room. Apparently the door was still closed.

GORMAN

Gorman is a community in northwestern Los Angeles County has, as far as I have been able to determine, one ghost active. Many years ago, a little girl died and was buried on the spot where later the Gorman School was built. In fact, it is said that the school cafeteria was built over her grave. It is also said that the cement over the exact spot where she was interred is still wet and never dried. The spirit of that little girl has also been seen running around the school.

GRANADA HILLS

Granada Hills, a district in the San Fernando Valley region of the city of Los Angeles, appears to also have only one resident ghost, rather a family of ghosts. When people drive eastbound on the freeway at Granada Hills, some have reported seeing a man, a woman and two children standing forlornly on the side of the road. When some good samaritans stopped to help them, the family had up and disappeared. No one seems to know who they are or how they became ghosts.

HARBOR CITY

They say that if you want to sell your soul to the devil, go to Harbor Park also known as the Duck Pond. Look for a well mannered man who smells pleasant. They say he may be the devil and he is willing to make you a deal. Local legend claims that a famous Rap star made such a deal at the Duck Pond. But I would be very careful... VERY CAREFUL!
In fact, I would not make any deal, even in fun! You have been warned!

HAWTHORNE

Nyman Hall at Hawthorne High School in the city of Hawthorne in southwestern Los Angeles County has a mysterious visitor, an old woman dressed all in black who wanders the campus. She may also be responsible for some of the other strange happenings. Lights in the buildings go off and on by themselves. Faulty wiring in not thought to be the problem. The sound of an unseen girl or woman can be heard in the girl's bathroom in Building 17. The water taps in the bathroom turn on and off and the toilets are flushed by unseen hands.

HERMOSA BEACH

The Prospect Street School in Hermosa Beach in Los Angeles County is closed and apparently used for storage. People in the building has heard the disembodied voices of little children just as if kids were still in school. I have experienced this phenomena myself when I was a school teacher and stayed after hours. It may not be ghosts but just residue energy from all those active children. Never the less, it is disconcerting to hear sounds and voices made by people who are not there.

HIGHLAND PARK

Highland Park is one of the oldest settled areas of Los Angeles city and the county. The ghostly form of a girl in white has been seen by many at Frankland High School In Highland Park. No one seems to know who she is and why she haunts the area. Do You? Years ago, a female student fell to her death from a fourth floor balcony that overlooks the quadrangle at Franklin High School. It is said that if you stand on that balcony and look down, you will feel a presence beside you. When you look to see who it is, you will get a glimpse of the that poor soul before she disappears. Another student supposedly died at the school in the 1950's and is still hanging around the auditorium and nearby classrooms.

HOLLYWOOD

Nearly everyone has heard of Hollywood, the home of movie stars and movie studios. It is a neighborhood in the west-northwest of Downtown Los Angeles. It is also home to many ghosts, famous or otherwise.

Ghosts as well as the living frequent the All Star Cafe in Hollywood. The spirits of a little girl and a boy have been seen running around the place only to disappear. Cold spots and lights flashing out of nowhere happen in the Ladies Vanity Room. It must be an interesting place to visit.

The Avalon Hollywood at 1735 Vine Street, Hollywood, used be called the Hollywood Playhouse and then the Palace Theater until it received it present name. The place is haunted with, they say, amiable spirits that come out around 230 AM. Beautiful, jazzy piano music has been heard coming from the third floor comedy room. Once in the 1990's, security guards heard the music and checked to see who was playing. The door was locked and a mysterious light could be seen coming from under the door. When the guard unlocked the door and entered the room, the light disappeared and the music stopped. The bench was found out from the uncovered piano as is someone had been playing it. Another night the guard was locking up the second floor when he felt an unseen presence and smelled sweet perfume. Then he felt a tap on his shoulder and turned to see who it was. Of course, no one was there. On yet another night the guard brought in a german sheppard dog. They were in the main room on the first floor when the dog suddenly began to stare at the left side of the stage in front of them. When they approached the curtain, the guard saw a man dressed in a tuxedo. But the man had no feet and a transparent face. When the dog advanced on the apparition, it vanished. An older couple dressed in 1930's style clothing have been spotted in in the balcony talking but disappear when approached. A large shimmering mass has floated across the stage and back again before it disappeared. Last but not least, employees have found in the morning that the club's adding machines and cash registers had printed out strange messages which appeared to be sentences of words. But instead of letters, numbers were used. Very mysterious indeed! Were one or more ghosts trying to communicate something?

The Beachwood Drive Apartments in Hollywood may have a ghost resident, an old man who walks around the central staircase. His apparently not one of the living residents!

Many famous people have stayed at the Chateau Marmont at 8221 Sunset Boulevard in Hollywood and it has been the site of much phenomena. The usual unexplained cold spots, mysterious drafts, weird energy and tingling sensations on the skin are common there.

Ciro's Comedy Store at 8433 Sunset Boulevard in West Hollywood was a famous restaurant and nightclub in the 1930's and 40's owned by mobsters and frequented by by many of Hollywood's famous and infamous. From the 1960's to the mid 1970's it was a home to rock and roll. Then it became the Comedy Store featuring many famous stand up comedians. Its basement is thought to be haunted by an evil entity. In addition to what ever is in the basement, there are at least four other ghosts hanging about. They are most active during the early morning hours but have been known to cause trouble anytime during the day. Chairs have slid across the stage all by themselves. One performer's show was interrupted by a loud disembodied voices. The ghosts, apparently dissatisfied with his performance, messed with the lights and sound system. The performer, fed up with the interruptions, demanded that the spirits show themselves. All the lights promptly went out!

The misty form of a man in a WWII brown leather jacket has been seen several times in different parts of the building. When approached he disappears.

The basement of the club was said to have been used by the mobsters to torture and/or kill people. Thus, the basement is felt to be full of bad vibes and evil entities. In 1982, the Comedy Club was investigated by the UCLA parapsychology team. They experienced some unusual activity such as coins following from the ceiling in the back stage area and the leader, Dr Taft, suddenly felt great pain in his legs when they entered the basement. Was it the pain inflicted on a hapless victim when some mobster broke his legs that the Doctor was feeling?

A guttural growl was heard one day by an employee coming from the basement. When that employee investigated, he saw that a padlocked gate in front of the basement was bulging outward. Was someone or some thing unseen trying to get out? Suddenly, the bulging gate snapped back into place. Then a huge black shadow radiating evil was standing in front of the gate. The employee beat a hasty retreat. Can you blame him? Much more has happened here but you will have read elsewhere to find out.

Something lingers in the El Capitan Theater in Hollywood after an suicide in the balcony. Theater goers say there is a strong energy felt when they sit in the seat where the suicide took place. In addition, people have also experienced a weird feeling in the downstairs lobby. After a former manager died in his office, his ghost was seen peaking out of a window. The proprietors had to block the window above the entrance way to stop his appearances. Then, when the projectionist died, he apparently keep coming to work as his spirit was often seen in the building.

There are two ghosts who like to frequent Hollywood's El Compadre Restaurant. They have been spotted after closing walking near the piano. An unknown presence haunts the large wall mirror in the bar. Maybe they are seeking one last ghostly drink?

The Hollywood High School is said to be haunted by Toby, a young boy who killed himself by hanging in the auditorium after his girlfriend dropped him for another boy. He apparently opens and closes doors in the school, move things around and appears as an unexplained shadow that roams the auditorium. He is not alone as the spirit of another boy who drowned in the pool has been seen walking around the pool and the gym.

The Hollywood sign overlooking the city is famous. It has also been sightings of weird looking figures and mysterious lights around the sign late at night. Could the strange activity be caused by the ghosts of two people who have committed suicide at the sign?

Immaculate Heart High School in Hollywood reports that a shadow of a num can be seen in the drama room's closet when the door is open. The stage area is apparently haunted as disembodied footsteps have been heard on the stage. Sometimes a cold breeze out of nowhere is felt on the cat walk above the stage.

A woman and two children are said to haunt one of the studios at KCET. They are blamed for such shenanigans as moving heavy rolls of wire around as well as wooden beam props from one side of the studio to the other. Also, objects have drop from the ceiling close to employee's heads. Maybe these spirits want to be part of the show.

Over the years, people have seen an old carriage pulled by white horses dart out at a full gallop from Lookout Mountain where it intersects with Laurel Canyon. This phantom carriage and horses have been blamed for many auto accidents at that intersection.

Mann's Chinese Theater in Hollywood is famous for the hand imprints of stars in the sidewalk outside. It is also haunted. The actor, Victor Killian, was murdered on that sidewalk and his ghost is still looking for the man who did it. Inside, some strange things have occurred. Black shapes have been seen falling from the ceiling of the main theater between shows. Nothing was found when people investigated it. Unexplained flickering lights have been seen and strange noises heard near the employee's locker room. All these strange happenings are thought to be the antics of the ghost of a man who hung himself in the theater in the early 1900's.

Neighbors around the former Errol Flynn's former estate on Mullholand Drive have seen strange lights of all colors and shapes and heard what sounds like a big party going on at night, most often in August. This interesting because, apparently, only the foundation of the house and the tennis court remains. Does any one know if anyone had built on the site?

The house at 1822 Camino Palmero Road at the base of the Hollywood Hills was the home of a famous Hollywood family with their own family TV show, " The Adventures of Ozzie and Harriet", in the 1950's and 60's. The ghost of Ozzie Nelson, the father, has been seen a number of times in the house and on the grounds. Owners of the house have experienced the usual paranormal phenomena such ghostly footsteps, lights and faucets turning off and on by themselves as well as doors opening and closing. A strong loving presence has been felt in the house and a white, misty form has been seen floating near people.

If you take the Haunted Hollywood tour, you will visit the Hollywood Forever Cemetery, next door to the Paramount Studios. Many famous Hollywood people are buried there. It is thought much of the ghostly activity at Paramount is caused by restless spirits from the cemetery hanging around the sound stages and scaring the security guards.

The Hollywood Forever Cemetery has its own mysteries. A lady dressed in black is said to still place two long stemmed roses on the grave of the silent 1920's actor Valentino every night. Valentino himself is said to stroll the grounds. Perhaps he is looking for the lady in black and her two long stemmed roses. Then there is the grave of Virginia Rappe who was involved in a scandal and court case with Roscoe "Fatty" Arbuckle, a silent era actor. People have heard sobs near her grave and felt a chill even in warm weather.

A number of apparitions dressed in 1930's and 40's style clothing have been sighted on and around the locked sound stages 31 and 32 and who simply disappear into thin air. The large aluminum doors at the entrances to the stages have been found unlocked by someone inside - someone invisible. Sound and film equipment have lighted up and turned itself on in stages that were locked securely from the outside.

The Lemon Grove gate separates the studio from the cemetery. Heads have been seen peering right through the cement wall and guards have chased what they thought were intruders up to the wall only to see them disappear through that wall! A man in an all white costume, much like the Sheik's costume Valentino was buried in, has often been seen in the area.

The Hart Building, part of the DesiLu Studios once owned by Lucille Ball and Desi Arnaz, has a flirtatious spirit. Many, mostly men, have smelled a strong odor of perfume in the upper offices. The ghost has also a habit of knocking over furniture and shoving things off desks.

The TV show, "Happy Days", was shot on Stage 19 at Paramont. The show "Wings" was shot there in the early 90's and experienced some paranormal activity. Strange laughter was often heard during the shooting of the shows and the lights kept turning off and on by themselves. Disembodied children's laughter and the sound of someone running has been heard coming from the catwalk. Many feel that it is the ghost of little Heather O'Rourke who was the little girl in the popular movie "Poltergeist". She had died tragically at the age of twelve. She also played in "Happy Days" and loved to play on the catwalk.

In Studio 56, the ghost of a headless man who was found in a garbage bag behind the building in 1991, let a famous music Rocker that he did not like the man's music. His manager and his engineer had hired out the studio for a recording session with a band. When they played back the night's recordings, they could hear what sounded like a rumbling voice chanting a Gregorian chant. Later, when they were alone, his friend was pushed out of his chair by something unknown. This something unknown followed the man into a rest room and appeared as a man who then promptly disappeared. When they went down the hallway to the lounge, they were greeted by a disembodied voice that told them not to go in there as they were not invited. To make matters worse, a small mist-like cloud was seen out of the corner of their eyes that floated across the room. The cloud ran up one man's arm and down his body giving him an icy feeling, Both men beat a hasty retreat and left the building. Apparently, other people using the building have made the acquaintance of the music hating headless ghost.

The Pantages Theater at 6233 Hollywood Boulevard in Hollywood is one of the most beautiful theaters in the world. The ghost of a female theater goer, who died in the mezzanine in 1932, may haunt the theater. When the building is closed during the day or night, the disembodied voice of a woman singing can be heard. Some feel that the woman who died hoped to become a singer and perform on stage before she died. In 1994, she may have even tried to accomplish her dream. Her ghostly voice was picked up by a mike during a live performance as she sang alone with the cast. Howard Hunt, who once owned the building, is said to haunt the second floor. Cold spots have been detected and the apparition of a man has been spotted going around a corner. The sounds of desk drawers being opened and closed and the clicking of brass handles as well as the smell of cigarette smoke indicated that something unusual was happening. Alexander Pantages, the original owner of the building, apparently haunts the ground floor and has even helped an employee who had fallen to her feet.

The Roosevelt Hotel at 7000 Hollywood Boulevard in Hollywood was a twelve storey luxury hotel for the rich and famous. The place was apparently quiet paranormal wise until it was renovated in 1984. Since then ghosts became very active. Maybe they like the changes. For instance, a strong unseen presence began to be felt in and around Room 928, where the actor Montgomery Clift stayed in 1952. Many feel that the ghost of Mr. Clift has come back to stay at the hotel. His spirit has been spotted pacing the hallway outside Room 928 and he has even practiced on his trumpet in the hallway. People have felt something cold brush by them and felt an unseen presence watching them. Some have felt a pat on their shoulder when they were alone in the room. The shadowy outline of a man has been spied sitting in a chair in a corner of the room. The ghost, thought to be Montgomery Clift, then got up, walked towards the washroom and disappeared into thin air.

Carol Lombard and Clark Gable used to stay on the 12th floor and her ghost still puts in an appearance on that floor. A mirror from Suite 1200 that now hangs in the lower elevator foyer sometimes shows the sad reflection of Marilyn Monroe. She is not the only long departed guest to be seen in a mirror. Other mirrors in the hallways seem to have their resident ghosts. The Blossom Room is said to be home to at least two ghosts. The room has a cold spot about 10 degrees colder then the rest of the room and 30 inches in diameter. A very anxious man in a tuxedo has appeared in the room from time to time. Piano music has also be heard coming from the empty Blossom Room. The apparition of a man in a white suit has been spotted standing beside that piano. When approached the man in white dissolved into thin air. Security cameras have detected the man in white in the pool but guards found the room empty when they check, even thought the camera still showed the ghost there. A five year old girl, who calls herself Caroline, sings and skips around the fountain in the lobby in the early morning hours before disappearing. Ghosts are often seen taking dips in the pool late at night. These are only a few of the paranormal antics that have occurred at this hotel.

The Todd A/O building in Hollywood has a ghostly resident, that of a worker who committed suicide back in the 1970's. He has been seen by security guards in the hall and making a quiet mumbling sound. He has also been blamed for the lights turning off and on by themselves and chairs rolling around the floor on their own.

Hollywood Universal Studios has at least two phantoms on its premises. The ghost of the actor Lon Caney Sr. is often seen running in a phantom like cape along the catwalks high above the stage. He is known to open and close doors, turn lights off and on and even for the ghostly tinkling of a long removed chandelier. Cleaners of the Back To The Future Ride have complained that after cleaning and closing the Ride rooms, they would a few minutes later discover the doors open and the place littered again. A little girl died on one of the rides and is still there somehow in her ghostly state consuming real candy bars.

The Vogue Theater at 6675 Hollywood Boulevard in Hollywood has been the scene of much paranormal activity. There are at least nine spirits hanging around there. One is Fritz, a film projectionist who passed away on the job in his booth. Then there is a maintenance engineer as well as a school teacher with some of her students who died when there was a school on the site before the theater was built. Maybe the ghosts like the films shown there, like "Ghost" with Patrick Swayze.

Sam Warner died before the Warmer Pacific Theater was completed in 1927 at 6423-45 Hollywood Boulevard in Hollywood. His ghost has been seen numerous times going about its business in the lobby, the second floor offices and riding the elevators.

The ghost of a woman has been seen at night on the grounds of the Wattles Mansion in Hollywood. A bus stop in front of the mansion was moved because of the many complaints of disembodied screaming and the phantom sounds of horses whinnying and galloping. Passengers waiting for the bus found it all unnerving.

One would expect a wax museum to be scary in and of itself. But The Hollywood Wax Museum has an extra delight! There are the usual cold spots, the lights go off and on by themselves and mysterious voices are heard by the Last Supper display.

HUNTINGTON PARK

The St. Mathias Mission House in Huntington Park, Los Angeles County, was once owned by an elderly couple who passed away many years ago. It is like they have never left their home. The vision of an old person has appeared in the living room mirror while disembodied footsteps, weird sounds and moans have startled visitors. Lights turn off and on and things fall from shelves in other wise empty rooms.

INGLEWOOD

Inglewood Park Cemetery is located in the city of Inglewood in southwestern Los Angeles County. A number of ethereal forms have been seen there including a lady who when approached disappears. Unexplained noises have also been heard by people visiting the cemetery.

LA HABRA HEIGHTS

Hacienda Golf Club in La Habra Heights in Los Angeles County may have a numbers of members long since passed away. There is the usual paranormal activity. Dark shadows are seen on the greens and in the halls of the club. Lights seemingly go off and on by themselves and unexplained noises are heard. If you tee off at this club you just might have a ghostly companion golfer.

LAKE BALBOA

Lake Balboa is a district in the San Fernando Valley region of the city of Los Angeles. Birmingham High School was a World War II hospital before it became a school. Many soldiers died there of their injuries. That might explained the strange goings on. They say that at night , if you stand on the quad, you can heard what sounds like rusty squeaking like that of metal bed springs. Also if you stand on the steps of the Performing Arts building and in the front entrance, you may sense the presence of someone unseen.

LAKE HUGHES

Lake Hughes is a community in the Angeles National Forest northwest of Palmdale in Los Angeles County. Weddings are often hosted at the Willowbrook Estates. To add a little excitement, they say that if you stay in the guest house, you might hear rustling noises and experience doors opening and closing by themselves as well as the lights turning off and on. But if you are a newly wed couple, you might be too busy to notice.

LAKE TAHOE

The community of Lake Tahoe also lies in the Angeles National Forest in Los Angeles County. The specter of a woman dressed in fine clothing from the late 1800's has been spotted a number of times floating below the surface of Lake Tahoe itself. Was she a drowning victim? Or worse? No one seems to know.

LAKEWOOD

Lakewood High School in the city of Lakewood in Los Angeles is said to be haunted by a swim coach who died when he broke a blood vessel screaming at his students. Now, apparently, he turns the lights off and on in the pool area and his wet footprints are often found by the pool when no one else has been in the water.

LA MIRADA

Creek Park in La Mirada, a city in southeast Los Angeles County, has a set of haunted steps. Go across the bridge to the right and up the stairs between the bushes. At the top you might encounter a gray shape that looks like a person with a hood on. If you are walking on the horse trail or down the steps nearby, you might hear the screaming of a little girl. When you go by an opening in the trees, close to the stairs, you might even glimpse that long passed away little girl looking back at you.

If the Taco Bell/Pizza Hut is still on Roscrances Avenue, and you go in there, you might see the ghost of a man sitting next at the table in the back. He apparently does not bother anyone. When you alone next to the window in the bath room (They do not say where it is the men's or the women's) the lights might flicker and you may hear disembodied voices. I would not stay too long in the washroom.

LANCASTER

Lancaster is the eighth-largest city in Los Angeles County. Staff on the fifth floor of the Antelope Valley Hospital have experienced an eerie feeling, saw doors move by themselves and heard unexplained noises. Staff have also experienced eerie feelings on the fourth floor. If you walk through the cemetery in Lancaster, (I think there is only one) you may be unfortunate or fortunate, depending on how you feel, to see the phantom of a little girl in old fashioned clothes. There is, if the land has not been rebuilt on, a demolished Insane Asylum with some concrete slabs remaining. Very courageous people have ventured onto the site late at night and reported hearing voices, screaming and the sound of something hitting metal. Some of these courageous investigators say they have been chased off the property by something or someone. They were not very specific. They just wanted to get out of there.

In the Lancaster High School theater, someone or something keeps turning the house lights off and on randomly when no one is in the lighting box. Bad wiring? Maybe. They also say that if you sit in the theater in the dark, a white figure will walk across the stage towards you. They do not say what happens when it gets to you!

Now a certain hotel, the oldest building in the city of Lancaster, is apparently so haunted, that, understandably, the owners do not like to talk about it. It has many of the usual phenomena such as phantom footsteps on the wooden floors, the scent of old flowers and vanilla in the air and ethereal music from an old scratchy record. Remember! Do not tell any one about this haunted hotel. The Lancaster Performing Arts Center on Lancaster Boulevard was the scene of a deadly accident when it was being built. An elderly woman fell off the stage and broke her neck killing her. Her ghost, apparently a black figure, has been seen on the staircase and in the green room downstairs. Seeing her has caused a number of people to feel that they had to get out of there pronto! And there is speculation that she is never seen upstairs as she, even in her ghostly gab, is afraid that she may fall. Staying downstairs is a lot safer. Can you blame her?

A ghost named George hangs out at the building housing or that used to house the Shamrock Carpet Cleaners in Lancaster. Carpet rolls and a telephone have seemingly moved by themselves or was it by George? Phantom footsteps have been heard in the back of the building.

LA PUENTE

Tyhe Hurley Elementary School tetherball courts is said to haunted by a boy who choked to death when a chain broke and wrapped around his neck some years ago. If you are hanging around there late at night, you may hear the sound of the chain hitting the pole and what sounds like someone choking. When you check the courts, you will see that they are empty - of the living at least.

The father of an owner of Nogales Burgers in La Puente was killed in a grease fire many years ago but still walks around the building at night. He apparently did not like a photo on the wall and threw it across the restaurant.

The spirit of a young student who was killed on the near by train tracks wanders the grounds late at night at the Nogales High School in La Puente.

LA VERNE

Damien High School in the city of La Verne in Los Angeles County has at least one unusual type of ghost. Around sun down, a large, white, mist-like cloud has been spotted floating swiftly across the school grounds towards the football field and even on to the football field. The 400 building located near the gym has something or someone spectral that turn the lights off and on and is manifested as a shadow moving down the hallway.

LENNOX

Buford Elementary School in the community of Lennox supposedly has a tombstone of a teacher who passed away right there were you enter the school. People have claimed that they have seen the dead teacher walking around the school and heard voices by the bathrooms late at night. Nyman Hall at Hawthorne High School in Lennox has two ghostly residents. One is a phantom lady that can be viewed by going on stage and looking up towards the stage lights. Look carefully and you may have the ghostly distinction of seeing her. The other ghost is that of a former drama teacher who thinks he still has a class to teach.

LINCOLN

The elusive ghost of a four year boy on a big wheel has been seen by a few people in Teal Hollow in the community of Lincoln. What would possess any ghost to be seen on a big wheel? Beats me!

LONG BEACH

The city of Long Beach in Los Angles County lies on the Pacific Coast. It has a good number ghost stories. A Navy hospital from WWII used to exist where Brooks College and the Cal State dorms are now. After the war, the hospital was torn down and the college and dorms built. Students are all the time seeing the ghostly forms of men in Navy uniforms wandering around. There is also the specter of a man in doctor gab hanging out in the area.

Casa Bonita on 6th Street in downtown Long Beach was once a hotel and is extremely old. As such, one would expect it to be haunted and one would not be disappointed. Mysterious noises are heard in the laundry room in the basement. The disembodied screams of a woman are often heard in the hallway. Hanging lamps swing from no known cause and cold spots abound in the halls and apartments.

Black forms float around DeForest Nature Trail accompanied by the eerie sounds of moaning and the laughter of spectral children. As you approach the end of the riverbed trail, you may feel cold spots and hear screams.

In DeForest Park itself, rapid ghostly footsteps are heard as well as spooky voices exclaiming people's names and asking for help. You may come upon a spot where there is complete silence. Then suddenly you may feel a blast of very cold air. When there is a thick fog at night in the forest, a mysterious and unexplained beam of light lights up the fog.

Residents of the Long Beach Job Corps have seen an older woman in a white wedding dress walk through the halls late at night.

A large number of people died of the plague at Los Ceritos Ranchos years ago. They do not however seem to haunt the place. Instead, the builder and founder Don Juan Temple is said to haunt the building. Then there is also a lady in white spotted in the men's washroom. Maybe she is a gender confused spirit.

Room 217 in the Marriott Hotel in Long Beach has a spirit that likes to keep the TV on and tugs at the bedspread. It also likes to touch the top of your back with its phantom hand.

The Queen Mary, a world famous luxury liner, was after decommissioning docked at 1126 Queens Highway, Long Beach and turned into a hotel and a museum. Now you can experience the luxury of ocean traveling without leaving the dock. Visit the museum and see how the rich used to travel. And say hello to the many ghosts like the male ghost in the engine room. He was killed there while the ship was still an ocean going liner. Ethereal children have been heard playing in the pool complete with the sounds of splashing water and wet foot prints by the pool made by apparitions. On the balcony of the pool room, the ghost of a young female bather in a green bathing suit is often observed passing right through solid columns.

The ghost of of a man crushed while trying to flee an engine room fire is often observed by Door 13. A mysterious woman in white and a phantom couple have been seen walking near the front desk in the hotel part of the liner.

Room B340 located in an abandoned area is now apparently closed due to the unexplained happenings. Lights would flicker and the whole area felt like a deep freeze.

In Shaft Alley, the apparition of a bearded young man with dark black hair dressed in blue-gray over-alls has been spotted. He may be the man who was crushed in Door 13 during a fire or a fire drill. The cooks and busboys have a ghostly helper in the Queen Mary's kitchen. The specter of a man dressed as a ship's cook has often entered the kitchen only to vanish into thin air. Dinnerware has moved by itself or by unseen hands. The lights flicker off and on - standard in most hauntings - and utensils keep disappearing. Another ghostly individual dressed in a white boiler room uniform still works hard at keeping the engines in ship shape. A transparent navel officer in dress whites marches around the pool area to the surprise of tour guides and their charges.

LOS ANGELES

The city of Los Angeles is a sprawling cosmopolitan with a large population of people and ghosts. Several years ago, a movie was being filmed in the Ambassador Theater. Several film crews saw a ghostly figure lean out of a fourth story window and then disappear in front of their eyes. Something or someone turned the lights off and on and cold spots abounded. There was also unexplained lights shooting around the halls.

The Angel Brewery in Los Angeles used to be known as Pabst Blue Ribbon and houses one of the largest artist colony in the world. It also has some paranormal activity. Disembodied voices can be heard on the stairs leading to the roof. It sounds like a hundred conversation being murmured at the same time. There is a freeway and train yard close enough for you to hear the noises from them in the building. But if you go up onto the roof, there is dead silence - no sound whatsoever can be heard.

The AON building on Wilshire Boulevard in downtown Los Angeles which used to be called the First Interstate Building caught on fire some years ago. An engineer riding the elevator supposedly burn to death when the elevator door open on the 12th floor where the fire was. At least two people committed suicide by jumping from the roof. Some superstitious people claim the building is cursed. It may just be haunted as janitors have heard unexplained noises in the building and have witnessed the lights on the 11th and 32nd floors going off and on by themselves. Why only those two floors? Nothing paranormal has apparently happened on other floors or the roof. Or has it and no one is talking.

A house on Ardmore Boulevard has a sad history and is thought to be haunted. After a wild party some years ago, a girl apparently died in the house. They also say that a man was murdered there. Residents have heard the sound of a champagne cork popping and the champagne being poured into an invisible glass. Loud raping in groups of three have awaken residents, who, when they checked found no one in the house. In addition the sounds of door knobs turning, someone whistling and heavy phantom footsteps heading towards the garage but never away have been heard.

Strange things seem to happen in schools and Bancroft Middle School in Los Angeles is apparently no different. People in the building late at night or very early in the morning have reported hearing whispers and footsteps on the third floor of the main building when they were alone. During Physical Education in the gym, the lights often without explanation go off and on by themselves. The janitors have also seen the climbing ropes move as if someone invisible was climbing them. In addition, the volleyball nets outside would shake very hard. There was no earth quake in progress at the time.

Arabella, a young girl who attending the Private Belmont School for Girls in the 1900's, died after that school burnt down, now haunts the auditorium. She apparently follows the actors and stage crew around during rehearsals. She is blamed for the opening and closing of doors by unseen hands, flickering lights, faucets in the dressing rooms turning on and off and curtains moving by themselves.

A number of cabins and bungalows were built at 2401 Laurel Canyon Boulevard in Los Angeles. The movie star Bessie Love bought one in 1918 to live in. She had some unexpected guests, two ghosts whose human forms had been killed on that spot when they tried to look for a Mexican bandit's hidden treasure. She heard a low moaning sound as well as men's voices. She had the usual trouble with the lights, doors opening and closing by themselves and cold spots in the living room. A female guest one night heard a man's voice and saw a transparent man wearing a cowboy hat walk though the wall of the living room and into the kitchen. Other owners of the cabin have experienced similar phenomena.

A storage room that was a student's room until 1999 in Phase II of the dorms at Cal State campus in Los Angeles is haunted. There have been loud moans, screaming and unexplained knocking coming from that room at all hours. A ghostly blonde lady has been seen on that floor and has even asked resident that she encounters do they think that she would not know? Abouit what, no one knows.Urban legend claims that tired and emotionally exhausted from exams, she found her boyfriend and roommate in bed together. She then hung herself in the hall outside the door of her room.

Cathedral High School is yet another school with ghostly presences. Cold spots can be experienced near the seniors, patio. Staff, while alone in the school, have heard noises from the floor above them. The Year Book room is thought to have a lot of negative energy in it. The room used to be a chapel and is said to still have a stain glass window. They say that the school was built over a graveyard. The football field has some problems. They still find coffin nails there and there is a spot that remains dry even when it rains. Then there are unspecified things happening in the gym during theater performances. Oh yes! A chair flung by unseen hands flew across a floor. It must be interesting attending that school.

An apartment on Centennial Street in Los Angeles' China Town may have a ghostly tennant. Disembodied footsteps are heard in the living room, unexplained noises are heard by the baby's crib, doors open and close by themselves and it often feels like someone unseen is standing by you as you sleep in the living room.

A man fell to his death off the top floor of the Los Angeles Coliseum at 3939 South

Figueroa Street in the 1960's. While some think that he was pushed, it was ruled an accident. But they say that near the end of games on game night, the apparition of a man is often spotted on the top floor of the Coliseum accompanied by screaming followed by the sound of a loud CRUNCH!

Ghosts have been sighted in the Cypress Park Branch Library in Los Angeles since it opened in 1924. A translucent man has been seen floating near the old fireplace. Cold spots abound especially near the occult book section (of course) and the fireplace. Spectral voices have been heard in the men's room.

Echo Park, a hilly neighborhood northwest of Downtown Los Angeles and southeast of Hollywood in Los Angeles, is where Charlie Chaplin Mansion sits on a hill overlooking the park. This mansion is thought to be haunted, not by Charlie but by the murdered family of a man who bought it Later. For some unknown reason, the man came home one day and killed his family. Screams are said to still heard coming from that old victorian style house. The phantom of an older woman thought to be the grandmother of the family killed has been seen in the house. Then there is the strange sightings of wild animals like lions on the property. People have also reported seeing a lit lamp sitting on a table shinning through a window.

An old Spanish style house on El Centro Avenue is haunted also. Residents of the home have felt that they were never alone in it. A transparent young man has been seen in the bedroom. He was seen a number of times and then was joined by a transparent female friend. When one resident, who had psychic powers contacted the ghostly couple, she learned that they had committed suicide there and could not leave. Interestingly, a check of the records confirmed the spirits story. The psychic lady wanted to helped the couple pass on. She prayed daily for weeks. Then one night, the male came and thanked her for her efforts and then disappeared never to return.

Elysian Park in Los Angeles has been the site of many ghost sighting dating back before the 110 Freeway and the Dodger Stadium. The stadium itself has a ghostly fan that sits in the seats still enjoying the game. The White Lady wanders the park crying for her children whom she drowned in the nearby river. Sometimes headless dogs are seen near her. No one knows how they are connected to the White Lady. There is a tunnel under the 110 Freeway at Solano Avenue where human like figures have been seen entering one entrance but not seen coming out the other side. There is apparently no place in the tunnel in which to hide. Mysterious light flickers on the hillsides in the area of the Lodge.

Fairfax High School has its share of ghost stories. Shadows from unexplained sources have been seen in the school's rotunda and cold spots abound. Students claim that when they walk on or near the third floor balcony, they get the urge to jump off of it. Two people supposedly hung themselves from the balcony. Then there was a man who died when he fell off a ladder while trying to fix lights in the auditorium. Now the lights flicker all the time and people blunder into cold spots.

The elevator in the Figueroa Hotel in Los Angeles stops on certain floors for no apparent reason. There is never anyone there when the doors open when the elevator does this. Maybe I am wrong but I thought that elevators normally did this. But then other mysterious things happen in this hotel. Mysterious sounds are heard coming from empty halls and rooms. TV sets turn on by themselves and can not be turned off. Maybe the hotel is a little haunted.

Another high school, Fremont High School may just be haunted by someone unknown. Mysterious shadows are seen on the stage in the auditorium. Some people have complained about having strange feelings when on that stage. Is it just stage fright?

Urban Legend has it that the previous owners of Griffith Park had died mysteriously and that the park's camp road was closed to traffic because of unexplained strange happenings. Some people have reported seeing at night what appeared to be witch like ceremonies and possible sacrifices in the park. But when someone investigated, nothing was found. Were these weird scenes ghostly re-enactments, real events or just someone's over active imagination?

The Harlow House at 9820 Easton Drive in Los Angeles is thought by some to be jinxed. Movie star Jean Harlow's husband killed himself there. Two other people drowned in the swimming pool. It is here that the young actress Sharon met her terrible end at the hands of Charles Mansion murdering clan. Apparently, Sharon may have been warned of her fate by a ghost. One night around 1960, she was startled in her bedroom by the apparition of a little man who entered the room and seemed to be looking for something. Sharon, they say, dashed out of the room and down the stairs only to encounter a ghostly figure with a cut throat that appeared to be tied to posts. Looking for something to steady her nerves, she pushed on a bookcase and found a hidden bar. For some unknown reason, she tore the wall paper at the base of the bar and uncovered a solid copper base. The next morning she realized that it was not a dream when she saw the hidden bar and the copper base. Some people speculate that one of the people who died there was trying to warn her of what was to happen. I do not know. All I know is that the story is spooky. What do you think?

The mansion owned by the famous Houdini may be haunted. Disembodied footsteps have been heard on the mansion's large stairs. The ghostly form of a man have been seen walking around the building. Is it Houdini or someone else?

The old I. Magnun/Bullocks building on Wilshire Boulevard near Vermont was converted into a law library for the Southwest Law School. Back in the 1930's a little girl was apparently pushed down the elevator shaft and killed. Now her voice can be heard crying in that elevator shaft.

During renovation, construction workers are said to have found secret passages from Mr. Bullock's old penthouse. The place also exhibits the usual signs of a haunting. Lights turn onc and off, windows and shades open and close and phantom footsteps are heard on the stairs. Several workers supposedly quit the site during renovations because of the paranormal activity occurring in the building's clock tower. The building may still be haunted.

The story about the third floor south of the J.F.K Library may or may not be true. Some visitors used to get stoned in the third floor bathroom. Someone had a bad trip and two people were bludgeoned to death. Now, as the story goes, after closing and before opening in the morning, there is an eerie feeling in the area as well as locked doors opening by themselves, faucets turning off and on, cold spots in the area and worst of all, the laughter of someone stoned on drugs.

The Knickerbocker Hotel at 1714 Ivar Ave., Los Angeles, is now a senior citizen community, the Hollywood Knickerbocker Apartments. A number of people have past away from various causes in the old hotel and several ghosts have been reported. Unfortunately I have not been able to find out anything more.

The ghost of an old woman has been seen in one of the empty, windowless back dinning rooms of Mrs. Knott's Chicken Dinner Restaurant at Knott's Berry Farm. The staff however claim it was just a fog. A fog inside a windowless room? I would like to see that for myself!

The ghost story told about the LA County Museum of Arts (LACMA) is very, very interesting and might induced some men to take up ghost hunting. A woman who was shot by her jealous husband for sleeping with other men is apparently asking men to have sex with her. She also plays with the electrical system causing all sorts of problems. Contractors have walked off the job because of her and her antics.

Someone haunts the boy's locker room in the uphill campus of the Le Lycee Francias. Students have seen the lights go off and on by themselves, lockers open and close by invisible hands. Doors slam shut and then are locked from inside in an empty room. Or are they empty?

The Los Angeles Airport Marriott Hotel may be haunted. Apparitions have be sighted on the 18th floor lounge and in the parking garage. Strange sounds and smells have also been experienced.

Los Angeles City Hall has numerous reports of ghosts on the 2,3,4,27 and 28th floors between the hours of 1:30 and 5:00 AM. Many strange noises have been heard on the second floor late at night and people have reported the feeling of being watched when no one else was around. Ghostly figures have been seen on the floor also. When you walk alone on the 3rd and 4th floor it feels like someone is walking beside you and , of course, no one is there. A life-like painting of a man in the Tom Bradley Room on the 27th floor is said to be eerie. The man in the painting seems to follow you with his eyes around the room. CCTV cameras on the 28th floor have picked up images of human figures, but when security checks there is no one there. I would advise you not to snoop around that building without permission,

A number of movie stars' pets are interred in the Los Angeles Pet Cemetery. If you visit the cemetery, you might hear the panting of Kabar, a Great dane that belonged to Rudolf Valentino, and feel its playful licking of your hand as it cavorts around its grave.

Los Angeles Senior High School has a male specter that wanders the theater singing Frank Sinatra songs and often sits in the audience section clapping his hands. He also likes to open and close the elevator's doors.

The field house at Loyola High School in Los Angeles is thought to be haunted. People have heard strange noises and sensed movement inside the building at night. An old student dormitory, now a class room, is home to the ghost of a student who committed suicide in a trap door in the room's ceiling. His eerie presence is felt there. The phantom of a nun has also been seen in the Jesuits' living quarters.

Loyola Marymount University has at least two haunts. The Strub Theater on campus has the ghost of an old lady who likes to sit in the back seats and watch the stage. Students in Rains Hall have seen several apparitions especially that of a girl who passed away in 1998 of heart problems.

The teacher who first taught in the print shop of Manual Arts High School in Los Angeles may still be trying to teach his students. Present day students often feel that someone is looking over their shoulders when they are alone developing film in the darkroom. Some could see out of the corner of their eye a man standing near the film drying area outside the darkroom.

Is the Neutrogena Corporation building in Los Angeles haunted?. Security guards have reported seeing a woman in a white dress walking around late at night. A child has also been spotted playing in the factory. Apparently children are not allowed on the site. Then there is a strange growling noise heard at night. Is it some type of ghost or just a very hungry security guard's empty stomach?

Occidental College has a number of spirits on campus. In Erdman Hall, two ghosts haunt a room in the center, front side of the 2nd floor. A young person plays tricks on the living trying to get their attention. The usual ghostly phenomena of water taps and lights turning off and on by themselves, occur as well as the chain on a door is taken off and on and messages are written on the walls by unseen hands. The other spirit is an unfriendly, large, dark man who stands by the doors of the students room and watches them sleep. Years ago a female student, depressed at being away from home, hung herself on the second floor. Fire alarms seem to go off by themselves and an unseen presence is felt there on the second floor.

The Olive Hotel at 750 S Olive Street in Los Angeles has several ghost stories told about it. The most popular one seems to be about a certain room which has a haunted closet. When visitors rented this room and open the closet door, they were shocked to see a man's body hanging there. This body was supposedly that of a man who hung himself fifty years ago. Note that in my research, I found that this hotel was said to be in either Los Angles County or Orange County. Maybe the ghost is trying to confuse me. It has happened before.

A spectral lady with red heels has been seen walking down a second floor hall at Our Lady of Loretto Elementary School in Los Angeles. Disembodied laughter has been heard in the girl's bathroom in the auditorium. Lights in the building seem to have a mind of their own. They go off and on by themselves. A student in the fifth grade jumped off the school roof in the 1970's. Some feel that his ghost may be trying to get someone to join him as several students claimed they got the urge to climb to the roof and jump. Hopefully no one has given into that urge.

A nun who taught at Our Lady of Talpa Catholic School in the Boyle Heights area of Los Angeles is still doing her job long after she past away. They say it is her when footsteps are heard and movements are seen behind the stage curtains. Of course, no one is there when the area is searched. The sound of an invisible person running in the halls is often heard. The num loved to play the piano and, guess what? The piano in the auditorium will play on its own.

Some stage workers and theater goers still like to be in the vaudeville era Palace Theater at 6th and Broadway in Los Angeles long after they have shucked their mortal bodies. A man caught and supposedly killed when he was discovered with another man's wife still sits in a seat neat the front. Two spectral stage hands still argue in the wings like when they were alive. If the spirits do not like a play, they make their opinion known though apparently the smell of invisible rotten eggs on the stage. You know that they are rotten eggs by the smell. Researchers have investigated the building and claim to have identified close to two dozen spirits in the Palace.

An overpass on the Pasaden Freeway in Los Angeles is the recurring scene of a murder. Again and again, the same woman is seen being chased by a man until they reach the edge of the overpass. Then he is seen strangling her before tossing her over the edge. When people rush over to her rescue, she and her assailant have disappeared into thin air.

Nineteen Chinese immigrants were murdered in a race riot many years ago where the El Pueblo de Los Angeles Historical Monument is in downtown Los Angeles. The largest building there, the Pico House Hotel may be haunted. Some paranormal investigators picked up some strange voices on their equipment. A security guard was apparently kicked down a flight of stairs by some unseen presence. He quit his job after that.

The Los Angeles Quantos Freight Warehouse is haunted by a warehouse worker who died while doing his job in the bypass section. A number of times, other workers have seen him at his old spot. When they approach him, he turns around revealing bloody and mangled hands and face before disappearing. This ghoulish ghost also appears in the cooler room where human remains are kept.

They say that the R building at Roosevelt High School in Boyle Heights used to be a four story building before a fire destroyed the top floor and killed a student. Now teachers working alone late at night on the third floor have heard ghostly foot steps, the sound of doors opening and closing and the TV's turning off and on. That is not all. Students hiding in the gym while trying to skip classes claim to hear strange whispering and clapping noises that scare them into leaving the building. Maybe it was the ghost of a gym teacher telling them to get back to class.

Silverlake, a hilly neighborhood in Los Angeles, is east of Hollywood and northwest of Downtown Los Angeles. Late at night there has been sightings of a crying little girl hiding behind brushes at the Edgewater Terrace. When people investigate, no one is there ! If you jog late at night in this area and by the lake, you may have a companion - the ghost of the Midnight Jogger. Not much else seems to be known about the jogger except that he or she jogs at midnight.

The ghosts of two former owners of the Silent Movie Theatre at 611 N. Fairfax Ave., Los Angeles, liked working there so much that they can still be seen there. One, John Hampton, hangs out in his old apartment now used as a lounge. The other, named Austin, can be found in the lobby. Neither ghost seems to bother anyone.

Someone or something unseen fools around with the showers on the tenth floor of Dykstra Hall at the University of California. When no one is anywhere near them, the showers come on full force. The students turn them off but the showers turn back on by themselves. Investigation of the showers have revealed nothing.

When the University of Judaism was first build in Los Angeles, young people used to hang out at night on the soccer field. Local legend says that a young girl was raped, her tongue cut out and then murdered in cold blood. Now, on certain nights of the year during the months of September and October, her ghost is seen wandering the soccer field trying to call out the names of her killer and trying in vain to scream. The legend also states that if a male is on the field when she is, they will not be able to speak until they leave. Boys, you have been warned!

There is a story told about Building 26 at the Westminster Avenue Apartment Building in the Venice Beach area of Los Angeles. The silent Film Star, Charlie Chaplan, did a lot of filming in and around this area. While making a film in 1915, Chaplin's stunt double disappeared from the film set and could not be found. A week later, the stunt double was found dead on the floor of Charlie's dressing room. The man had apparently been dead for several days and was covered with wet sea weed. An investigation as to how he died and then turned up on Chaplin's dressing room floor a week later was unsuccessful. These days residents of Building 26 hear strange noises like someone struggling through shallow water as well as moans and faint cries for help. The specter of a man, tied hand and foot and dressed the same way Chaplin's stunt double was the day he disappeared, has been seen standing in what witnesses described as luminous corners of the building. Did the stunt double fall into a time warp, drown in the ocean and then was transported back by another time warp and now haunts Building 26?

A student, years ago, is said to have hung himself from a pipe in a bathroom stall at Virgil Junior High School in Los Angeles. Student and staff there apparently have seen rope hanging from that same pipe and heard low moaning sounds coming from empty rooms. Doors also are known to open and close by themselves. To confuse things, there are reports of of a glowing clown-like phantom. Is this glowing ghostly clown causing the problems or is the specter of boy who hung himself.

While no actual ghosts are active at the Vista Linda Hospital in Los Angeles, people say the building should be. The elevators open and close and run up and down the floors by themselves. People have complained of terrible odors like the smell of sick people. But then again it is a hospital. Lets not forget the sudden chills and cold spots people have experienced there. Then there is the crematory said to lack air and feels eerie. Isn't that what you would expect from a crematory?

Three ghosts are said to plague Westchester High School. One is a sixteen to eighteen year old boy who died while playing basketball in PE class. Someone knocked him down and he cracked his head on the floor. Now late at night he still plays basketball. If you go into gym you might encounter his ghostly form who will ask you if you got game. He then laughs and disappears. As for the other two, they are a ghostly couple seen all over the school at different times. They usually disappeared when spotted by some living person. Occasionally they apparently take a dislike to some of the living, following and harassing them.

Four different entities are active at Wilson High School. The spirit of a boy pushed from a high window to his death can still be seen at times sitting in the window. Years ago, a person used to run around the school track late at night. One terrible night he was killed by gang members who ran him over with their car. The runner is said to still run that track late at night. The third ghost is that of a football player who died when he fell backwards while sitting on a bar near the school's loading dock. He is often seen sitting on the same bar. Last but not least is the unknown thing in one of the darkrooms that likes to push people around and lock them in the room.

LYNWOOD

In 2003, a young man riding a bike during the day in Lynwood Park in Lynwood, Los Angeles County, was killed brutally. Now both day and night he has been seen riding his bike and then disappearing a short distance away. At the spot where he was murdered, his spirit has been seen lying on the ground and asking for help before disappearing.

MALIBU

Malibu is a sea front city in Western Los Angeles County. A ghost may be to blame for a small problem at the Moonshadows Restaurant there. The water faucets in the women's restroom like turning on by themselves.

MARINA DEL RAY

The ghost of a man supposedly murdered by a jealous lover some years ago has been seen roaming the 3rd floor, the stairs and the roof of the BuyCheapSoftware.com building in Marina Del Rey, a sea side community in Los Angeles. Is he looking for his killer or some cheap software?

MENTRYVILLE

Mentryville was once an oil drilling town in the Santa Susana Mountains in Los Angeles County, next to Stevesonville. In the late 1800's, a nearby dam broke and drown many people. They say that their ghost are seen and heard in the oak trees that now grow in the area.

MONROVIA

You will find the city of Monrovia in the foothills of the San Gabriel Mountains in the San Gabriel Valley of Los Angeles County. The phantom of a lady in gray or white haunts the Azteca building on Foothill Boulevard near the corner of Myrtle. Unexplained noises are also heard in the building.

A ghost walks in the Band Room at Clifton Middle School in Monrovia late at night while the chorus girls are getting ready. Is he guarding them or hoping to get a peak?

At Monrovia High School at night in the main hallway on the second floor, staff feel that someone or something unseen is watching them and trying to sneak up on them. When I taught school and stayed late at night, I could always hear what sounded like people walking and talking in the deserted hallways. If I had felt that something unseen was trying to sneak up on me, I would have got out of there and never worked late again!

MONTEBELLO

The city of Montebello in the southwestern part of the San Gabriel Valley in Los Angeles County had a number of haunted places. When AMC Montebello 10 Theaters first opened, legend say, a person was stabbed there and killed. Now this spirit haunts the building, in particular theaters 6 and 9. When movies are showing in Number 6, a shadow shaped like a person is often seen on the wall. Patrons have found Theater 9 very cold even in warm weather or when the heat is on. When employees turn off the lights in the projection booth over Theater 9, the lights turn back on by themselves. No electrical fault has apparently been found when the wiring was inspected.

The Battle of the Rio San Grabriel took place in 1847 near the present day intersection of Bluff Road and Washington in Montebello. Phantoms that look like Spanish soldiers are seen walking around that area and they often seem to follow people passing by.

Some Park Rangers and employees at the Montebello Parks and Recreation Office claim that when they are alone in the building they often hear footsteps and voices in the men's restroom and the hallways. No explanation has been found.

For some unknown reason, a woman supposedly hung herself in the C building at Montebello High School in the late 1980's. They say that if you walk the halls of C Building late at night and listen carefully, you can hear the sounds of the woman struggling. Sit in the auditorium late at night with no lights on and you will hear disembodied footsteps and what sounds like people laughing at you.

MOUNT SAN ANTONIO

Mount San Antonio, also known as Old Baldy or Mount Baldy, is the highest peak in the San Gabriel Mountains in Los Angeles County. The sky lifts are haunted by a man with a mustache and dressed in all white including his hat. No one knows who he is but some feel that he seems to be from the days that the mines were open years ago.

NORTH HILLS

The district of North Hills in the San Fernando Valley region of the city of Los Angeles has at least one haunting by an unseen presence. Students and staff at James Monroe High School have heard the sound of loud footsteps and the opening and closing of doors in an empty hallway. Lockers in the girls gym room have open and closed all by themselves in front of students when no one else was there. This phenomena seems to be common to a number of schools.

NORWALK

The suburban city of Norwalk in Los Angeles County is home to at least three spirits, maybe more. Chavez Elementary School is haunted by a child and a former Principal. Balloons from out of nowhere have floated down the halls while someone unseen tries to turn door knobs and slams doors. Then there are the disembodied screams and cries of a child. To make matters worse, alarms go off for no known reason late at night in the school. Is the moving around of the dead principal and/or the ghostly child setting them off?

Ghosts have been sighted in one of Metropolitan State Hospital buildings. A woman walks through the walls and often stands near the shower room. A mist often floats at knee high level down a hall before disappearing into thin air. Dark human-like forms roam the office areas while some unseen thing makes noises in the kitchen.

In the 1980's, a boy was killed in a weight lifting accident in the weight room at Norwalk High School. They say that you can still hear him working out at the weights late at night.

PALMDALE

The city of Palmdale can in the north-central area of Los Angeles County. There are several ghosts in the Palmdale area. They say that if you go to the railway tracks behind Joshua Elementary School, supposedly late at night, you will see a black figure there. No one seems to know what or who it is or why it appears there. The ghost of a fisherman warns people away from what is apparently his lake - Lake Una - at Ave S and Sierra Highway in Palmdale and is very vicious about it, lashing out at the living. In addition, black figures have been observed climbing nearby trees and vanishing into thin air.

PALOS VERDES

Palos Verdes is a group of coastal cities in the Palos Verdes Hills on the Palos Verdes Peninsula, in southwestern Los Angeles County. They say that if you go to the Lighthouse at Palos Verdes, you will either hear or see a woman screaming. She killed her baby and then committed suicide and is now doomed to hang around the lighthouse.

The Wayfarers Chapel designed by Frank Lloyd Wright Jr. overlooks the ocean at Rancho Palos Verdes. At night, foggy shapes appear in garden behind the church. Visitors hear disembodied voices call their name. An old Indian man, often seen in the distance gardening, disappears when someone approaches him. A mysterious, giant white owl often puts in an appearance only to disappear into thin air. A rumored small cemetery hidden in the hills behind the church is blamed by some for all the paranormal activity at the church.

Rocky Point at Palos Verdes and about three miles south of Redondo Beach is said to be very scary what with dead skin divers appearing in ghostly forms, mysterious lights that roam around the area and disembodied voices disturbing the your peace and quiet.

The Vanderlip Mansion in Palos Verdes was the scene of a terrible tragedy. Mrs. Vanderlip is said to have killed her entire family including the dogs and burying their bodies in the walls of the house before hanging herself from a wooden beam in the living room. The dogs, as glowing apparitions, haunt the yard, still doing their job - scaring away trespassers. The woman and her dead family have often been seen staring out of the abandoned house windows. If you listen carefully, you can hear the dying screaming for help.

PANORAMA CITY

Panorama City is a district in the San Fernando Valley region of the city of Los Angeles. There is an Optometry office in that city that may be haunted by a little boy who likes to caress patients hair and to laugh out loud in the examination rooms. Employees feel that at times someone is standing behind them but find no one there when they look. When alone in the office at night, staff have heard people talking in the empty lobby.

Supposedly, you can hear a little boy, who is not there, crying in the rest room of Rose's Beauty Salon in Panorama City. Customers have also complained of a cold spot by the cashier desk in the lobby. Just think, for the price of hair cut you may have a paranormal experience that you can tell all your friends about.

PASADENA

The city of Pasadena in Los Angeles County has or used to have an abandoned asylum off Green Street under what is known as Suicide bridge. Its real name is the Colorado Bridge. Disembodied voices, strange orbs of light, doors moving by themselves and the distinct feeling of being unwelcome there as well as cold anger are all part of the ambiance of the old asylum. It is a wonderful place NOT to visit.

A murder occurred at the bridge of Fair Oaks Exit on Highway 101. They say that you can see, if you look carefully you might see the ghosts of a man and a woman fighting. Do not let it distract you from your driving! There is also a front yard of a house near by, where supposedly the ghost of a little girl about two or three years old runs around holding a doll in her hand.

The Castle Green Apartments in Pasadena are also said to be haunted. Heavy perfume has been smelt and the rattling of chains has been heard. Door knobs seem to turn by themselves and shadows pass under closed doors. Voices come out of thin air. Yes, it sounds like it may be haunted.

The specter of a woman in white has been spotted on the top floor of the Green Street Hotel. Why is she there? Maybe she can not find her room.

There is a small forest in or near Pasaden that is haunted. Where it is exactly, I have not been able to find out. But people claimed they have heard unexplained and strange noises coming from it. They have also claimed that they could hear unseen people following them. By explanation some say that there is a haunted house on one of the hills as well as a mental hospital. OK, I can accept that but more information would be nice. Do you know anything about the place?

A haunted mansion is hidden up in the hills overlooking the Colorado Bridge (Remember? It is also known as the Suicide Bridge). The rundown place was closed and board up awhile back making it a prime candidate for a haunting. So, people claim that there are unspecified ghosts living there and mysterious voices are heard. Then there are the phantoms of wild animals hanging about here also. Hmmm! That I would like to see for my self, if I could find the place.

If you just happen to be in the Pasadena Rose Bowl parking lot around midnight, with the owner's permission of course, you might see a woman dressed in a white wedding dress walking towards you. Then she will up and disappear in front of you.

The specters of coyotes surrounding the ghostly figure a man in Indian head dress have been seen in the area of the Colorado Street and Scoville Bridges. The sound of galloping invisible horses have been heard and strange apparitions are seen by the bridges. Are they scenes being recreated from the past?

The Pasadena Historic State Landmark Theater, once a College of the Performing Arts, is haunted by its founder, one Gilmore Brown. The elevator in the classroom tower building used to stop all by itself at the floor Mr. Brown's office was on. A distinct male voice could be heard saying hello in an otherwise empty room. Actors and the staff felt that his friendly spirit was always watching the goings on in the building.

PARAMOUNT

Paramount West Campus High School has a certain amount of paranormal activity that indicates it is haunted. The screams of a girl are often heard as well as a deep laughter in the school's auditorium. The lights there also go off and on by themselves. A ghostly flute is often played by someone unseen. The shadow of what looks like a young girl is often spotted in hallway running from the music room to the auditorium.

Some years ago, a girl was supposedly murdered and her body thrown in the showers. People have claimed to have seen her bloody murder reenacted time and and time again and have heard her screams for help.

PICO RIVERA

Pico Rivera is a city located in southeastern Los Angeles County. The Little Theater, aka the Drama Room, at El Rancho High School in Pico Rivera is haunted by a former teacher, a Mr. Letty, whose wake was held in the school. Apparently his spirit has never left the building, in particular, the Drama Room. Costumes are often found mysteriously pulled off the racks and thrown on the floor. The lights are dimmed and turned off and on by themselves while mysterious noises spook people late at night. A ghostly face has been seen peeking through a curtain in the Little Theater's office during a drama class.

A battle must have been fought back in the Spanish era in the Rio Hondo riverbed in Pico Rivera. In fact there appears to be an audible reenactment as screaming and musket fire can often be heard there.

In Room 9 at the Pico Revera St, Hillary School, there is a boy who loves doing homework, even after he died in a horrible car accident according to the locals.

POMONA

Pomona is the fifth largest city in Los Angeles County. They say that if you are in the Ganesha High School in Pomona and you hear the wind, don't be surprised to feel that someone is watching you. Someone is! The apparition of a girl with red eyes!

There are apparently a number of ghostly entities at Charles Grill at the corner of Garey and Holt Street in Pomona. There are ghostly footsteps, doors slamming by themselves, the sound of arguments out of thin air, apparitions wandering around and displays of paranormal activity such as the tops of potted plants bending over all by themselves towards the floor and then springing back up straight. Here is your chance to dine with some ghostly friends.

The Lanterman Developmental Center in Pomona is thought to be very haunted as it has a morgue in the basement for clients that have died. Some of their spirits may be responsible for the disembodied voices and footsteps heard in the residences, keys spinning in locks and the locks themselves locking suddenly and just as suddenly unlocking. Ghostly forms have been spied washing their hands as they go down the halls and are even said to try and play with the staff. I wonder how the staff feel about that?

The band room at Pomona High School has at least two ghosts hanging around there. Band and drama rooms in schools seem to be really popular for spirits. One of the two, apparently a peeping tom, hides in a closet and watches people undress. He or it has never been seen but people changing there feel like someone is watching them from what is supposed to be an empty closet. The spirit likes to hang out at the back left door of the school, swinging it open and slamming it shut. Sometimes this invisible presence likes to stop people from opening the door. Once upon a time, the Palomares Cemetery sat where an empty lot now exists behind the school. It is, of course, blamed for the strange activity.

The Spada Cemetery in Pomona was the original Old Settlers' cemetery from the mid 1800's and sadly is now closed to the public due to vandalism. The place is haunted by the ghost of a man who, at night, walks through the cemetery until he disappears into a tombstone. Even though the place is under a freeway, it is said to be very still and quiet. In the pass this silence ended when someone started to act up. Then a hot wind comes out of nowhere and is only felt in the cemetery and nowhere else. Do not go into the cemetery without permission from the owners. Please respect the property and the dead.

RANCHO PALOS VERDES

Rancho Palos Verdes, or RPV as it is sometimes abbreviated to, is a city in Los Angeles County. The Point Vincent Lighthouse has been featured on the TV show, Unsolved Mysteries. The ghost of a woman supposedly is still waiting for her loved one to return. It is said that the Coast Guard finds it hard to keep the place staffed due to the ghostly antics of this woman.

There is a lot surrounded by houses at the end of Lunada Bay called Spike that has a sinister reputation. The name Spike apparently comes from the iron gate with sharp black spikes on top that used to be there. It remains vacant even though some people has tried to build on it unsuccessfully. Legend say that if you try to go on this lot, you will get the feeling of wanting to throw up. Your car may also stop dead in front of the lot. Some have reported seeing a house on the lot and hearing screams whenever there was a thick fog. When the fog lifted, the house was gone. Legend also says that, once upon a time, a boy living there killed his whole family and now haunts the lot.

REDONDO BEACH

Redondo Beach is one of the three Beach Cities in Los Angeles County. The now closed General Cinema Theater I had a problem with a ghost that used to open boxes and scattered the contents on the floor in the Stockroom It also like to turn the taps off and on. Staff working behind the concession stand often felt that someone invisible would brush pass and bump into them. Locked cabinets would be found unlock in the morning and their contents strewn about. Guess that ghost did not like the movies they were showing.

A ghost named Jack haunts the Redondo Union High School Auditorium where, they say, he died in the 1940's. He is said to walk up the walls because people have heard his footsteps - that's right! Right up the walls! Other strange occurrences are also blamed on Jack such as loud unexplained knocks on the wall, paper airplanes falling from an empty catwalk, lights turning off and on by themselves, something being seen and making sounds going up the staircase to the sound booth, cold spots on the one of the sound booth stairs. The tiles where he is said to have died is supposedly still stained with his blood.

ROSEMEAD

Years ago, a student shot himself in the parking of Don Bosco Tech in the city of Rosemead in Los Angeles County. He still seems to hang around that parking lot as many people have reported seeing him. Students have reported hearing someone invisible crying in the washroom of Buildings 400 and 600.

A few years ago, at the corner of Rush and San Gabriel Boulevard in Rosemead, a passenger in a small car was killed when a bus slammed into it. A scar from the accident apparently still remains. A shadowy form has been seen standing under a nearby tree. It appears to be waiting for something. People waiting at the crosswalk where the terrible accident occurred have reported that they can feel or hear someone near them that is not there - at least to the human eye.

ROWLAND HEIGHTS

The community of Rowland Heights in and below the Puente Hills in the San Gabriel Valley, in Los Angeles County, has one known ghost story. A female faculty member was killed in a car accident in front of the Rowland High School. Ever since then, a lady wearing torn up clothes and bearing scars on her face stands in the middle of the street at night.

SAN DIMAS

The Extended Stay Hotel in San Dimas in the San Gabriel Valley in Los Angeles County has a ghost haunting the first floor. He was a depressed guest who committed suicide in a room. Apparently if you enter that particular room, you will be greeted by his invisible presences. Many guest are unable to sleep in that room and it is rarely rented out.

Several years ago, a girl drowned in the Wave Pool at Raging Waters and was taken down to the First Aid Station that used to be on the lower plaza food area. That spot is now a freezer. The ghost of that girl is often seen there. Other paranormal activity includes the ringing at all hours of the park phones. When answered, the line is nothing but static. Most calls seemed to have come from the Wave Cove. When security personnel check those phones, they usually find the phone itself swinging just as if someone had just dropped it. But there was no one anywhere around. Guards at night have reported hearing their names called while checking the upper pavilion food court and have also heard a young girl calling for help. They never did find who it was.

Waitresses at the Pinnacle Peaks Restaurant in San Dimas have seen a little girl with long hair and Native American in appearance walking with customers into the building and then, apparently, disappearing. In addition, glasses seem to fall on the floor by themselves or is it the little girl? Sometimes people are tripped by someone unseen. The building was one of the original stagecoach stops in the 1800's. An old picture of cowboys may still hang on the wall at the bar on the west side. It is said that sometimes a huge face replaces the cowboys as if one of the cowboys came up real close to the front of the picture to see what was going on in the bar.

The San Dimas Mansion built in 1887 has some paranormal activity. You can hear invisible things sliding across the floor, someone trying to pull open a locked door, banging on the windows and the door bell ringing by itself.

SAN GABRIEL

Gabrielino High School in the city of San Gabriel in Los Angeles County is rumored to have been built on the site of a Native American burial ground. Sports teams and staff returning to the school late at night after games have seen a body-like mist in the hallways which disappeared when approached. They have also heard children crying when no one else was around, let alone children late at night. Spooky!

The Red Cross Mansion in San Gabriel is also a site with paranormal action, maybe by a polite ghost. If people leave doors open, someone or something unseen closes them softly. Soft disembodied voices often whisper as if they were trying not to disturb any one. Even thought certain rooms are empty, phone calls originate from them. The electricity goes off and on in the kitchen all the time. A man's face has been spotted in some of the windows after the building was empty and locked. Some believe that it is the spirits of a long dead servant who may be responsible.

There are many stories of hauntings at the San Gabriel Civic Auditorium. I will only relate a few here. When it was built, underground tunnels were added running the length of the building. This allowed the owner, nicknamed Uncle John, to go from backstage to the foyer unseen. After he died, the tunnels were not used until the Depression. Then the tunnels were used to house dead bodies. Why, I do not know for sure. That is just how the story goes. The tunnels were sealed when they were full. They say that there is a door in the front men's washroom besides the entrance door. When opened, all there is is a brick wall. As the story goes, some people tried to remove the brick but gave up after five feet. What does this have to do with ghosts? Be patient and I will enlighten you. A theater down or background scene was preserved from the original set. During the Temple City High School musical some years ago, the drop started to sway all by itself. There was no draft and no one was seen anywhere near it. Now, someone brought in a psychic who claimed to see a man swing on that drop. Of course, no one else could see him. Wait! There's more! They have tv monitors on stage left that show what is happening on the stage. During the showing of Music Man in 2003, many of the crew saw on the TV monitors and even the audience saw a man in the second story window of the fake house on stage. Many wondered how he could be up there as there was no ledge or platform behind the set. The kicker is that the mysterious man was thought to be Uncle John. You remember him. He was the original owner who died long ago. Oh, yes! There are two other ghost present, an old stage manager and a little girl both of who roam the halls late at night. As for the connection with the tunnels, you will have to ask Uncle John. They are his tunnels.

At San Gabriel Mission High School the ghost of a girl who hung herself in the school library can sometimes be seen dangling from that balcony. Someone unseen is heard using the bathroom towel dispensers.

Some visitors to San Gabriel Mission claimed that there is a feeling of foreboding in the old church. It often gets very cold suddenly and a presence is often felt. When people look around to see what is there, there is no one there.

There is or was an old farmhouse on Palm Street in San Gabriel with an old pantry that dark and hollow. The residents of the house felt that something was in that pantry watching them. One day the lady of the house saw a small gray/green face with red mouth twisted in a weird grin. She immediately left the house with her child. I do not know if she and any member of her family returned to that place. I know I would not!

SANTA CLARITA

Santa Clarita is the third largest city in Los Angeles County. The Space Ordnance Systems is located off Highway 14 at the Sand Canyon Exit. Explosives were mixed at the old ordnance facility and several explosions ocured there. They saw that nights guards often saw ghosts with only their shoes and belts on their charred bodies running screaming across the filed. Many guards found it a bit too scary to keep working there. I do not blame them? Do you?

Both the Cottage on Walnut and the Egg Plantation next door were converted from old homes and are thought to be haunted. Tags in the store seem to flap all by themselves and things have been heard being shifted around as well as disembodied steps. Loud clangings can also be heard in the hours before the store is opened. Apparitions including that of an angry cook have been seen in the restaurant next door.

The home of the silent film star William S. Hart in Santa Clarita is haunted by Mr. Hart and his sister, the ghost of their nurse as well as Mr. Hart's dogs. Add the smell of invisible coffee in the museum and you have an interesting place to visit.

Santa Clarita's Lake Elizabeth was said to once be the home of a sea serpent and various demons. The Spanish who settled the area reported dead cattle, ruined crops and sickness as well as a sulfuric smell in the region. No creatures have been reported recently but the smell apparently still lingers. That sulfuric odor may explain the sickness, bad crops, etc., but it is said that an eerie presence is still felt in the area. Oh oh!

In the 1980's, teenagers on the way to a prom crashed their car at the intersection of Sand Canyon Road and Warm Springs Road in Santa Clarita. I have not confirmed that anyone died in the wreck but people see a young woman signaling for help before vanishing into thin air.

SANTA CATALINA ISLAND

Catalina Island as it is often called is a rocky island off the California coast but is part of Los Angeles County. Banning Inn at Two Harbors on the island is said to be haunted by the Lady in White, but little is known about her. A long passed away fisherman still lingers on the island. If there is a strong smell of fish and/or tobacco and no sight of either, that will be him just hanging around. The ghost of the movie star, Natalie Wood, has apparently been seen around the area where she drown years ago.

SANTA FE SPRINGS

St. Paul High School in Santa Fe springs, a city in Los Angeles County, has at least three ghosts there. If you are near the football field at night, you may hear the football players (unseen of course) practicing for a ghostly game. The ghosts of a female in her prom dress and her date, who, they say, hung himself in the 100 Building, wander the halls. Why he hung himself is not at this time known. Why her ghost is there is not known. Something strange happens in the boys' bathroom in the 500 building. The motion activated sinks and toilets activate all by themselves when no one is near enough to trigger them. Is it some ghost doing his thing?

SOUTH EL MONTE

South El Monte is a city in the San Gabriel Valley, in Los Angeles County. History comes alive again at Whittier Narrows Park. The ghost of a Spanish conquistador on horseback appears sometimes near the intersection of Lincoln Avenue and San Gabriel Boulevard where he drown looking for the gold he had buried near a beach on the river. Locals also claim that mysterious fogs roll in and out of the area. Reminds me of the movie "The Fog".

SOUTH GATE

In 1968, a young man died unexpectedly in the Hahn Auditorium at South Gate High School in South Gate, a city in Los Angeles County. Students claim that they can hear his ghostly footsteps and have encountered cold spots in the auditorium. Stanford Elementary School in South Gate was the scene of a tragic murder when a young girl with green eyes was killed for some unknown reason by her boyfriend. Now her ghost complete with green eyes follows people around the school and, some times at night, she can be heard crying eyes out.

SOUTH PASADENA

They say that the ghost of a WWII soldier in the penthouse Apartments in South Pasadena is trying to get a message to his son but, so far, been unsuccessful. No one seems to know what the message was.

The Rialto Theater in South Pasadena is at least seventy years old and has at least two ghosts stories attached to it. Many years ago, a young girl slit her wrists in the girl's bathroom, climbed up to the balcony and bled to death in the seats. You would think her ghost would haunt the seats, but no! The doors to the girl's washroom are said to shake, supposedly by the unseen presence of the the young girl. The apparition of an older man, maybe the one they say went crazy in the projection booth, has been seen sitting in the seats and walking up and down the balcony stairs.

SUN VALLEY

Sun Valley is a district in the San Fernando Valley region about ten miles away from Downtown Los Angeles. When the DWP, Valley generating Station was operational, a ghostly figure was often sighted at night on the second deck. Night operators would see it pass by one of the electrical rooms. They followed it and were startled when it would disappear through locked doors or pass through solid walls. Employees working on the lower and second decks have reported the feeling of being watched by unseen people. Some speculate that the ghost may be the victim of a former employee who was one of the two Sunset Strip Slayers.

An unidentified building on Roscoe Boulevard in Sun Valley is haunted by the ghost of a mysterious man who seems to be protective of children. He is only malevolent towards anyone over twelve years old.

SYLMAR
Sylmar is a district in the San Fernando Valley region of the City of Los Angeles. Glen Haven Memorial Park in Lopez Canyon has a very unique statue beside the mortuary building. They say it likes to walk around the park late at night.

TORRANCE
The city of Torrance is found in the South Bay area of Los Angeles County. I do not know what happed at Bishop Montgomery High School but there is apparently some para normal goings on. People have had visions of blood on the hall ceiling while others have seen a passed away teacher in the drama lab and the spirits of old nuns hanging around the hallway of the third building.

A male apparition has been seen in the Del Amo Mall near a skateboard shop and visitors have reported the unsettling feeling of being watched as well as experiencing cold spots in the area.

Years ago a woman and her two children were brutally murdered on the grounds of the Zamperini Stadium in Torrance after a game. Now neighbors often hear a woman crying and children laughing late at night. Some have even seen the dead woman and children appear and then vanish into thin air.

VALENCIA
The community of Valencia is located in the city of Santa Clara in Los Angeles County. The two story Olive Vista Hospital was once closed but the ground floor was reopened again as a hospital. The top floor remained closed. Speculation has it that the top floor is very haunted but no details are available at this time.

Six Flags in Valencia is thought to be haunted. The ghost of a child dressed in a striped shirt has been spotted running thought the supports beneath the Colossus ride at night. Even if the ride is shut down for the night, workers can often hear lift chains running and the anti -rollbacks clanking. Visitors and workers at Magic Mountain have reported feeling an unseen presence and have blundered into cold spots. A girl working as an attendant on the Revolution roller coaster, once known as the 76er, was killed by incoming cars when she accidentally stepped out onto the track. Her ghost has been spotted by the track in the train station or in the tunnel just after the loop. Disembodied screams have also been heard.

VAN NUYS

The district of Van Nuys in the San Fernando Valley area of Los Angeles has at least two possible ghostly presences. Judge for yourself. The DWP Utilities Building on Van Nuys Boulevard has some sort of malevolent spirit there that likes to touch people and give off a feeling of strong negative energy. Several cold spots have also been experienced in the building. The second place is said to be the Right Side Up where unexplained electrical malfunctions occur and cold spots abound.

VENICE

Venice is a district on the west side of Los Angeles. The Fourth Grade classroom at St. Mark School is said to be haunted by the ghost of a nun. She apparently taught the fourth grade there and was seen several times after she passed away. Now the classroom door slams by itself and someone unseen opens the classroom windows. I bet the students in that classroom are very well behaved.

Some sort of entity haunts the Venice High School. Many feel that the decor of the old school is a bit eerie and may be blamed for the weird feelings some get when they walk into the empty auditorium. Then there is the other phenomenon such as the lights and the sound system turn on by themselves. Disembodied (I like that word) screams have been heard coming from the empty control room. The place also gets very cold at times. Yes, I would say something unseen lurks there in.

WALNUT

They say that St. Mary's Catholic School in the city of Walnut in Los Angeles County was haunted. The school doubled as an orphanage. Some years ago, some children snuck out one night to play in the small play ground outside. They were found dead the next morning by the nuns. No one knew how they died. They say that if someone goes to the site late at night they will hearing the sound of running feet coming from inside the building, the eerie sound of swings swinging and see the unlikely sight of children's toys moving by themselves. Others stories claimed that devil worshipers wrote anti-Christ slogans in blood on the walls. Another claims that someone was killed in one of the bathrooms and you can still see the bloody hand prints on the walls. This all may be urban legend. Decide for yourself.

Some years ago, a woman was killed by a car while crossing Lemon Street in Walnut. Now her ghosts supposedly crosses at that same spot between 9:00 PM and 3:00 AM. Be careful if you drive down that street and see a lady crossing it. She may be a ghost but then she may not!

WEST COVINA

Galster Park with its three entrances is located on a hill in the city of West Covina in Los Angeles County. It is said to be closed due to the multiple rape and murder of children. Late at night, people claimed to hear the children pleading and screaming. The phantom of a boy sometimes young sometimes older has been seen standing at the first or second gate to the park. The ghoul apparently invites people into the park to see what's there. Most locals say that the park is dangerous and people should stay out of it at night. You should stay out of any park any where at night if you are smart!

Three women were killed in a car accident some years ago in front of South Hill Elementary School in West Covina. Their apparitions have been reported standing in front of the school at night. Is this just another ghost story told to keep the kids from hanging out around the school yard late at night? I remember as a kid, when I was told stories like that, I was only too eager to check them out. But, then that was me. I am sure your kids would not do that. Or would they?

WEST HILLS

The district of West Hills in the western San Fernando Valley area of Los Angeles has several ghosts stories told there. Take Capistrano Avenue for instance. The apparition of a lady with long dark hair hangs out on that street late at night. Then there is a hooded form with glowing red eyes that stands under the dark trees lining the avenue. The ghostly sound of creaking stairs, jangling keys and heavy footsteps have been reported at an unspecified house in the same area.

A young boy was killed and almost decapitated some years ago at the old ranch house at the Shadow Ranch Park recreation center in West Hills. Now, they say, at night you can see his almost decapitated body staring down at you from a second floor window.

The Target store in West Hills has a number of ghost stories told about it. When the storage area behind the dressing rooms is empty, they say you can hear loud music and voices from there as well as lights showing under the door. Mysterious fires have seemingly broken out by themselves in various areas. The ghost of a dead employee is often seen walking in the garden area and then walks through the door to the store and dissolves into thin air. A female employee in the food area used to leave the store at 3:00 PM. For several months after she died suddenly, door alarms would suddenly go off for no reason. And in her work area, alarms would go off, power would shut done and doors seemed to lock by themselves. The ghost of another worker, who had hung himself, has been seen walking around the receiving area. Other phenomena includes turned off phones that ring at night, disembodied footsteps and voices are heard on the stairwell. Cold spots are encountered and stock put on the shelves end up on the floor even if no customer is around. I have worked in a "big box store" and have experienced such things including towels shooting off the shelves all by themselves and just straightened stock getting all messed up by unseen hands. Thus I feel that this store just might be haunted but don't quote me!

WEST HOLLYWOOD

A janitor at Melrose Elementary School in the city of West Hollywood in Los Angeles County hung himself in the auditorium supposedly because no one liked him. He must have liked working there as his ghost has been spotted walking the halls and on the stage. He is also thought to be the cause of window curtains moving by themselves, the sound of scratches on the classroom doors and in the ladies restroom. The restroom door would also shake but no one was found outside when they checked.

WEST LOS ANGELES

West Los Angeles, a district in the city of Los Angeles, is also known as West L.A. The area around Quicksilver TOWS-O.P.G has been the scene of many fatal accidents. Now they say that people in that area have experienced cold spots, eerie feelings, seeing phantom children, hand prints from unseen hands appearing on cars and dome lights inside cars turning on by themselves. That is what they say about the area. Enough said.

WHITTIER

People at the California High School in the city of Whittier in Los Angeles County keep seeing a ghost in Room 10. No one seems to know who it is or why it is there.

At what some people call Dead Man's Park in Whittier, the old Quaker cemetery was made over into a park. That is probably why they now call it Deadman's Park. Even though the grave stones were removed, the names of the dead were engraved on a large marker placed in the second half of the park. They say that the dead are not happy with the changes. A strange fog often settles in the park but does not go pass the surround streets. In fact, the fog does not appear on the road that runs through the park. Some claim that the fog is physical manifestation of the dead's anger. There are other strange happening occurring such as joggers reporting that they feel like someone is always watch them when they are in the park. Dead cats are often found there.

The four floored King Richards Antique Center off Whittier Boulevard near the Historic Whittier district has been the site of some strange happenings. It was once a citrus packing plant where two employees apparently died. One locked himself accidentally in an old basement freezer room and froze to death. Falling machinery fell on another employee. Now, around closing time, dark shadows are seen. There has been reports of a black figure watching cleaners on the bottom floor. Battery-less electrical devices have started and pictures on the walls have fallen and ended up feet from where they were hung. Objects like saucers and other items for sale roll off the shelves or are thrown by unseen hands. Customers have complained about a cold spot where stairs used to be and many sense an invisible presence there.

Some strange sounds are heard at La Serna High School in Whittier. Students and staff, while in the wrestling room, heard have the disembodied sounds of a basket ball game such as shouting, sneakers squeaking on the floor and the bouncing of basket balls on the floor coming from the empty women's gymnasium next door. What is even weirder is the sound of feet on the roof. Is there a ghostly basket ball game going on in the women's gym and are some ghostly fans are trying to get a better view from the roof?

The ghostly figure of a man or teenager running laps around the track at the stadium at Pioneer High School at Whittier will often disappears into thin air when people approach him.

Years ago a number of children were killed in a bus accident and apparently buried in Rose Hill Cemetery in Whittier. I say apparently because if they were buried anywhere else, why are they said to be haunting that cemetery?

The restroom in the 100 building at Whittier's St. Paul High School is haunted. When people are alone in the restroom, sometimes one or more taps will turn on by themselves. Then, at other times, the stall doors open and close by themselves or do they? The place is haunted by something unseen! Right?

Turnbull Canyon Road at Whittier has several strange stories told about it. Human like shadows lurking in the roadside bushes have been reported. At a certain section of the road, something unseen will seemingly push your car up a slight rise if you leave it in neutral. Some have heard a knocking noise coming from under their car but that could be something mechanical. May be! To add to the eerie mix, satanic cult activities and UFOs have been reported in the area. That is a good place to stay away from at night but you probably won't listen to me.

A ghost named George haunts the Whittier High School Auditorium, in particular the Green Room downstairs. He supposedly hung himself by accident in the auditorium and still likes to hang around the place.

The Women's Club on California Avenue in Whittier has a bit sad and perhaps lonely spirit that patrons feel holding their hands and brushing again them.

WILMINGTON

Ghosts of Civil War Generals apparently think that war is still on. Their spirits have been spotted in one room of the Banning Residence Museum in Wilmington, a district of Los Angeles. They appear to be planning an attack. They are not the only apparitions as the ghosts of some people who used to live there also put in their appearance.

The spirit of a blond, blue-eyed man, the victim of yellow fever or cholera during the Civil War, has been sighted by visitors and maintenance staff at Drum Barracks. The phantom looks confused, wandering around the place before he ups and disappears.

WOODLAND HILLS

A young couple in their final school year in 1969 were brutally murdered in the football bleachers at Taft High School in Woodland Hills, a district in the city of Los Angeles. Their ghosts have been seen at football games. Apparently the ghostly couple like to pull on fans' legs before disappearing into the bleachers.

CHAPTER M
Madera County
CHOWCHILLA

The city of Chowchilla in Madera County is fifteen miles northwest of Madera. The Chowchilla Library used to be a bowling alley that had caught on fire in the kitchen. Unfortunately the cook died in the blaze. Later, when the building was renovated as the library, the ghost of a man in an apron and holding a spatula has been seen standing near the checkout corner where the kitchen used to be. People has also reported seeing a flash of flames and sometimes feeling heat. That must be an interesting library to work in.

They say that many students from Chowchilla High School who passed away for various reasons are still seen at the lockers in the halls, in the cafeteria and the gym as well as other places. Students have said that they feel that someone was always watching them in the classrooms. One ghost, in particular, a girl with long blonde hair called Michelle, will stop students and ask them what time it was before disappearing.

Now at the Chowchilla Minturn Cemetery, visitors at night appear not to be welcomed. Apparitions are said to chase cars on the the dirt road in the cemetery. Then there is an unseen woman who screams and children laughing or crying. Lets not forget the male phantom seen picking up trash around the graves.

RAYMOND

The town of Raymond in Madera County apparently has a haunted fire station that was used seasonally. Off season, when it was closed and no one was inside, the lights came on by themselves. Then there was a door that was found constantly open with no evidence of human activity. Did some fireman, long since passed away, want to keep an eye on the closed station?

Marin County
FAIRFAX

Camp Both, a Girl Scout camp in in Fairfax, was once an Indian reservation until the 1920's when it became a Tuberculosis Hospital. Some of the fixtures such as the sinks are still there. And, apparently, some of the long gone TB Hospital staff and patients. The ghost of a nurse still pushes her medicine cart in the halls and you can apparently hear disembodied moaning and screaming. There has also been sightings of Native American spirits possibly from the Indian Reservation days.

SAN RAFAEL

San Rafael is the county seat of Marin County. "Blue Boy" is the ghost of a student who drowned in a bath tub at the Dominican University in San Rafael. Wet footprints have appeared out of nowhere near the spot where "Blue Boy" is said to hang about.

Mariposa County

I could not find any ghost stories for this County. If you know of any, please email me at jamesfosterrobinson@live.com or jimrobinson@hotmail.com.

Mendocino County
FORT BRAGG

Fort Bragg is located in coastal Mendocino County and is said to be very haunted. Custer and the Seventh Calvary once passed through Fort Bragg and are still seen riding up a steep cliff at Pudding Creek in Fort Bragg. There is a path that heads towards the ocean and then to MacKerricker State Park. The specter of a young lady dressed in mid 18th century clothing approaches people on that trail and asks if they had seen her lover. He apparently died in the Civil War but she is still looking for him.

The Glass Beach Inn in Fort Bragg may have a cursed chair. The woman who owned the Inn apparently advised people that a number of people who sat in the chair have died mysteriously shortly after. I wonder why no one has gotten rid of the chair or does the curse cover that possibility?

Some unseen and probably long dead person hums the same verse over and over and over again several times on different nights in Green Acres Park in Fort Bragg. Some listeners have also reported feeling a strange chill at the same time. The chilling effect is one of the signs that a ghost is out and about.

Some people who have worked in the bar at Fort Bragg's Gold Coast Hotel feel there may be a ghost there. They point to the fact that glasses have moved by themselves on the bar. Maybe a thirsty ghost is trying to get their attention.

The Grey Whale Inn was once the Redwood Hospital and may be haunted by at least two phantoms. A ghostly lady roams around the garden area while the specter of a man appears often in one of the windows.

Mecred County
ATWATER

You can find the city of Atwater on U.S. Route 99 in Mecred County. Castle Air Museum was once part of Castle Air Force Base and houses one of the biggest collections of aircraft in the USA. An old B-29 in which a bomb exploded during a mission killing a crew member is said to be haunted by the ghost of that unfortunate man. He is blamed for the turning of the locked propellers and the landing lights turning on and off by themselves.

MECRED

Merced is, of course, the county seat of, Merced County. Years ago, a skater at Applegate Skate Park tried a fancy trick, fell on his head and broke his neck. Apparently he has not given up trying that fancy trick because his ghost has been seen there a number of times.

They say a terrible accident occurred some years ago at Girl Scouts Island on Yosemite Lake at Mecred. A woman and her daughter went for a boat ride late one night and the boat was sucked into some sort of whirl pool. The daughter drown while the mother survived. The poor woman grieved for years until she passed away. Now, they say, that the mother's spirit enters the girls' tents looking for her long lost daughter. Sometimes she strokes the girls' hair and sings to them.

When a young woman found out her fiancee died during WWII, she jumped off the tower peak on the Tower Theater in Merced killing herself. Since then, theater goers have encountered her in the building asking if they have seen her fiancee. Unfortunately no one has.

There ia another story told about Yosemite Lake, specifically the boat tower. In the 1970's, a mother had let her two children jump off the tower while swimming there. Tragically, both kids drowned after hitting the bottom in shallow water and their bodies were never found. Their mother went there every night thereafter looking for them. She has since died but you can still see her car pull up and a lady in a long, flowing gown gets out, open her arms and cry out for her children.

PACHEO PASS

The Green Man is often seen on in Pacheo Pass on Highway 152 near Mecred between Gilroy and Los Banos, if I am not mistaken. Who is the Green Man you ask? Sit down and I will tell you! From 1975 to 1980, A strange looking man or maybe a ghost dressed in a black cape, with a lime green face and a bald head, a stern look on his face and his arms folded was seen standing beside the southbound lanes day or night. Well, he must have been a ghost. He floated just above the ground!

Modoc County
WEST VALLEY RESERVOIR

The high winds in the spring can made boating on the reservoir dangerous. Several boats have deadly accidents. Now, some boaters claimed that the spirits of the accident victims sometimes hover overhead. Some might think that liquid spirits maybe be responsible for these sighting. But I am not going to check that theory out.

Mono County
BODIE

The ghost town of Bodie is located in the Bodie Hills east of the Sierra Nevada Mountains in Mono County near the community of Bridgeport and is a historical district recognized as a National Historic Landmark. It became a California State Park in 1962. People say that the ghost town is haunted. Unseen spirits can be heard walking up and down the stairs in most if not all the buildings. The ghost of an old woman still rocks in a rocking chair on the porch of the Gregory House working contently on an afghan. When accused of flirting with the master of the Cain House, the Chinese maid apparently killed herself. She loves children but torments teenagers and adults. She smiles at children and likes to appear to them in the upstairs bedroom. Some times, the disembodied music of a music box can be heard coming from the upstairs bedroom. It is a different story for teenagers and adults. Adult staying in the house have seen their bedroom door open, sensed something very cold enter the room and then felt a heavy suffocating pressure on their chests. Others have had the lights turn on by themselves in the bedroom. They would turn them off, get back in bed and something would turn the lights back on.

The Mendocini House in Brodie is said to be haunted by the spirit of a woman and and her children. The children follow visitors around. When rangers open the house in the spring, they are often greeted by the delicious smell of cooked Italian food. Some nights, the sounds of a party have been heard coming from the house but when checked nothing was found. Often the sound of children laughing and playing could be heard coming from outside the building. Of course, when people checked there were no children in sight.

BEWARE! They say that anyone who takes anything as a souvenir from the town will be cursed. How cursed, I do not know. And I am not aiming to find out.

Monterey County
CHUALAR

Chualar in Monterey County is located 10 miles southeast of Salinas. Anyone driving late at night near the end of Chualar Road might be surprised to see a woman walking along the shoulder. If you look back after passing her, she will be nowhere in sight! Be careful in that area! One night, a motorcyclist was riding at the end of the road when he saw the woman. As he passed her, he was thrown from his bike by something unseen, hitting his head on the ground and passing out. When he awoke, he saw a black haired woman standing over him. He blinked and she had just simply disappeared!

JOLON

The small village of Jolon is about 250 miles north of LA in Monterey County. The Mission San Antonio De Padua, is near Jolon and a miliary preserve in a remote spot in a long, dry valley. The ghost of a monk in a cowl is often seen in the courtyard at night and vanishes when approached. An Indian woman, beheaded for betraying her husband with another man, is often seen ridding a galloping horse and as been chased unsuccessfully by MPs in their jeep. Some students from an Archeology class reported seeing a cloud float through a mission arch to a fountain in the garden and then pass through a church door. A seven year old, who died of cancer, was buried at the mission as per her request. Purple violets mysteriously sprung up from her grave and when her mother died, a single white violet grew up in the center of the purple ones.

MONTEREY

The City of Monterey sits on Monterey Bay along the Pacific coast in Monterey County. The Stokes Adobe, a restaurant at 500 Hartnell Street in Monterey, is haunted. When employees lock up at night and head out to the parking lot, the inside lights often come on by themselves. Footsteps are heard in the unoccupied upstairs rooms. A young child can be heard crying in those upstairs rooms. Of course, no living child is up there to make those sounds. That leaves a ghost. Right?

California's first theater located in Monterey is said to be haunted by a ghost called Jack Swan who had built the old wooden pews over a hundred years ago. He often calls down from the attic costume and prop room complementing the actors for a good performance. You can recognize his voice as it sounds like it is coming over a tinny sounding PA system.

When the famous American author, Robert Luis Stevenson, visited Monterey he stayed in a boarding house that now bears his name. The place is haunted by the Lady in Black, the proprietor at the time of Stevenson's visit, who still mourns her grandchildren who died of cholera. She can usually be found in a second floor room that was a nursery.

The Colton Hall Museum is located on Pacific Street, between Jefferson and Madison in Monterey. As it was close to the jail, the second floor balcony was used to hang the condemned. Now they say that you can feel unseen entities watching you. Ghostly footsteps have also been heard coming from that balcony. Then there are the familiar cold spots, which, in this case, move around a lot.

The Naval Postgraduate School at University Circle # M10 in Monterey was once known as Hotel Del Monte. Be aware that visiting is restricted. The ghost of a middle aged man with a well groomed, grey beard, dressed in a neat grey suit had often been seen in the old hotel. He is thought to be a Charles Crocker who now haunts Herrmann Hall, the main building. He may also be responsible for other ghostly happenings such as chairs and trays that moved by themselves in the dining room. An old elevator that could only be operated by someone inside it often went up and down between floors all by itself. No one was inside it. A ghostly form has been spotted near the tower on rainy or foggy nights. Shades of the movie "The Fog!" You can read more about these hauntings in Randall A. Reinstedt's book, "Ghostly Tales and Mysterious Happenings of Old Monterey."

The Royal Presidio Chapel on Church Street in Monterey is also know as the San Carlos Cathedral. Thought the chapel was built in 1770, ghostly activity apparently did not start until the 1920's when a lighted candle began floating in mid air up and down the aisles, in the sanctuary and in front of the alter. The apparition of a priest who died unexpectedly in the 1920's has appeared before people in the church. Even the church bells have rung during the night by unseen hands. The Old Rectory, a two story building next to the Royal Presidio Chapel, has several entities hanging around. They touch people on their backs and turn off desk lamps when they are trying to work. The usual disembodied footsteps have been heard. Curtains moved and rocking chairs rock by themselves. Then there is the unexplained rattling noises heard.

PRUNDALE

The community of Prundale in Monterey County has supposedly experienced a number of accidents on Highway 101 due to the terrible scenes reveal by headlights in a group of trees to people traveling towards San Juan Bautista at night They say that if you flash your lights you will see children with bleeding eyes on the roadside, bodies hanging in the branches, dead animals on the roadside and the "coup de grace" - the horrible witch who is responsible for all this mayhem standing in the middle of the highway. Watch out that you don' hit her!

SALINAS

Salinas is the county seat and the largest municipality of Monterey County. An old stage coach road runs outside of Salinas and through some back roads of King City. Many stories are told about that old road. One tells of the rape and murder of a woman there in the late 1800's or early 1900's. The murderer cut her head off, threw it away and left her body in a field by the road. Now the poor woman holding her head walks down the road. Sometimes she walks the road wearing her head and drivers give her a ride. Imagine their surprise when the car goes by the scene of the crime, the woman vanishes into thin air.

Years ago, a distraught old woman hung herself in the living room of the Market Street House. They say that she, dress in black, now wanders the building trying to get people's attention even to the extent of seemingly choking them. That is what they say.

A long dead teenage girl whose name is thought to be Jennifer has appeared to students at Salinas High Bell Tower asking if they has seen her boyfriend named Adrian. She also asks them to tell him goodbye and disappears in front of the startled students.

SEASIDE

The city of Seaside in Monterey County was once known as East Monterey. The present day California State Monterey Bay was in the past the site of the old army base, Fort Ord. They say that some of the army activities still linger here in the form of disembodied (how I love that word) voices and the sound of breathing. The old officers quarters as well as the military prison are said to be haunted but no details are available at this time.

SOLEDAD

The Los Coches Inn in Soledad, another city in Monterey County, has the ghost of a very eccentric woman dressed in black roaming the grounds of the Inn. Have you noticed that most female ghosts wear either black or white? Besides her, they say that you can hear the screams of dead miners coming from an abandoned well on the property. Don't ask me what they were doing down there in the first place.

SPRECKELS

Spreckels is an interesting name of a community in the Salinas Valley of Monterey County. An old brick warehouse by the old sugar beat storage silos is haunted. If you go by there late at night you might be entertained by disembodied singing punctuated by screaming coming from that old warehouse.

CHAPTER N
Napa County
CALISTOGA

The bride of the original owner of the Elms B&B in Calistoga, a Napa County city, is still said to appear in the former master bedroom in ghostly form. No one seems to know why. Maybe she just likes it there.

NAPA

The city of Napa is the county seat of Napa County. A ghostly couple has been seen in the Napa Cinedome. You known that they are somewhere around if you sense a cold spot in a certain place in the theater and if you get a weird feeling of someone is watching you when you sit in a certain seat. Maybe you might be sitting in one of the couple's lap.

Nevada County
GRASS VALLEY

The city of Grass Valley in Nevada County was originally known as Centreville. The now rebuild Jack in the Box was said to have been haunted by a ghost named the Miner. He was blamed for the turning off of the drive-through soda fountain when the place was busy. After the place was shut down and locked, staff often heard children's laughter coming from inside the empty lobby. Toys left on the tables were moved by unseen hands or just disappeared. People seeing their reflections in the glass windows often saw what looked like a person standing behind them, but none was there when they looked. Was it the Miner standing there? The disembodied sounds of children's laughter in the vacant lobby reminds me of when I was a teacher and stayed late at the school. I often heard children running and laughing in the halls even though no one was there.

The North Star Mine Lodge in Grass Valley was a Christian boarding school from the 1960's until the mid 80's. During that time a ghost apparently kept things lively for the staff and students. Pictures kept flying off the wall and doors and windows opened and closed all by themselves. Often it got colder when these things happened. I wonder if the same thing is still happening there.

The Holbrooke Hotel in Grass Valley in Nevada County, built in the 1800's, has had many guests such as presidents and actors. Don't tell anyone but at one time it was a brothel. The downstairs reception hall is haunted by ghostly revelers who turn the lights off and on, and drag chairs across the floor. They say you can hear their phantom voices in the hall when it is empty of the living. The hotel dining room was named after Arletta Douglas. She apparently liked it so much her ghost haunts the room.

NEVADA CITY

Nevada City, the county seat of Nevada County, has in the past been known by several names - Nevada, Deer Creek Dry Diggins, and Caldwell's Upper Store. The National Hotel was built in the late 1800's and recently restored except for the left wing. Miners and tourists now come looking for the ghosts that are said to haunt that left wing. If you go into the left wing, you may experience creepy sensations, cold spots and watch in morbid fascination as the light flicker all by themselves.

TRUCKEE

Brickeltown was the name of Truckee before it was renamed in 1868. The old Star Hotel was closed down some years ago. Then passersby began to see people inside the locked building who disappeared in front of their eyes. Lighst were also seen inside the building at night when it was supposed to be locked and empty. There is a business there now and I wonder if they have had any problems with disappearing people?

Richardson House, a two-story Victorian in Truckee, welcome guests who don't mind a rumored ghost. One of the wives of original owner, Warren Richardson, likes to float through the rooms and a specter with long dark hair has been seen passing by guests' bed as they wake up in the morning. Her visitations make for an interesting stay.

Donner State Park, 12593 Donner Pass Road near Truckee was the scene of a terrible tragedy. A party of settlers led by a Mr. Donner tried to cross the pass in that area in late fall in 1847 and became trapped by snow. Some tried to survive by eating their dead companions. Very gruesome! They say that Donner's spirit is forced to roam the present state park. You will know it is him when you see a glowing, yellowish, transparent figure floating a few inches off the ground at night. Don't Worry! I do not think he could eat you.

CHAPTER O
Orange County
ANAHEIM

They say that the Anaheim Fairfield Inn By Marriott has two ghostly guests, who had been killed in a car accident on the freeway next to the building. Why they chose to haunt the motel instead of the freeway is anyone's guess. Maybe they thought it was better than hanging in all that freeway traffic.

The theater and auditorium at Anaheim High School may also be haunted but by who? It is not known. Mysterious footsteps have been heard up on the empty roof while disembodied voices and laughter have resounded in the auditorium.

Chain Reaction used to be a biker's bar and a Mexican restaurant before it became a club. It is said that years ago a bum was found dead in the back alley and there were supposedly many stabbings in the biker's bar. One of the dead still hangs out there. It is possibly the dead bum as disembodied laughter and voices have been heard late at night in that alley and in the washrooms.

The spirit of a little girl may be responsible for all the strange antics happening at Anaheim's Kmart on Euclid Street after it is closed. The little girl spotted in store is called either Isa or Isabel and is blamed for stock falling off the shelves by itself.

The Performing Arts Building used to a seniors' home and may still have some senior residents in ghostly form hanging around the joint. Many people have experienced cold spots, the weird feeling of being followed by some unseen presence as well as mysterious whistles and footsteps, all on the second floor.

Disneyland in Anaheim has thousands of visitors every day and a number of unwanted spectral guests. Many stories are told about these ghostly intruders. Here are a few of them.

A 19th century photo of young woman sitting on a shelf in the Christmas Store is said to have disturbed some of the stocking crew when they are working at night. Usually the girl in the picture has a straight face but then there are other times people swear that they have seen her frowning. At those times, a strange wind seems to blow through the store. Just vivid imaginations? I wonder?

Late at night and in the early morning, a tall man that looks like Walt Disney himself has been spotted walking around the Disney Gallery above the Pirates of the Caribbean. Many believe it is Old Walt. I almost forgot to mention that many visitors have complained of cold spots in the Gallery.

The second floor of Disney Land's Fire Station is empty and closed to the public. Yet, at night, someone or something knocks on the inside of the door to that floor and footsteps have been heard coming from that empty area. Some think it might be Walt again as the area used to be a fully furnished apartment for him to stay in when he visited the park.

The Haunted Museum at Disneyland is all about haunted things but somethings there are for real, such as at least three ghosts appearing there. They are the spirits of an elderly woman and man both of whom died of a heart attack in 1970 and a young man who thinks he is funny. In addition, some feel there is a nasty something in the attic. Apparently you can feel it just before your car heads out into the graveyard. People, while riding in a supposedly empty car through the Crypt, have had their hair pulled by an invisible someone or something. Others have had the back of their hand touched, again by someone or something unseen, spotted people walking up the Portrait Hall or Grand Staircase only to see them stop and disappear into thin air. Others have seen faces peer around the corner at the top of the Grand Staircase, heard phantom foot falls on the false floor behind the loading area, saw a man who was not there reflected in a mirror by the exit and experienced the frightening sensation of unseen hands touching their faces. Maybe there is more to Disney magic then we thought.

In It's a Small World there has been a problem with the dolls moving about when there was no power turned on. Then the lights seem to go off and on by themselves. You think it might be just electrical problems or maybe another ghost?

Some years ago, a woman named Dolly died when she fell out of her sled on Matterhorn Mountain and was crushed by the sled behind hers. Now she supposedly haunts the mountain. Have you seen her?

The Pirates of the Caribbean ride operators have spotted on the video monitors a young boy riding one of the boats late at night. They find no one there when they check the boat out. They say it is the ghost of a young boy who died from cancer. His last wish was to be cremated and his ashes be spread over the Pirate ride which he loved. Disney Park would not allow it because of health concerns but his mother secretly spread his ashes. Now the boy rides his favorite ride for ever!

Back in the 1970's, a male guest died on the Space Mountain ride. He is still riding it apparently. The large man with reddish hair and face is known as Mr. One-Way. He is often spotted getting into cars that have only one passenger. At the end of the ride, he is nowhere in sight. He is also known to hang around the women employees' locker rooms.

It is said that some years ago a young man died on the old People Mover Ride on Grad night. He had foolishly jumped out of the cabin and was dragged beneath the car. The poor boy tried to save himself by grabbing the long blonde hair of his girlfriend. Even, to day, it is claimed by some that he is still trying to save himself by grabbing at girls' long hair while they are on the ride.

At least three young men have drowned on different Grad Nights in the Rivers of America. Now people see several ghosts, thought to be these boys, wandering around Tom Sawyers

Island.

I wonder what menacing presence might be lurking at Tomorrow Land as people have reported feeling something strange there as well as the ubiquitous cold spots.

BLACK STAR CANYON

Many mysterious things have been reported to happen in Black Star Canyon which runs from the Santa Ana Mountains down into eastern Orange County. Now as to the strangeness. A giant crow that utters unearthly calls and flapping its huge wings with a strange swooshing sound has been seen in the area. It is often accompanied by a strong wind out of nowhere. A bullet proof small cottontail has also been spotted and shot almost point blank with little or no visible effect. A formation of all black creatures about two feet high were seen at least once marching up and down the side of the canyon. They were also accompanied by a strong wind out of nowhere. Visitors seem to have trouble at times starting perfectly good autos. The strange phenomena has been blamed on the massacres of Indian tribes living in the canyon by Spanish Conquistadors. The spirits of the dead Indians have been seen walking the creek or riding along the canyon rims before disappearing. Many visitors have felt a presence and in some case heard it as it paralleled them on the trail they were hiking. Chants, howls and screams have echoed through the canyon at night. If you plan to visit the canyon, you would be wise to check with the Orange County Sheriff's office before going there.

BREA

The city of Brea in Orange County has several ghostly denizens. Late at night, frozen food takes to flying across the room all by itself at Brea's Best followed fifteen minutes later by disembodied laughter. Weird shadows are often spotted moving on the walls. It seems that an invisible someone is playing pranks on the staff. At the Performing Arts Center in Brea Olinda High School, the ghostly form of man sometimes stands on the stage and stares at people. He sometimes help the staff by putting the seats back down after they had cleaned under them. Then there are the strange noises heard late at night in the auditorium.

BUENA PARK

Knott's Berry Farm in Buena Park in northwestern Orange County is said to be home to at least two or more restless spirits. Cries and noises have been heard coming from the Camp Snoopy's Peanuts Playhouse even when empty. People have complained of chills and the feeling of someone unseen following them. The lights would go off and on by themselves even if there was no power to them. A maintenance man fell to his death some years ago at the Kingdom of the Dinosaurs Ride. Now he apparently haunts the ride. The spirit of a young boy is often seen in the Ice Age area but at this time it is not known who he is or why he is still there. They say that in the early 1980's a distraught young man killed himself by jumping off the Parachute Ride. The ride is closed but the structure remains. People have heard the sound of a heavy object striking the ground but found nothing when they checked the area. This is what you might call an audible ghostly reenactment of his jump and subsequent thump.

COSTA MESA

They say that there is a female phantom who screeches at night behind the Back Bay School in Costa Mesa in Orange County. No one seems to know why she does that and I am sure not going to ask her! Something lurks in Estancia High School in Costa Mesa. It touches people, emits a strange smell and shine a flashlight beam in empty hallways at night. Faculty and cleaning staff, they say, are none to happy with this invisible presence. I do not blame them. Do you?

CYPRESS

Cypress is a small suburban city in the northern region of Orange County. The Photo Department of Cypress College has a benevolent spirit by the unlikely name of Photy. He hangs around one of the photo enlarger in the main darkroom often in the form of a light outline. He has been known to shake pictures on the wall in the photo-finishing room. Now, when he is around, students say that they experience a feeling of calm and well being. Apparently, earlier in his career, he was a bit upset and was blamed for faulty meter readings, exploding equipment and mistakes in film development. There is, of course, an explanation for his presence. And here it is. A human skull with a bullet hole was brought into the studio and photographed. That was when all the fun started. Apparently the previous owner of the skull did not like having his picture taken. He started pounding on the stock room door. The rest is ghoulish history.

A student was up in the attic of the Performing Arts Building at Cypress High School to get some equipment when she fell through the floor boards to her untimely death. Now her ghost haunts the place. Staff and students going into that attic claim that they get an eerie feeling that they are being watch. Of course, no one alive is around there. Often she was seen in a prop that was used for outplays. And she looked real angry!

FOUNTAIN VALLEY

Fountain Valley High School is yet another institute of learning that apparently has problems with unwanted spectral visitors. The screams of children are often heard at night coming from the darken interior of 100 Building. Often, when janitors enter the locked building, they find lockers open and their contents strewn about the floors. It is thought to be the work of an unknown poltergeist. But what about the reports of visions of mutilated dead students in the bathrooms? Something weird may be happening in that school.

The James H. Cox Elementary School in Fountain Valley seems to also be having paranormal problems if the stories are true. After 9:00 PM, the sounds of dogs barking can be heard coming from inside. Other weird things that happen include the appearance of dead cats on the grounds, human like shapes spotted in the windows late at night, interference on cell phones and radios near and in the building and the usual eerie feeling of being watched.

FULLERTON

The city of Fulleron is found in northern Orange County. The specter of a moaning old man with a cane has been spotted in Albertsons. He stares at people before fading away. He has been blamed for the mess workers find in the morning. Somehow during the night, cans of food fell off the shelves and splattered on the floor. They say that if you are in Cal State Fullerton dormitory at about 2:00 am, you might be witness to small, greening glowing balls roaming the building. Strange tapping, voices and clattering noises have been heard on walls of adjoining empty rooms. Many have experience the common ghostly phenomena of someone unseen watching them! The old Melody Inn, destroyed by fire years ago, sat on the southeast corner of Harbor and Commonwealth in Fullerton. Apparently the ghost of the former owner's father appears with a match box in hand and offers passersby a light for their cigarette. Then he smiles and vanishes into thin air. I wonder if the cigarette stayed lit?

The old Fox Theatre building in Fullerton is said to have a ghost guarding the kids in the neighborhood from violence. He is Michael O'Donnell, who, though he had a hard life and problems with drinking, loved the kids in the neighborhood and helped them where he could. He can often be seen in the theater lobby, standing against a wall reading a book. Beware all perpetrators who seek to harm children in that area, Michael O'Donnell is protecting them. I do not think you want to tangle with a ghost. Remember Patrick Swazee in the movie "Ghost"?

The Phi Kappa Tau Fraternity House is home to the ghost of a little girl found murdered in a ravine beside the house. Her laughter sometimes rings through the building on hot summer afternoons. She wanders the Fraternity House at night having fun opening and closing cabinet doors, flicking the lights off and on and playing with the water taps.

There are tunnels running under Fullerton that are apparently accessible from Plummer Auditorium and other places as well. Locals say that there are numerous ghosts from various eras down there. One well known phantom, a soldier from WWII, will follow you to the exit before he vanishes. Maybe he just wants to make sure you are safely out of his spectral domain.

A place in Fullerton called Ralph's Store is said to have the famous cold spots and the phenomena of boxes moving around the store on their own. Maybe there are some ghosts looking for a job. If the place is haunted, it might be a great draw for customers.

The cellar at Stadium Tavern has a ghost that has been seen by workers cleaning up after the place is closed. It often calls out their names. Someone playing a practical joke? I am not going to get a job there to find out. I will take the workers' word for it!

A paranormal investigation was done recently by the Valley Investigators of the Paranormal at the Cellar, 446 Clovis Avenue in Fullerton. They found that the place was apparently haunted! One investigator was touched by a hand on the end of an arm that projected out of a wall. Someone or something unseen also tried to pull a piece of investigative equipment from the hands of another member of the team. Some sort of male presence was found to be hanging around the female restroom. What is this with male entities hanging around ladies washrooms?

GARDEN GROVE

Garden Grove High School in Garden Grove, a city in northern Orange County, has the pleasure of having Lizzy, a female ghost, haunt the Heritage Hall in the E building. She was apparently killed when part of the building fell on her during the 1933 earthquake. I think she is still a bit upset by fact that she slams doors, trips alarms, pushes and trips people and has put in public appearances at night.

The Midnight Adult Books was once a nightclub where a man was stabbed to death when a drug deal went south. He is thought to be the man in a cowboy hat seen entering occupied viewing booths and disappearing. Strange noises are heard at night while objects fall off shelves, seeming all by themselves. Could the shadowy shapes often seen be the cause?

The Stanley-Ware House at 12174 Euclid Avenue in Garden Grove's Heritage Park may be certifiably haunted. A ghost has appeared to a staff member one night and advised him not to take any "Bull sh--!" The spector of an old man in clothes from the 1920-40 era often likes to watch rehearsals in the Heritage Barn Theater but disappears when approached. Strange bolts of lightning have appeared over the heads of the actors in pictures taken of plays. The cries of an invisible baby have been heard coming from the upstairs nursery in the Stanley House Museum. Visitors are often spooked by two portraits in the Museum. One is the solemn portrait of J.G. Handler which often smiles at people. The other picture is that of an unknown man. People are shocked when they see that he appears to be bleeding at the throat. Closer investigation shows tiny beads of blood forming just above his collar spreading out into a thin red line along his throat. Optical allusion or something else entirely different? Psychic investigators have checked the place out and seem to agree that the site is haunted.

HUNTINGTON BEACH

The city of Huntington Beach is by the ocean in Orange County. There is the phantom of a preteen boy, all dress in white of course like a good ghost should, that appears near an old bomb shelter. As soon as someone sees him, he takes off around a corner and vanishes into thin air. No one knows who he is or why he has not gone to the light.

If you happen to drive by Edison High School on Magnolia Street in Huntington Beach do not be surprised if you see mysterious lights dancing around the baseball field. And you might spy apparitions of people hanging around the back soccer field. Inside the school in the early morning is when apparently some ghosts stir. Lockers in the boy's locker room bang and rattle while showers turn on and off by themselves.

Ethel Dwyer Middle School is said to be haunted, of course, by, wait for it! - YES! - by Ethel Dwyer. She was a student, then a teacher at the school before she passed away. Late at night, lights are often seen in the school and strange sounds resound from the boiler room.

They say that George was a young man who, during a play in the auditorium, hung himself.

Any play performed there is apparently jinxed by George if certain conditions are not met. A paper signed by the play's performers must be put where his hanging rope is supposedly or else! Do not remove the rope or else the next play will suffer ruination. Apparently some performers did not pay attention and they lost their voices, forgot their lines and suffered minor accidents when sets toppled and lights fell. Oh and nooses that were used in plays always came undone all by themselves, or so they say!

IRVINE

In the 1970's, a talented drama student at the Irvine High School in Orange County died suddenly. Now his friendly ghost lingers in the school theater, sitting in the center seats. He is easy to recognize as he appears as a faintly glowing green area.

A previous now passed away oriental resident must have like living at the Orange Tree patio homes. He is often seen around 10:30 AM practicing golf swings, walking near the pool and taking a stoll with his spectral dog.

If you drive alone along Campus Drive on the University of California Irvine at night, your car may stall. If so, do not be surprised to see a woman standing at your car window. And do not be surprised if she asks you with out moving her lips for you to help her look for her daughter. You apparently hear her voice in your head. They say it is no use refusing as she will simply appear beside you in the passenger seat. I do not know what happens after that and I do not want to not want to find out myself. But tell me if you know. I do know her story. Her daughter was raped and killed and the woman very distraught started walking down Campus Drive to look for her. They say that the woman was never seen alive again.

Be careful if you happen to be in the Woodbridge High School in Irvine when a large black apparition puts in an appearance. If you do not run away immediately, the thing gets angry and starts throwing trash cans around. Maybe it thinks you will clean it all up? Right!

LAGUNA HILLS

The city of Laguna Hills is located in southern Orange County. At Top of the World School, the apparition of a little girl who died from hypothermia sitting on the swings all night can still be seen and heard in the playground. She had run away from her parents fighting at home.

LAGUNA WOODS

The ghost called Bud is said to haunt the Leisure World Theater in Laguna Woods. Staff in the offices below the film booth have heard footsteps overhead coming from the supposedly empty booth. During shows, technicians have felt like someone invisible was looking over their shoulders. Bud is thought to be a man who worked in Leisure World as its first technician the the mid 1960's.

LA HABRA

When you go back towards the hills in Esteli Park in La Habra, a city in the northwestern corner of Orange County, you might experience some strange things. Others have! They have heard disembodied voices, loud whooshing noises and found animal tracks with seven claws. You also might experience strong feelings of fear and not being welcomed. Some have reported seeing incredibly fast creatures with spikes on their backs emitting high pitched growls. Some also say that dark clouds will gather overhead and follow you until you leave the park. Hard to believe! But I, for one, am not going to see if it is true or not true.

Before the Friendly Hills Medical Group building was torn down and standing empty, security guards had to contend with disembodied voice in the empty hallways, the sounds of heart monitoring machines in the cardiac room, toilets that were flushed by unseen hands and a bunch of cold spots. Plus someone or something made them feel that they were not welcomed. Maybe the dead did not like being disturbed.

I am a little confused about the stories told about the La Habra Depot Theater and an Amtrac Train used as a dressing room. The stories say that loud footsteps could be heard in the theater when it was empty. And it seems that loud banging noises were heard coming from the Amtrac train. The ghost of a young girl has been spotted peeking around a wall, while the image of a Victorian couple appears in a mirror. Do you know anything about any of this?

Something ghostly may be happening at Serria Valley School. People wandering near the school late at night have reported being chased by something unknown and that "ghostly things" have been seen near the classrooms and in the back of the school. The swings supposedly start to swing by themselves and all sorts of creaking noises are heard in the area. Then there is the spirit of a little girl seen often in the one of the girls' washrooms. Just your usual spirits having a little fun?

LAKE FOREST

I am also not too sure of the reports of unease, EVP recorded by ghost hunters plus some photos taken in a room on the ground floor of the Best Western Hotel in Lake Forest and cold spots in the room's kitchen alcove. Haunted? Maybe. But remember that reality is often in the mind of the beholder. Sorry. That is a lousy paraphrase.

NEWPORT

The city of Newport is ten miles south of downtown Santa Ana in Orange County. Balboa Island is one of three artifical islands in Newport Beach Harbor. Two kids drowned off the island in a rip tide in 1993. Since then people have reported seeing flashes of light beneath the waves and have heard some mysterious sounds. Are the ghosts of those two children still trying to get help?

The ghost of a woman is said to haunt an apartment on the first floor of the M building in the Coronado Apartments. The kitchen seems to be the focus of the phenomena. Phantom music and muffled voices have been coming from the area. Someone unseen opens cabinet doors and turns lights on and off. Some feel that she may be the person who was killed in the apartment some time ago. But that is puzzling as the full body apparition that has appeared was dressed in clothes that were popular before the apartments were built.

In the 1990's, three boys, who had been drinking, snuck into Robins Hall at Newport Harbor School and were fooling around on the stage when two of them fell on their heads on the gym floor killing themselves. The third boy fled and told no one. The police later found the dead boys. Now the two dead boys are still wondering where their friend went. They say that at night you call hear they calling "Where is he? Is he here?" At those times, even though all the windows are closed, there is a cold wind blowing.

John Wayne's boat, the Wild goose, is or was docked in Newport Harbor. Harbor staff and passersby have seen Wayne's ghost on the decks of his beloved "Wild Goose" walking or waving at people.

ORANGE

The U.S.. Naval Weapons Station Seal Beach was built over an old Indian Burial ground and the historical site of an early 1800's seaport, Anaheim Landing. Around 1900, it was a public beach and boardwalk and the Bolsa Chica wetlands and marsh areas are partially with in its boundaries. Why am I telling you all this? Read on and you will understand. The place is haunted by all sorts of spirits, ghosts and phenomena. Spectral Indians wander the area. Strange shadows are often seen moving about at night. Someone unseen turns lights in the complex off and on while disembodied footsteps follow security guards. Late at night, ghostly knocks are heard on security vehicles. Strange whispering can also be heard there. Apparently nature spirits such as a water diva are getting in on the act. Other ghosts have been creeping around the site and spine tingling moans and bloodcurdling scream have rend the darkness.

They say that a young teenage ago killed herself about thirty years in the girls bathroom of the Theater at Orange High School. Many feel that the tormented spirit of that young girl is still there. The bathroom door usually is slow to closed but, often, something unseen slams it shut. The lights in the theater seemingly shut off and on by themselves or is it the ghost doing it. When people are alone in the theater, they often feel the very air thickening and then a cold wind seems to be blowing towards them. Of course no one is there, alive at least!

A woman dressed all in white is said to haunt the Holy Sepulcher Cemetery at 7845 East Santiago Canyon Road. She roams the ground but rests in one particular spot. A lit candle which does not flicker and seems to change color and shape is often seen seen all night and is not extinguished by any wind. Its shape would transform from a complete circle to a half circle to a tear drop shape and back to a complete circle.

The La Verta train tracks in Orange County is haunted by a hostile phantom who, when he was around twenty years old, was killed in the 1940's in an accident by the tracks. People walking by the tracks at the location of his tragic demise have heard disembodied whispering. One victim says he heard the mysterious whisperer say "I see you!" Many have experienced strange rushes of air as if someone had just dashed past them as well as cold spots. The angry spirit has also been seen and seemed to be wearing clothes from around 1950's. The ghost hangs out in a very small territory in a narrow passageway between two buildings and a nearby dumpster. He apparently does not like visitors and will slam the open lid of the dumpster shut if anyone dares to come near him.

PLACENTIA

The Girls' Bathroom in Crook Park in the city of Placentia in northern Orange County is haunted by the spirit of a girl who was raped and killed by an unknown person. They say that every afternoon she stirs things up by turning lights on and off (or is then on?) and scaring passersby with chilling disembodied screams!

Late night joggers in Tri-City Park in Placentia have heard what sounded like an old lady's voice screaming for her lost children. They also observed what looked like someone invisible walking through the water in a pond.

SAN CLEMENTE

Something strange has been seen at San Clemente's Shore Cliffs Golf Course. Images have been observed of what appears to be children floating through the walls of sewer pipes and often walking in some tunnels on the course. Then there are the mysterious sounds of laughter, crying of people as well as growling, snarling and whimpering of invisible animals fighting and dying.

The very faint specter of a Native American woman is often seen in the brush in the morning and very late afternoon between the par 5 uphill tee and fairway apron of the Talega Golf course in San Clemente.

A surfer was killed while trying to cross the train tracks at Cottons in San Clemente to get to the water. Blood from the terrible accident some times reappears on the tracks. The ghost of the surfer has also been credited with saving the lives of other surfers who got into trouble in the waves off the train tracks.

SAN JUAN CAPRISTRANO

The city of San Juan Capistrano is about 23 miles southeast of downtown Santa Ana in southern Orange County.

The El Adobe de Capistrano Restaurant building was originally two separate structures. The northern half, the Miguel Yorba Adobe, was a private residence while the south half was a jail and court house. When the two buildings were joined to make the present building, the jail became a wine cellar. Employees of the restaurant working down there felt that they are being watched by someone unseen. In addition, the phantom of a headless monk often strolls the street outside the restaurant. An evening at the restaurant could be exciting!

The two room Montanez Adobe can be found on a side street across from Mission SJC. You may easily be able to identify it by a ball of light that often appears in the living room.

Some think it is the ghost of a previous owner, Dona Polonia Montanez, who taught local children there.

A large, old pepper tree On Rios Street is where the White Lady of Capistrano has often been seen when she is not walking Rios Street. She often has the company of several other ghostly ladies. One of her friends is known as the Phantom of Del Obispo (or the Del Obispo White Lady) and is accompanied herself by a black dog. The Del Obispo White Lady was Dona Bernadino before she passed away and was either a healer or bruja (Spanish for witch). Railway tracks run through the historical Los Rios Street area and other ghostly figures have been known to walk that area.

They say that if you go to the railway tracks in Old Town San Juan in San Juan Capistrano, look for a lone drinking fountain. You just might see the spirit of a woman in white kneeling in prayer there. She will rise slowly, turn and flow towards you before disappearing. That is what they say.

There is a memorial to an Indian girl in the cemetery at the San Juan Capistrano Mission. At this time I have no information as to who she was or why there is a memorial. Her ghost has been seen at her memorial. The small cemetery is very crowed with graves and it is not surprising that ghostly shadows roam the area and that the disembodied voices of crying children are often heard.

SANTA ANA
Santa Ana is the county seat and most populous city in Orange County.

There is a story that a man died in the boy's locker room at Costa Mesa High School in Santa Ana and his ghost supposedly hangs out there. Little else is known or told about this haunting.

A lot of stories are told about a now torn down place at the corner of Hazzard and Euclid. The place was supposed to be haunted by multiple victims of gang shootings. Some claim that the place was built on an old Native American burial ground and that the spirits of the dead came out at night and chased people out of the premises.

Now, I do not know if this is true but people claim that a large man can be seen floating around the boiler room of a place called Ralph's Grocery Company. Ralph or who ever owns the building, please let me know if the story is false and I will remove it from the book. I would also like to know if it is true.

Alice, a young female student actress at Santa Ana High School, died when she fell from a balcony before the play opened in the auditorium. They say that the sounds of someone walking around and making knocking noises came be heard coming from the auditorium's attic. The story also relates that a sort of good luck charm appears on the floor just before the opening act starts. The good luck charm disappears when the play is over.

In the early 1970's, a little girl's body was found in the back of the Sports Authority store. Now her ghost is often see walking through the place and is heard giggling when the premises is closed at night. Many people in the store feel that they are being watched by someone unseen. Does the spirit of that murdered girl watch over the store?

STANTON
Some people say that the city of Stanton in western Orange County has a possible poltergeist at the Stanton Industrial Complex. This malicious creature rips up ceilings, punches holes in pictures, throws plastic sheeting and knives at people, mutilated one person's dolls. A TV set flew off a wall while others go off and on by themselves. Cups have flown out of opened cabinets and people have felt tugs on their clothes. The sounds of someone sawing wood have been heard in an empty apartment. Sure sounds like poltergeist to me!

TUSTIN
The apparition of a little boy throwing marbles and the ghost of a lady all dressed in white have startled passersby on Mitchel Avenue in the city of Tustin. Who the kid and woman are is not known at this time.

WESTMINSTER
Apparitions of cowboys or country folk from lone ago have been spotted in the Country Harvest Buffet or around the shopping center in Orange County city of Westminster. Any one have any idea who they might be and why they have not gone into the light?

CHAPTER P,Q
Placer County
LINCOLN

There is something strange, and I mean more than usual for a cemetery, at the 18th century Manzanita Cemetery in Lincoln in Placer Country. Besides the dark shadows that seem to roam the site and the strange sounds that erupt around dusk and last until dawn, an interesting incident occurred some years ago. Firemen were fighting a local wild fire that burnt up to the back of the cemetery. The firemen were surprised when the fire burnt all around the edge of the graveyard but touched nothing inside it. Are there some fire fighters from long ago buried there?

I hate it when I have only a small tidbit of a ghost story! There is the ghost of a four year old boy on some sort of a big wheel bike seen a few times in Teal Hollow near or in Placer. That is it! Do you have any information on this ghost story?

ROCKLIN

Ghosts of play writers from twenty years ago are said to still haunt Finn Hall, a playhouse, in the city of Rocklin in Placer County.

A ghost called Billy hangs around the Rocklin High School theater. Students and teachers one night were touching up paint on the theater's wall when the word "Help" appeared on an unpainted section of the wall. In another incident, a student found a cell phone and locked it in a cupboard for three days. On the third day, he heard it ringing but was now able to retrieve it in time. To see who called he punched *69 and called the person back. He was very surprised when the person who answered claimed that his cell phoned had called her phone the day before and that she had not called just minutes before. Who was doing the calling? Was is it Billy? Was he trying to call for help?

ROSEVILLE

A ghost named Mac is blamed for a number of accidents in the theater at Wood Creek High School Roseville in Placer County. Light fixtures have fallen from the ceiling. Doors in the theater have locked all by themselves and someone or something unseen keeps tripping actors backstage. Maybe Mac is or was a wannabe actor.

Plumas County
KEDDIE

Eddie Resort in the community of Keddie was the scene of an unsolved murder years ago. Cabin # 28 where the murder took place, visitors experienced chairs moving by themselves and other unrelated phenomena as well as some sort of mysterious writing appearing on the walls. Cabin # 28 was supposedly torn down before 2003 but some people say it still exists. If you know either way about the cabin or anything more about the haunting, and indeed any haunting, please email me at jimrobinson@hotmail.com.

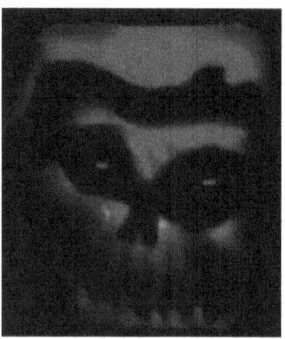

CHAPTER R
Riverside County
BANNING

Payless Shoe Source in Banning in Riverside County apparently has the specter of a little boy who keeps showing up in the break room in the back of the store. Urban Legend has it that when the boy was refused a new pair of shoes in the store by his mother, he got angry and ran out of the store right into the path of an automobile and died. Now the angry little boy is doomed to appear right before the store's opening and closing. Let that be lesson to all you little boys and girls of all ages who get angry when you do not get what you want. You may end up just like that doomed little boy!

Sunnyslope Cemetery in the city of Beaumont in the Greater Los Angles area of Riverside Country has some serious paranormal activity. There is the usual cold spots, unexplained noises, and eerie feelings as well as touching by unseen person or things. People alone in the graveyard have reported seeing what they thought was a groundskeeper but he would disappear into a shed and never come out. When the witness checked the shed he was not in it. He seemed to have disappeared into thin air!

CATHEDRAL CITY

A young man wounded in a drive by shooting in the Riverside County's Cathedral City ran into a nearby vacant lot. He died later in the hospital. People living in the house next to the vacant lot began to hear banging noises on the outside wall facing the vacant lot. The faint cries of a man in pain could also be heard but when they checked outside no one was there.

CORONA

The city of Corona in Riverside County has a haunted Gravity Hill. Do not know what a Gravity Hill is? It is supposedly a spot in the road where if you stop on the road facing up the hill and put your car in neutral, it will roll up the hill. Corona's Gravity Hill is haunted by a distraught girl who had been dumped by her boyfriend and had driven too fast and crashed at that spot. They say that her ghost pushes your car uphill and that, if you car is dirty, she will leave hand prints.

If you go into Horse Thieves Canyon Road, you may experience things that you not want to. Travelers on this road have reported that their eyes seemed to burn, felt dizzy and the eerie feeling of something pulling them towards a wooded area. Hikers camping in that woods have encountered floating black apparitions that do not like flashlights as they reportedly push and kick those who have them turned on. These phantoms also kick up dust and make strange noises. Then there is the spirit of a blonde woman that runs between trails in another part of the woods. Finally, hikers have experienced very cold breezes from out of nowhere at certain spots on the trails.

J J Live Oak Steakhouse in Corona used to be known as El Cerrito - Live Oak Inn. In 1988, Michelle, a young waitress was murdered and her body dumped in the trunk of an old car behind the Inn. Michelle haunts the site of her tragic death. She is apparently a nice but shy ghost. The only complaint peopole have about her is that she used to continually flush toilets just before closing time. In 2004, she stopped flushing toilets and has started ringing the food bell at all hours. Disconnected shadows are often seen in the place and a man in black is often seen walking around the building. One more macabre detail - an old tree in the front yard was used to hang people. They say that the hanging rope can still be seen even though the tree has grown mostly around it.

There are many stories of ghostly goings on at Marie Callender's in Corona. Things fly off shelves and sail across the room. Trays are flung at servers's heads by unseen hands in the dishwashing area. Strange unidentified sounds are often heard. Balloons float out of nowhere. TV's turn off and on by themselves. Empty salt and peppers shakers miraculously fill themselves. These are just a few of the ghostly things...

HEMET

The city of Hemet is situated in the San Jacinto Valley in Riverside County. Christine is the resident ghost of the Hemet High School Theatre. She often appears as a white blurry figure wandering around the stage and back stage area. Christine likes to leave messages on walls and on the roof. Why on the roof? I do not know. What did the messages say? Again, I do not know.

The valley surrounding Hemet was cursed in the 1800's by the wife of a man who was shot to death. Anyone born and raised in the valley would be unable to leave. At that time, there was only three ways out of the valley. A fourth way was built later. They say that anyone born and raised there and left through one of the original exits felt overwhelming urges to return. Once they did, they suffered financial losses that prevented them from ever leaving again. However, any that left by the non-cursed fourth exit had no problems and hardly ever returned. I wondered what would have happened if one of those cursed simply tried to walk out the non-cursed exit?

Mysterious lights, accompanied by strange feelings of being electrified, have been spotted in Hemet's Santa Fe Menlo Cemetery. It appears that no one knows what may be causing the phenomena. Do you?

IDYLLWILD

The town of Idyllwild is nestled in the San Jacinto Mountains in Riverside County. McNeale Hall, the main boys dorm at Idyllwild Arts Academy is said to be haunted. Residents and visitors have reported hearing strange, disembodied voices and something or someone unseen running in the halls. Someone or something unseen touches people and moves things around.

INDIO

Indio High School in the city of Indio in Riverside County has at least one ghostly re-enactment. Some teenagers were killed in an auto accident back around 1980. Two of them have been seen by a caretaker sitting in the rain at an old fountain in a garden outside the school. The girl was wearing a prom dress while the boy was wearing a varsity jacket.

When he approached them, he saw a curious thing. Neither of them were wet from the rain. They stood up turning towards the caretaker. Then they vanished!

LAKE ELSINORE

Lake Elsinore or LE as it is also known is a city in western Riverside County and has several ghostly tales attached to it. A freshman hung herself in the back of the theater stage in Elsimore Middle School after being deeply embarrassed in a hazing by the soccer team. People working alone in the theater have heard what sounds like a girl choking. Many feel that the sounds are made by the ghost hanging herself over and over again.

Visitors and possibly staff have felt cold spots near the shelves containing china dolls in the Home Interiors store in Lake Elsinore. The store used to be called the Chimes. Supposedly the spirit of an unfortunate person who drown in a pool on the property has been seen wandering around the basement. Certain spots appear to be cold and very creepy.

There is or was an abandoned hotel on Main Street in Lake Elsinore. Every Saturday night, they say, screams can be heard coming from the boarded up building. A man looking like a janitor has also been spotted on the roof during the early morning.

LA QUINTA

I have found only one ghost story so far in La Quinta, a resort city in Riverside County. Employees at the local Walmart there have told others that they often hear the disembodied laughter of a little girl late at night and that toys fall off the shelves seemingly all by themselves.

MORENO VALLEY

Years ago, a bus full of children broke down on an overpass on Nason Street in the city Moreno Valley in Riverside County. A large truck hit it, pushing it over the side of the over pass. No one survived. Now, they say that if you park your car leaving it in neutral and heading south at the bottom of the overpass, the ghosts of the children will push the car UP the overpass. In addition, small hand prints have been found on some cars. They also say that phantom footsteps and laughter can sometimes be heard there late at night.

There is or was an old hospital off Nason Street in Moreno Valley that they say was changed into a small school for the lower grades. The school was supposedly the scene of a terrible tragedy when a deranged gunman shot and killed all the students and the teacher in sheds out behind the school. Even though the school is closed, a number of people with morbid curiosity have entered it and claimed to have seen the ghosts of the murdered children and heard their dying cries.

Priest Hill in Moreno Valley is another one of those haunted mystery hills. A priest's car apparently broke down there one day and was he was hit and killed by another driver. If you stop your car there, put it in neutral and sprinkle powder (before hand of course and not when the car is stopped, silly) the priest will push your car up the hill and will leave hand prints in the powder.

MURRIETA

The city of Murrieta in southwestern Riverside County has at least two or more ghosts stories. At the Boston Scientific Company building in Murrieta, the ghost of a young girl likes to wander around cubicles in a restricted area of the office. A faucet in the woman's restroom next to the lunchroom turns on and off all by itself. The sound of someone unknown unrolling toilet paper in the last stall can be heard. They say that the product coming out of bio machine in the clean room is thrown through the air by someone or something unseen. To add insult to injury someone unseen keeps blowing in people's ears.

The KEA Milling building was closed up in 2005 by cementing the window and doors. No one is readily able to enter the building and there are no stairs inside. And yet, a teenage girl in a light blue dress is often seen at night sitting on the ledge of the middle top window. If you happen to see her, they say you will perceive a great sadness come over you. Who is she and why she is there, no one seems to know.

Murrieta Valley High School is an example of a ghost story with little information but nevertheless morbidly tantalizing. The specters of children have been seen there and school equipment seems to move about all by itself. Why? Do you know?

PALM DESERT

At the Palm Desert High School in the city of Palm Desert in Riverside County, in the Coachella Valley, approximately 11 miles east of Palm Springs, the ghost of a young girl who drowned in 1990 hangs around the school's pool late at night. Some people feel that she is still trying to fulfill her ambition to be on a swim team again.

RIVERSIDE

Riverside is a city in Riverside County with a very large population of ghosts - at least stories about them. Years ago, a man killed himself at Station 3 at the Alta Vista Convalescing Home. Now his ghost is often seen around Station 3 and is blamed for the call light turning on in an unoccupied room where the resident had just passed away. The heavy medication door at Station 3 also closes by itself. Or does that ghost close it?

At the Villa is an antiques store just north of the Mission Inn at 3563 Main Street. The old building was the original mercantile for the city. A female shop owner at this location was violently killed in a car jacking in the mid 1990's and appears to be still a little upset about it. You know when she is around when you can smell a strong scent of perfume and objects move on their own, often disappearing and reappearing later in a different spot.

The old mission style buildings of Riverside's California Baptist University housed an insane asylum from the early 1900's to the 1950's. Beneath the buildings are catacombs or tunnels used by the asylum staff to come and go when the place was locked up. Unfounded rumors claim that some patients were tortured in the catacombs. One of the tunnel entrances to the catacombs was in the basement where offices are now located. They say that knocking can be heard on the door to the catacombs at night and that the basement is unusually cold. Supposedly secret entrances to the catacombs are found mysteriously open with very cold air flowing out of them. Those who were unafraid to enter the catacombs have seen the ghosts of long dead patients roaming the tunnels - or so they say.

Castle Park in Riverside has several ghostly patrons. One is a lady in white who hangs out there. Another spirit stands on the balcony above the Plaza Cafe and reportedly flies across to the room when disturbed. Someone or someone pushes people inside the Big Top Restaurant. In the arcade, the door by the prize counter opens and closes by itself. If you cross the tracks to the tunnel near the cafe you may see the silhouettes of Indian women roaming about. The area from the Tyler Mall to La Sierra Boulevard is said to have been an old Indian Burial Ground. If you go there and see what appears to be a fire burning in the far corner, do not approach it as it will simply disappear - maybe! Another surprising fact - but maybe not - is that only males can see these spirits, who are, they say, all females.

The old mansion known as the Aviles House sits in the Indian Hills section of Riverside. Reportedly the spirit of an old woman walks the hallways at night and knocks on the laundry room door.

The older Mission Inn hotel in Riverside has a number of ghostly guests staying there. They say that closed tunnels run beneath the building towards Mount Rudidoux. A lady has been heard singing in an otherwise empty room in one of the upper floors. The ghosts of the the first owner, C.C. Miller, his son, Frank and sister, Alice, are thought to haunt the place. Blue lights the size of bowling balls has been seen inside room 215. Alice Miller's room is in the south east corner of the fourth floor. Many have sensed the strong presence of 'Aunt Alice' and have encountered other apparitions, been touched by unseen hands and have shivered in cold spots. Across from Alice Miller's room is the two level Bridal/Honeymoon Suite. Something there likes to push people down the spiral staircase. The catacombs under the hotel were once an underground museum and been closed since 1992. Late in the evening an apparition has often been seen near the foyer. Frank Miller's Room in the north east corner of 4th floor was not renovated during the closure of the hotel from 1985-92. People have reported sensing Mr. Miller in his old room at the end of Author's Row. The hallways are very active with ghostly visitations of long departed guest especially the covered hallway near Alice Miller's room, along Author's Row on the 4th floor as well as the 2nd floor, and the service area in back of the Dinning Room. A phantom has been spotted several times floating near the ceiling and traveling from the entrance wall near the patio to the far back in a south to north direction. There is more recorded phenomena but I think you get the ghostly picture.

The spirit of an old lady walks the hall near the old pressroom of the Press Enterprise. As she passes the pressroom door, she ups and disappears. She may be responsible for the stall doors in the restroom slamming shut and locking by themselves. She may also be the entity who taps people on the right shoulder leaving them feeling instantly very cold.

While this is not a ghost story, I thought that you might be interested in reading about it. Awhile back, a green monster - yes I said a GREEN MONSTER - lived under the Riverside

Bridge. One night it supposedly came up onto the bridge and attacked a passenger of a car, leaving a mysterious green residue on the vehicle. As the river bed is now dry, it is likely the creature has moved on to wetter climes.

Years ago an old man died of natural causes during a performance of his favorite play, the Nutcracker, at the Riverside Municipal Auditorium. They say his ghost is still spotted in the building possibly hoping to see his favorite play again.

In the spring of 2006, for some unknown reason - at least to this writer - a young man hung himself late one night in the Lothian dormitory. Now staff at the UCR Lothian Dining services have been visited by him and have had to work with unusual cold spots in the building late at night.

Most of the huge University of California Rivera Library was remodeled during 2000-2001. The ghost of an unidentified female haunted the untouched areas on the first and second floors usually at night when the place is closed. Night staff have experienced cold spots and an obnoxious smell in the basement and have heard strange sounds as well.

Another story tells of blurry black shapes wandering the area of Dufferin and Victoria. They also tell of hearing strange sounds like that of children being tortured! Did something happen there once upon a time?

RUBIDOUX

If you visit Mount Rubdioux near the community of Rubidoux in Riverside County at night, you just might get the dubious pleasure of seeing what some people think are the "Little People" running and playing around the east side of the mountain. Do not get too close as they like throw rocks. You might, in your wanderings in the area, find what looks like a tint portrait of Jesus embedded in the side of the mountain. Now get this? They say that it was a picture of Mary, the mother of Jesus before it changed.

SAN JACINTO

Lauis's Pet Store "Feathers and Fur" in San Jacinto, a city in Riverside County, has more than just pets and supplies. It also, apparently, has a ghost or two. Strange shadows appear in different spots before disappearing. Disembodied whispering has also been heard while the specter of an old man in a military unform staggers as if drunk in the aisles usually at night.

San Jacinto's Vosburg Cafe/Hotel may still be there. Years ago it was boarded up but passersby kept seeing mysterious lights flickering off and on in the building.

TEMECULA

Temecula ia a city in southwestern Riverside County and has at least three ghost stories. The ghost of an old Indian woman is often seen in the mirror in the woman's restroom in one of the local McDonald's. A woman alone in the room and standing before the mirror may be startled by seeing the apparition behind her in that mirror. Then the spirit will push the woman (the living one) on the shoulder and then laughs. When the living woman turns the Indian woman disappears!

Some people find funeral homes creepy to begin with. The Stout Family Funeral Home has apparently some creepy things such as the lights going off and on, mysterious knockings on the doors and disembodied whisperings. Then there is the black form often seen in the embalming room.

The area under the bridge that the 15 Freeway crosses in Temecula is called the Gallery. It is a favorite and apparently famous place for graffiti artists. Taggers from around the world visit there to leave their mark so to speak. Some years ago, an unnamed tagger was shot and killed by the police. Now his ghost in a hooded sweat shirt is seen down there and people have heard him rattled his ghostly can of spray paint to get it ready to spray.

WIDOMAR

In 1983, a car crashed in a field next to Catt Road in the city of Widomar in Riverside County. The man and woman who were killed in that terrible accident roam the field on warm full moon nights as - you guessed it - Ghosts!

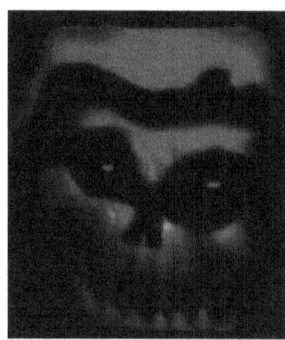

CHAPTER S
Sacramento County

ELK GROVE

Old Downtown Elk Grove Boulevard in Elk Grove, a city in Sacramento County, is where you might see the spirit of a lady in white with no face at all who walks the streets. She often walks up to the railway tracks before disappearing.

FAIR OAKS

Many drownings have occurred in the American River in Fair oaks in Sacramento County near the Sailor bar. One drowning victim still in his wet clothes often approaches people in the area and then vanishes before their eyes.

FOLSOM

The city of Folsom in Sacramento County is perhaps better known for Folsom Prison than for its ghosts. A little girl has been seen running around the pool table and disappearing in Yager's Tap House and Grille Pub on Trader Lane. She likes to play games such as hiding the eight ball and popping it out onto the table at unexpected times. Footsteps in an otherwise empty attic and the laughter of a girl have been heard. Another ghost haunted the building. She is an old woman who hangs out in an old bomb shelter built years ago under the pub. The old woman sometimes startles people by touching them.

SACRAMENTO

Sacramento is both the county seat of Sacramento County and the capital of the State of California. The city is home to a number of ghosts. The spirit of an unknown child has been seen around the Ashford Apartments. No one seems to know who the kid is and why it still has not past into the light!

Patrons and possibly staff at Sacramento's Crocker Art Museum have seen the apparition of a man as well as feeling a presence and have heard unexplained squeaks on the floor board as if someone unseen was walking around.

The Delta King River Boat, an old paddle wheel boat docked at Old Sacramento, is now both a theater and restaurant. The spirit of the original river boat captain has been seen sitting in the theater's balcony when a play was in progress. He may have showed his displeasure at one production when a glass of water mysteriously spilled onto the sound board in the sound booth. Disembodied footsteps has also been heard on deck.

A ghostly re-enactment of the shooting of a Burger King manager on Florin Road and the subsequent suicide of the gunman may be occurring on certain nights. Staff and patrons have heard mysterious gun shots and screams but have found nothing to account for it.

It is said that some workers at the Freeport Factory in Sacramento died on the job and haunt the place. People warn you to hold on to any door there that you open as the ghosts will try to slam it shut. There has also been heard the laughter of unseen children.

Pops Kerth, the original owner of Iceland, Sacramento's oldest ice skating rink, is still look after the place even though he passed away years ago. His spirit is often seen at around 4:00 AM patrolling the building as always.

A house at Jackson and Bradshaw Streets in Sacramento was built before the Gold Rush and is a prime candidate for haunting. In fact, unseen children can be heard whispering, crying and screaming. Unexplained shadows have been spotted floating around the rooms and various items have moved from one location to another seemingly by themselves. It is not ghosts that causes this strange activity.

The Martinez House at H and 22nd St. in Sacramento was the site of a huge murder years ago where the demented head of the household killed all his family and staff. The Martinez family bought it later in 1976 and began to experience all sorts of paranormal activity. Unseen persons struggled in the kitchen at night. An invisible presence made panting noises and the ghosts of an oriental man in a white lab coat, some children, a woman in a flower print dress and even the dead family cat began to appear and disappear. Apparently the house was shut up in 2000 and lies empty except for its ghostly residents. As with any site listed in this book, make sure you have permission to visit. The owners of a lot of haunted sites do not like trespassers.

Ghost lights appear from time to time at Sand Cove Park in Sacramento and an invisible woman can be heard saying "Te papa" near the river. Who she is and why she is saying those words is anyones guess. Some figure that it might have do with the area maybe being an Indian burial ground or long shuttered mine shafts. Take your pick!

The Sacramento City Cemetery has several apparitions hanging around the grounds. There is a couple all in black accompanied apparently by a pit bull who follow people around before disappearing much to the relief of the persons being followed, I bet! The ghost of a little girl likes to play near the headstone on a grave where a little girl is buried. Do you think it is her playing?

There is something strange happening in the Sacramento Room on the 2nd floor of the Central Library. It sounds and feels like a person at the back of the room in the California section but they remain not unseen. The sound of mylar rustling, the pulling and shelving of books and someone bustling around the copy room are often heard. This invisible person often misplaces books that the staff are looking for. The shutters on the door to the copy room rattle and the front door sounds like it was opening and closing by itself late at night when the place is closed.

Five ghosts that hang around the Sacramento Theater Company building make what many people claim is the most haunted place in the city. A former stagehand affectionately called "Pinky" because of his glowing pink aura often appears near cold spots. The specter of an unknown man has been seen walking through the halls and disembodied footsteps have been heard on the stage after the building is closed.

They say that the Sutter Middle School was built where an old Indian burial ground used to be. In the middle of the night, doors slam by themselves and things are moved around by unseen persons.

The Leland Stanford/Governor's Mansion is at 802 N Street, Sacramento, in the Leland Stanford Mansion State Park two blocks west of Sacramento's Capitol building. The son of Leland Stanford is said to have appeared before his father and asked him to build a university to help young men become something better. Mr Stanford and his wife then built Stanford College.

San Benito County

I could not find any ghost stories for this County. If you know of any, please email me at jamesfosterrobinson@live.com or jimrobinson@hotmail.com

San Bernadino County

ADELAIDA

Adelaida Cemetery lies off Chimney Rock Road in the community of Adelaida near Paso Robles in San Bernardino County. If you hang around that cemetery between 10:00 PM and midnight on a Friday night you just might make the acquaintance of a female ghost named Charlotte Stiton dressed in a long, white gown. She apparently places flowers on the grave of one of her children who died in the Diphtheria epidemic many years ago. Wait! There is more. Shadowy human-shaped figures of mist with glowing red eyes wander the area. Footsteps by unseen things or people are often heard at night. Car batteries fail and the electromagnetic field meters used by ghost hunter fluctuate all over the place. You will feel cold off and on even in warm weather. Be careful. Hooded black shapes may try to chase you off the property. I do not think that they are human.

AMBOY

Amboy is a small community in San Bernardino County. Amboy School, closed in 1999, had one or more ghostly students. Or maybe it was a long gone staff member. Someone unseen would come in the front door but when the staff checked, there was no one there. The back playground swings moved by themselves when the wind did not blow. Things in the gym seemed to move around by themselves. When put in one spot, they were then found in another spot apparently moved by someone unseen. Teachers working late at night got the creepy feeling that someone was watching them. When they looked to see who it is, there was no one there. Locals say that several Indians died in 1868 when working on the nearby railroad. Apparently, their ghosts roam the town of Amboy and may have been the unseen presences in the school.

APPLE VALLEY

The town of Apple Valley lies in the Victor Valley of San Bernardino County. A new restaurant and several other businesses now exist where the Neurology Clinic which used to be the old Apply Valley Inn was located. At least a trio of ghosts used to haunt the site and maybe still do. A man who hung himself used to sometimes take a walk across the parking lot. A woman who was murdered used also put in an appearance. A third ghost dressed in white apparently hung out in a certain part of the old building. Are they still there?

BLOOMINGTON

The community of Bloomington in San Bernardino County has two good ghost stories. The first one takes place in Bloomington High School. A female drama teacher was working alone late one night when she was either pushed or fell into the orchestra pit and died. Now workers in the building can hear screams and mysterious footsteps. Some times, something or someone unseen would try to push a person down the stairs.

There is a table between three marble chairs in the southeast area of the Green Acres Cemetery in Bloomington. They say that every year on Halloween (of course) blood appears on that table. No one seems to know why or how it gets there.

CALICO

The former mining town of Calico in San Bernardino County is now a ghost town in more than one sense. At the Calico Mines behind the town a small road stops in an open area. On the day of the winter solstice, there occurs a strange scene. A bear moves slowly cross the area followed by a bizarre collection of ghostly animals and humans. Again no one seems to know why it happens. Apparently it just does!

Then there is the old Calico School House where an old school teacher is looking for more students to fill her class room.

Wyatt Earp still walks its street, tipping his hat to those living that encounter him. Some men who died in an old mine searching for gold are apparently still there. One in particular carries a pick axe and warns the living not to enter the mine shaft. Is he guarding a stash of gold dust? I, for one, am not going to try to find out!

CHINO

The city of Chino in San Bernardino County can be found in the western end of the Riverside-San Bernardino region. Years ago an escaped prisoner murdered three members of a family in the Chino Hills but, for soon unknown reason, only cut the ears off of the little boy in the unfortunate family. Now the ghost of the murdered family members are often seen in their home and bloody prints are still visible, or so they say.

COLTON

In the Agua Mansa Road and cemetery area of the city in San Bernardino County, the despairing spirit of a woman still searches for her lost children. Over time, the facts behind the haunting seem to have disappeared. Like wise the facts about the haunting by a little boy and five girls in the "BIG" room at Carrows Rest in Colton seem to have evaporated into thin air!

DEVOURE

The community of Devoure in San Bernardino County is near the northern junction of Interstate 215 and 15.

When the Treehouse Fun Ranch was being cleaned for new owners some years ago, a worker stayed alone over night and got the fright of his life. He was not apparently alone! He heard mysterious noises, saw the lights shake and flicker and the fire pit suddenly turned on by itself. He spend the night outside the building. In the morning, he told the other workers all about his night. While they were cleaning up, they found a urn full of ashes. It apparently contained the cremated remains of a trucker that used to love the place. How did the urn get there? Was it the ghost of the trucker who scared the worker? No one seems to be talking - not even the dead!

EAST HIGHLAND

The Bethany House in East Highland in San Bernardino County is and may still be an old abandoned Insane Asylum set back in some orange groves. It is a favorite spot for teens to party. They however stayed outside because of the many stories told about the eerie place. They say that one young fellow was stupid enough to go in for a look and never came back out. Apparently his body was never found. Perhaps the phantom of a middle aged woman seen occasionally has something to do with his mysterious disappearance? When she was a patient in the asylum, she was known to be very violent and attacked people who came near her.

FONTANA

The city of Fontana in San Bernardino County is home to around 200,000 living residents and a number of ghosts. Something unknown resides in the A.B. Miller High School Theater as witnessed by the banging coming from inside the walls and the weird blue lights that are often seen. Strange looking figures have also been spotted appearing and disappearing and disembodied voices have been heard coming from the cat walk. Do you suppose that it might be the ghost of a teenage actress who climbed up onto the cat walk to try and fix a light as a favor? She fell off a ladder and died.

The Big Lot's store, formerly Pic N Save, near Sierra and Foothill Boulevard is said to be haunted by several spirits. Unexplained noises like someone or something falling on the floor in both the men's and women's washrooms when no one else was in there have been heard often. Restroom lights flick off and on by themselves. Unexplained voices and mysterious noises have also been heard coming from inside the empty and darkened break room. Like wise, several unknown voices and sounds like stock falling have been heard in the warehouse.

The old auditorium at Etiwanda Intermediate School in Fontana is now apparently a cafeteria. There is supposed to be a narrow staircase going up to what was a small dressing room back then. The story goes that occasionally people outside see a young Indian girl standing by the single window in the room. She hung herself in the room back in the 1970's and was only spotted when someone looked up at that window.

Foothill Boulevard in Fontana used to be part of the famous Route 66. If you drive down the street between Cherry and Citrus cross streets, you just might see a young man in a stripped shirt and carrying a walking stick crossing the street right in front of you. When you slam on your brakes to avoid hitting him, he ups and disappears. He is sometimes spotted walking with a black dog on the side of the road. No one I know knows who he is or was and why he is still trying to cross the street. Do you?

Mango Elementary School in Fontana has a sad ghost story attached to it. Years ago a little girl, to avoid her parents fighting, used to climb to the top of a tree behind the school. It became her refuge and her friend until one day... One windy day she fell to her death. Now they say that you can hear her at night calling for help and sometimes see her, dressed in a little white dress and wearing straight hair, fall to her death.

At Mary B. Lewis Elementary in Fontana, something ghostly stirs between 11:00 PM and 4:00 AM. Disembodied footsteps walking around and the sound of an invisible toilet flooding as well as a conversation can be heard in both of the locked bathrooms. Loud banging, strange whisperings and the sense of an unseen presence adds to the weirdness.

A construction worker is rumored to have died when Fontana's Tokay Emementary School was built. Now possibly the ghost of the that dead worker is still trying to get his work finished as the sounds of invisible construction work is often heard.

If you happen to be in the quad at Fontana's Sequoia Middle School around sun down and no employees are around you might encounter the ghost of a little girl at the lunch tables. She will be crying and bouncing a ball. She is known to ask people to play with her and if they say no, she starts to shed tears of blood and follow those people. Has anyone said yes and what happened then? Do you know?

FOREST FALLS

The woods around Fallsvale Elementary School in Forest Falls in San Bernardino County are home to the Ghost Children. No one seems to know who they were before they died and haunted the woods but there may be some connection with the historical landmark - the fenced-in old school. These little ghosts do not seem to pose a problem and are friendly to the living children in the new school. Some of the living children supposedly know the name of some of the ghostly children.

JOSHUA TREE

Something or someone unseen has made its home in the Joshua Tree Inn in the community of Joshua Tree in San Bernadino County. Things disappear and reappear later. Some times the objects start to shake and move mysteriously all by themselves.

KELSO

Kelso is now a ghost town and was old railroad depot in the Mojave National Preserve in

San Bernardino County. After Kelso Depot was closed, the ghost of a man, who hung himself in Room # 6, was seen a number of times walking up the stairs. Local legend says that to this day you can see a stain on the wall of Room # 6.

LOMA LINDA

Loma Linda is Spanish for Beautiful Hill and is the name of a city in San Bernardino County. People hanging around the Monticito Graveyard in Loma Linda at 2:00 AM might encounter a ghost dressed in white. There is a warning that you should not look at the gate or you will hear a disembodied voice behind you. The voice will stop if you turn back from there and not enter. If you go near the cemetery at night on Halloween you will see a fog.
I wonder if the fog is seen any other night or if it is just that type of weather that time of the year.

NEWBERRY SPRINGS

The community of Newberry Springs lies at the foot of the Newberry Mountains in San Bernardino County. They say that you should not walk the Mojave dry river bottom from Harvard Road to Minneola Road at night or the Hatchet Lady might get you! The terrifying ghost carrying a hatchet roams the river bottoms and is supposedly responsible for the unexplained disappearances of a number of people who foolishly walked the bottoms. You have been warned!

ONTARIO

A little girl about 7 or 8 years old who was raped and killed in Bon View Park in the city of Ontario in San Bernardino County is still often seen around 10:00 PM hiding behind trees. She apparently wants to play Hide-and-Seek.

Lights in the auditorium of Chaffey High School in Ontario flick off and on by themselves. If you venture into the auditorium basement where the old bomb shelters are, do not be surprised if mysterious green light follows you. The antics in the auditorium and the green lights are attributed to the ghost of a student who died one night when he fell into the orchestra pit. He has a neighbor. She committed suicide for some unknown reason by jumping off the balcony to her death. Now she hangs around the light room.

There is something weird about a tree that was and may still be in a field between an airport and a freeway in the city of Ontario. After an airliner crashed, the bodies of the survivors - sorry - the dead- were laid out in the field. Thereafter, that poor tree grew twisted and grotesque. If you approach that tree, they say that you can heard the ruffling of thousands of unseen crows in its branches. Ghosts of crows! Now I have heard everything.

The 2nd floor of Ontario's Hotel Beverly is plagued with disembodied footsteps and shadows in the southwest corner window. As for the rest of the hotel, lights flicker unexplainably, cold spots abound in the basement and fire alarms like going off by themselves at any time of the day or night

If one of you ladies happen to visit the ladies room back in the lay-away department in Kmart on 4th Street in Ontario and no one else is there, do not be surprised if you hear the door of one of the empty stalls slam shut! Ghost have to go also.

If you happen to be alone at night in Vince's Spaghetti Restaurant in the city of Ontario and hear phantom footsteps, it may be the ghost waitress who has been seen walking into the back of the new room. She may not like company as the ice machine has been known to fling ice out at people. This spectral waitress has also been overheard talking to invisible customers. They also claim that if you go into the restrooms (they do not say men or women's - probably both) and sit in the center stall, the other stall doors will flip open and closed very quickly. You may also hear the toilets flush and the taps turn on. You might think someone else (alive) is there but if you look, you may find you are alone - except for the ghosts of course! Staff cleaning at night have heard scratching and thumping noises coming from the ceiling. It is a fun place to eat and work. Reserve me a table, please!

The Antique Underground in Ontario has a mirror that if you look into it you may see the apparition of a young girl, six to seven years old, giggling and smiling. The sound of glass breaking and a woman screaming can be heard coming from the basement but when people check it, there is no one there and no broken glass.

PARKER DAM
The community of Parker Dam in San Bernardino County seems to be bothered by only one ghost story. Workers at the Intake Pump Plant, Metropolitan Water District, apparently can hear the jingling of invisible keys and someone unseen whistling. They are lucky that there is nothing more happening.

RANCHO CUCAMONGA
Rancho Cucamonga, a city in San Bernardino County, has an interesting but ghastly men's restroom in Red Hill Park by the Auditorium. The bloody corpse of a dead dog is often seen there between 3:00 AM and 3:00 PM. The ghost of a boy scraps his knees as he slides across the floor. But why would anyone go to the washroom in that park late at night?

The Sycamore Inn in Rancho Cucamonga along the famous Route 66 is said to have great steak. It also has a ghost - a man dressed in cowboy style clothes.

REDLANDS
The city of Redlands in San Bernardino County is said to be the ultimate ghost town with its old victorian style houses on the south side and the many ghost stories told about it. There is supposedly many devil worshippers in the community.

The Fox Theater in Redlands is said to have a violent presence but little else is known about it.

You can hear, they say, unseen women talking in the ladies' dressing room, the dressing room slamming shut and heavy footsteps on the roof of the Harris Department store when it is closed.

Some strange happenings have been reported at Hillside Cemetery in Redlands. Throw a ball over the graveyard wall and someone or something unseen will throw it back. Do not be surprised if the horn on your car goes off by itself. The ghosts in the cemetery seem to have a sense of humor.

The House of 1,000 Stairs in Redlands was once a covent but is now a large house with, they say, at least one hundred stairs inside and three hundred outside. That sure is a lot of stairs. They also say that the living are not the only ones in residence there. Apparently, the ghosts of some of the nuns like staying in the house of 1,00 Stairs.

Local Legend has it that if you go late at night to a place called Kimberly Crest you might be honored with a view through the top window of the house of the ghost of a woman sitting in a rocking chair. Some feel that it might be Kimberly for whom the house is named.

There is an urban legend told about the Mariposa Elementary School in Redlands. Supposedly in 1950's or 60's, a boy named Billy was hit by a school bus and taken into the school's nurse's office where he died. They say that his last wish was to go back to school. He now supposedly hangs around the nurse's office. If someone knocks on the door, he returns the knock. Sometimes he is heard walking in the empty room and sometimes he wants people to play with him. A recent theory suggests that the returned knock is simply the chunking of a time clock in the office. Maybe! But what if it is not the time clock?

The privately owned Morey Mansion was once a Bed and Breakfast. It is also home, apparently, to at least three ghosts. Both a little girl and a boy have been seen along with an old man who used to be the caretaker there. Sorry folks, that is all the information that I have.

Ghostly figures have been seen on the stage in Prospect Park in Redlands. One of the phantoms is thought to be that of a teenage girl, a performer in one of the plays, who raped and murdered late one night.

A senior student at Redlands East Valley High School was killed the night before he was to graduate. His ghost lingers around the school, maybe waiting to graduate before entering the light.

When a teenage boy lost his girlfriend in a tragic car accident, he became so distraught that that he climbed up into the air ducts at Redlands High School and composed and wrote poems in her remembrance on the walls. Later, he too died in a tragic accident in the school's theater. His ghost haunts the theater.

They say that on late rainy nights at Sacred Heart Church and School on Fourth Street, an immense and mysterious fog sometimes forms. Multiple transparent forms have been seen wandering around inside the fog. When that strange fog dissipates, the figure of a woman, still wrapped in fog, walks slowly towards the church before she too disappears.

Two black iron gates that used to stand along the roadside of Sunset Street in Redlands are called the Gates of Hell. Many frightening and scary things were said to happen if you pass through those gates. A bloody head of a bull may roll down the driveway towards you and specter of a headless cat may come running after you for starters. The gates now apparently long gone, but I wonder if the strange happenings still go on.

The ghost of a man in army clothes wanders the hallowed halls of Merriam Hall at the University of Redlands. He likes to sit late at night in a bathroom stall next to one used by a living person. You can tell that he is there when you see boots showing in the next stall and you known it is empty. If you are not sure, check the stall. It will be empty and the boots will be gone, or so they say. The man has also appeared in mirrors where some girls are brushing their hair. When they turn to confront him, he is not there.

RIALTO

A depressed boy shot himself on the grounds of Rialto High School in the city of Rialto in San Bernardino County some years ago just before graduation. He is now, apparently, a ghostly student hanging around C, E and G Buildings late at night. There are disembodied footsteps, cold spots and flickering lights just like in any good ghost story.

Rialto's Blockbuster Video has an invisible specter that turns off the power in the building, leaving neighboring buildings untouched. It opens the drop box doors and can be heard walking around the store.

There are at least two ghosts cavorting at Rialto Public Pool. A young and pregnant looking girl dressed in 1920's style clothing and an older man have been seen walking across the top of the water in the pool. That is why people know they are ghosts! They also parade around the pool deck and in the office area. They have been a bit of trouble because they often fling chairs and papers around in the office. The staff apparently does not like to be alone there after dark. Can you blame them?

SAN BERNARDINO

San Bernardino is a city located in and is the county seat of San Bernardino County. La Llorona or the Weeping Woman is the ghost of a beautiful woman who drowned her six kids years ago and is doomed roam the streets around Agua Mansa Cemetery in San Bernardino. In addition, the ghosts of two people murdered execution style on the road leading to the cemetery haunt the area. Are they or La Llorona to blame for all the unexplained car crashes in the area?

There are or were some abandoned apartments on Marshall Boulevard in San Bernardino that were thought to be haunted by the appariton of a little girl. I wonder if she is feeling abandoned? If you try to find out, please be careful and make sure you get permission from the owners before venturing there.

Some time ago, a student at Aquinas High School in San Bernardino hung himself from a beam between the stairs in the school. Now, they say, that after dark, his ghost is often seen floating in the school and for some unknown reason in the library.

A few days after Will Rogers performed at the California Theater in San Bernardino, he died in a plane crash. His ghost apparently haunts a practice room in the theater. The room is cold all the time and his reflection is seen in a small window in the room.

There are stories that the ghosts of passed away nuns roam the halls at San Bernardino's Holy Rosary Catholic School at night. This is not definite as only the nun who opened the school at 6:30 AM saw them and she apparently told few people about it.

The ghost of a nun walks mostly at night in the halls of the old areas of St. Bernadine Hospital in San Bernardino. A covent is attached to the hospital and some of the nuns living there and working at the hospital passed away on the site. One is apparently still trying to do the good work to which she dedicated her life.

Once again we have an institution of learning inhabited by a ghost. A student trying to fix lights on the second floor balcony of San Bernardino High School's auditorium fell to his or her death. Now weird figures are seen in the auditorium while its doors open and close and lights go on by themselves. The ubiquitous cold spots are found on the stairs leading to the second floor balcony.

Park Poad is located in the San Antonio Heights area of the city of Upland in San Bernardino Count. The ghost of an old man often stands in the middle of the intersection of Mountain Avenue and Park Road. If you should stopped at the intersection, be warned! They say he will approach your vehicle and start shaking it while groaning and moaning like all good ghosts do.

Here's another haunted hall of learning. A ghostly form has been seen wandering the hallways and in the unused darkroom at Upland's Pioneer Junior High School. The spectral figure has been blamed for books falling off the shelves and the disembodied voices heard in the empty school office.

VICTORVILLE

The city of Victorville can be found in the Victor Valley in southwestern San Bernardino County. The phantom of an elderly man in a top hat and with no legs walks slowly very late at night and early in the morning at the corner of Condor and Tawny Ridge. The sight of him is so eerie that a cold and scary feeling remains after he has pasted. Then there is the specter of a woman dressed in 1800's style of dress that stares down the street late at night. No one seems to know what she is staring at. If they do, then they are not talking.

Drivers on El Evado road in Victorville late at night may see a number of ghosts. One in particular is that of a little girl killed by a car. Also drivers may hear the unexplained crying and yelling by invisible people and experience a chill down their spines.

YUCAIPA

The city of Yucaipa lies 10 miles east of San Bernardino in San Bernardino County. The ghosts of four kids dressed in white clothes are said to hang around a certain unnamed housing development next to a golf course late at night. They also are said to like to mess with golf carts on that course.

The ghost of Jamie Petersen haunts Flaghill Park in Yuciapa. When she was alive she used to sit in the park a lot enjoying the squirrels. Then, one day, she was found dead by the cross in the park. Now she wanders the park in ghostly form asking strangely to be smoked out? What she means, I have no idea. Do you?

A boy named Andy Garcia was walking his dog one day at Mill Creek in Yucaipa when his dog went crazy and dragged the boy into the water. Just before he drowned, the boy supposedly screamed out the name of his gay lover, David. Now his ghost is seen around the area screaming out his lover's name. This could just be an urban legend.

The area around Oakglen Road in Yucaipa is supposedly cursed by a woman many thought to be a witch. A group of teenagers apparently died in a crash because of the curse. There were and may still be stairs at that spot that led to her house. Now the hill where all this happened is a haunted gravity hill. If you leave your car in neutral at this spot the ghosts of the teenagers will push your car up the hill out of harms way. This is of course an optical illusion. But it makes for a nice ghost story.

A woman known as the Red Lady of Pendleton Road died in a car accident on Pendleton Road in the 1950's. Her body was found about one half mile down the road. She had apparently crawled out of the wreck to that spot before dying. This story could put a twist on the song "Lady in Red"!

The story goes that a pool boy got jealous of the older sister of four young girls at the Wildwood High Lands mansion in Yucaipa. He stabbed all four girls to death and threw their bodies out of the top floor window into the swimming pool below. Some say the bodies are still there and will try to drag you down if you swim in the pool. I do not believe that the bodied are still there. But I am not going to try to swim in the pool to see if they try to drown me!

San Diego County
CAMP PENDLETON

The main United States Marine Corps base on the west coast is at Camp Pendleton in San Diego County. A second story room in a barrack in Area 41 is said to be haunted by a marine who shot himself after his fiancee left him. He is known to sing the theme song to the TV show "Jeopardy", striking sleeping marines and moving furniture. Residences of that room often feel they are being watched by someone unseen.

CARLSBAD

Carlsbad is a coastal Pacific Ocean resort city in San Diego County. Plaza Cinema 4 apparently has a ghost or two who like to scare the staff by rolling a trash can up the hallway and whispering a name in an otherwise empty Theater 3. An unusual accident in Theater 4 was blamed on ghosts when a large piece of ceiling fell and crashed on the floor a few feet from an usher. Faulty ceiling? Or did the ghost not like that usher? Ever have a ceiling fall on or near you? I could tell you stories...

CAMPO

The ghost of a young woman in a long white dress startles campers in the woods at Lake Morena Campground in Campo. The spot were she sometimes appears has a cold, eerie feeling to it. Her ghostly singing and laughter has also been heard as well as heavy footsteps coming and going at night outside campers' tents. When the campers checked, no one is seen. Interestingly, a large orb of light that was not visible when a picture of a camper was taken appeared in the finished photograph.

CHULA VISTA

Chula Vista is the second largest city in the San Diego metropolitan area of San Diego County and the seventh largest city in Southern California.

According to local legend, a sailor who went crazy at sea came home to Hilltop Road in Chula Vista and murdered his wife, daughter and son. Their house burned down years ago but a chimney is said to still stand there. If you go there at night, they say that you will experience a sense of dread and chills as well hearing the screams and crying of the dead children.

Proctor Valley Road in the Eastlake area of Chula Vista is haunted by a woman in a long white dress walking along the road side. Some concerned people have stop to give her a ride but she quickly disappears.

CORONADO

The ghosts of Hotel Del Coronada (check location) in Coronado have been featured on several ghost hunting shows. Room 3327 that used to be numbered 3312 is home to the ghost of Kate Morgan. Kate was partnered with a con artist who got her with child in 1892. After an argument about settling down and going straight, he left her and supposedly promised to meet her in Coronado at the Hotel Coronado. He never showed. Kate fell sick and brought a gun. Then she was found shot in the head on the steps to the beach. Everyone thought she committed suicide. However, a man named May researched and wrote a book on the affair and felt Kate was murdered by her partner. Room 3312 at that time was numbered 312 and her ghost has been spotted there as well as walking down hallways of the hotel and standing at windows. Room 3502 is also said to be haunted by a maid who lived there. Both rooms have trouble with electrical equipment, lights flickering off and on by themselves, curtains on closed windows moving by themselves and the ubiquitous cold spots. The above are only some of the paranormal activity experienced in the hotel.

DE LUZ

The community De Luz lies in San Diego County six miles northwest of Fallbrook. The Santa Margarita River Bridge in De Luz has a number of ghosts stories connected to it. A small wagon train was ambushed near there during the California Gold Rush and everyone was killed. In the early 1900's, six teens attending a prom at the newly established Fallbrook Union High School disappeared and their bodies were found in the river by the bridge. The ghosts of the wagon train people and the six dead teens are siad to haunt that bridge.

EL CAJON

They say that balls of light and strange smokey smells occur every night in the city of El Cajon in San Diego County. Where exactly in that city has not been reported. Have you seen the great balls of fire?

One of the mobile homes in El Cajon is haunted by a very pale old man who does not like people praying. He gets angry when he hears them and throws things off the shelves. He also tries unsuccessfully to open doors by twisting the knobs and sometimes borrows things. They say you can see only the top part of his body, making him easy to identify.

The apparitions of two cowboys often appear on the old dirt road at the back of Rios Canyon in El Cajon. The story goes that they are still looking for some lost gold. Good luck, partners!

ELFIN FOREST

Elfin Forest is an residential community in San Diego County in the Santa Rosa Mountains foothills. There seems to be a mixture of myth and truth in the stories told about this area. Most of the stories center around a mysterious place called Questhaven. Let me known if I have somehow included other stories from other places. It is a bit confusing. Well here goes!

Some years ago a band of gypsies were driven out of the area by locals. Some gypsies were killed and the band put a curse on the area. Now stories are told about a cult house and an abandoned insane asylum. Supposedly nooses hang from burned trees, unearthly crackles are heard and broken bones and skulls crunch under foot. A ten foot ghostly white owl haunts the area looking for victims. A witch supposedly lives in the woods since the expulsion of the gypsies and floats along on a black station on the forest roads. Dressed in a black cloak, she searches for unwanted intruders. Do not look into her eyes as a ray of green light will shoot out of them killing you. She is blamed for a number of suicides by people who were followed by her. Other phenomena include a lady in white following hikers, trees that bleed, orbs and the phantom of a man missing an arm who guards the gates to Questhaven. Enough said! Even if the stories are not true, there must be a reason why so many are told about the area. I for one do not wish to investigate that place.

FALLBROOK

Fallbrook is a community in the northern part of San Diego County. The press room of the Fallbrook Enterprise Newspaper was the scene of a tragic and fatal accident in 1962. A worker's sick daughter was knocked into the presses, supposedly by an unseen force, and died. Now, they say that the ghost of that little girl will warn you that you are getting to close to the presses by pulling on your pants.

Back in the 1960's, as the story goes, the employees at Jack in the Box in Fallbrook were all murdered by a gang of drug crazes hippies. Now, they say, hippy music, workers talking and the sound and smell of burgers cooking is common after the place is closed late at night. In addition the ghost of a worker can be seen outside a window cleaning it and the bathroom doors keep opening and closing by themselves. It is also claimed that at 4:34 AM the lights go on and the people who died there can be seen walking around.

When the Fallbrook Union High School was remodeled in 1999, a native Indian Chief's grave was uncovered next to the new library building. Since then, some strange things have happened. Smoke is often reported on the school grounds but no fire was ever found. Orbs of light have been spotted as well as a pack of phantom coyotes and even a teepee.

In Live Oak Park are a couple of big rocks that Indians used to grind corn on. The ghost of an Indian girl grinding corn on the rocks has been seen at different times of the day.

There are reportedly some hot trees in Fallbrook's Masonic Cemetery. Some people reported a strong surge of heat when they touched certain trees there. Sounds like a hot time in the old cemetery tonight!

A malevolent male spirit apparently did not like the construction of a new wing at the Silvergate Retirement Center in Fallbrook some years ago. One guard swore that the violent spirit tried one night to force him over an opening in the second floor. Obviously the phantom was unsuccessful. Other guards reported hearing the disembodied voice of little children in the new wing late at night.

HIGHWAY 94

Strange spherical lights emitting blue electric-like glows have been spotted singly or in pairs on and around Highway 94 in southeast San Diego County. Motorists must be startled by these mysterious lights. I wonder if the lights have caused any accidents. Please be careful when you drive that highway and send me pictures if you see those lights!

JULIAN

The Julian Hotel in the historic gold mining town of Julian in hills of San Diego County is haunted by a ghost by the name of Albert Robinson, a freed slave and his wife who set up the original hotel in 1897. Back then, it was called the Robinson Hotel. In 1915, Albert died and some prejudiced town people did not want him to be buried in the local cemetery. He was buried in another cemetery exclusive at that time for African Americans. The insult by the townspeople is believed to be the reason why Albert's spirit lingers around the hotel and is blamed for the balls of fire that fly around in the building, shattered glass, doors and windows opening and closing by themselves, disembodied footsteps, the smell of cigar smoke when no one was smoking and furniture moving by itself. After an exorcism was performed, the violent activity stopped and, they say, Albert makes a quiet appearance once in a while.

LA JOLLA

The hilly seaside resort community of La Jolla lies on the Pacific Ocean inside the northern part of San Diego in San Diego County. Muirlands Middle School may be haunted as people have heard voices behind them in the hallway but saw no one when they looked. Someone or something unseen keeps turning the lights in the auditorium off and off. No apparent electrical fault has been discovered. Can you tell me why do ghosts like to play with the lights so much?

LAKESIDE

There is a screaming tree at the end of Willow Road in the suburb of Lakeside east of San Diego. Drive down the narrow dirt Willow Road pass what looks like a slaughterhouse until you see a clearing with a tree in it. If it is the right tree, when you sound your horn three times, the ghost of a girl will start screaming. Who she is and why she scream at the sound of not one, not two but three blasts on the horn is not known at this time. It is better not to go alone in the area as it is supposedly a hang out for dangerous characters.

LEMONGROVE

The Kentucky Fried Chicken establishment in the city of Lemongrove in San Diego County is haunted by Rudy, an employee so dedicated to his job that he continued to go it after he died suddenly during his shift. He is blamed for the security back door being found open when the store was closed and dirty dishes being found cleaned by an unseen person. There was also the usual haunting phenomena such as cold spots, flickering lights, items disappearing and showing up later in a different place and well as the eerie feeling of being watched.

OCEANSIDE

Oceanside is the third-largest city in San Diego County. A student hung himself from a tree beside the 400 building at Oceanside's El Camino High School in 1990. The rumor is that his ghost is sometimes seen hanging from that tree. Where the Hunter Steakhouse in Oceanside sits on a hill above the Buena Vista Lagoon was originally the site of the Buena Vista Cemetery. When the graves were moved, some of the ghosts may have decided to stay. A female spirit likes to hang around the bar area. She must like the company. Others spirits seem to prefer a locked storage room above the lower dining area and entrance when the joint is busy. Patrons and staff when outside are drawn to look up at three windows in the room as if someone was up there trying to get their attention. An apparition has been seen from the second floor floating in mid-air across the room from the fireplace. Disembodied male and female voice often call out people's names. There are unexplained power surges and objects moving by themselves or maybe by ghost power. Once the friendly face of a man formed out of the solid chimney.

SAN DIEGO

The city of San Diego is, of course, the county seat of San Diego County and home to over thirty apparitions. The ghost of an older man likes to appear suddenly in the back seat of cars driving along Bonita Road in San Diego. He was run over and killed on the road and is apparently looking for a ride home or maybe to the hospital.

Something or someone stirs late at night at Abraham Lincoln High School In San Diego. There be strange whispering heard in the empty girl's washroom by the band room and feet are often seen in a supposedly empty stall. There is no one there when the stall is checked. Sound familiar? The girl's bathroom by the main office is often the site of the sound of toilet paper unraveling and it not those blue bears in that silly commercial on TV. The activity is often blamed on the fact that a girl was raped and killed in a room by the cafeteria.

Someone or something unseen is also bothering people at San Diego's Bonita Vista High School. The showers in the boys locker room turn off and on when no one is near them. Loud whispering is often heard coming from the empty boy's bathroom in the front room of the gym and some people complain of a malevolent feeling in that room. Cold spots appear on the bleachers and an unseen hand often grabs at people's ankles or shoulders.

Janitors at Brooklyn Elementary School have apparently seen children running in the halls at night and have heard child crying. When they check, no one is there. There are also the usual cold spots. When the janitors try to leave after finishing thier work, they often have to push hard on the doors to get out. It is like there is someone who does not want them to leave and is trying to push the door so it will not open.

San Diego's Solar Turbines, once the Global Power Company, is located on Harbor Drive near the Airport and Kearny Mesa on Ruffin Road. Some devoted workers, who passed away years ago, still report to work in ghostly form at the engineering factory. Unintelligible whispering has been hard in the office area. Elevators with no one on them and no one (alive that is) pushing buttons move up and down by themselves. The sound of doors opening and closing have also been reported. It must have been a good place to work.

The Machado Family once owned the land on which the El Fandango Restaurant in San Diego's Old Town Historical Park now sits. One of the Machado woman died in a fire in 1858. Her apparition, a wispy white female in Victorian attire looking sad or angry, sits at a table in a dark corner near the front window but only when the shade is drawn. Often she will float around the place, passing through walls and closed doors. She seems to not want to be bothered with the living and wants to be left alone.

Casa de Estudillo Museum is also in San Diego Historic Old Town. Some of the ghosts inhabiting this building manifest themselves as human faces in the mirrors on the walls. Other entities appear as dark forms floating from room to room. One wears a brown monk's robe as he hangs out near the chapel. There are the usual cold spots plus flashes of red light in the master bedroom. A music box lid lifts all by itself and music starts to play. Other ethereal music has also been heard by the staff. The ghosts must like the music as they are often seen dancing across the floor. Physic researchers have reported the red flashes and one person was apparently attacked by an angry spirit that broke the ma's camera lens. The group also recorded an angry voice admonishing them to get out! Other researchers have reported similar phenomena.

The old El Campo Santo Cemetery in the Old Town San Diego Historic Park shrunk over the years as the town grew and encroached on it. As a result of roads and building being constructed on cemetery land, graves were moved and some were lost. As you probably suspect, the buildings and roads around the cemetery began to experience strange phenomena such as problems with their lighting, electrical power, appliances and alarm systems as well as a variety of apparitions hanging around within and on the outside of the brick walls of the small remaining graveyard. Some entities dress like the period costumed staff of the historical park fooling the foolish living. Others like to float around with only the top part of their bodies showing. Hispanic and Native Indian ghosts also get in on the fun floating around the area above the gravestones. There are the usual cold spots. What is a haunting without them? Do not park your car in front of the graveyard as the playful spirits like to foul up electrical starting system. After a number of graves were found under the pavement in front of the cemetery and under the parking lot, and two plagues were mounted memorializing them, the ghosts have seemed to quiet down a bit.

The Horton Grand Hotel in downtown San Diego may be haunted as people have reported experiencing unexplained cold spots and sighting apparitions. In 1843, a man called Roger Whitaker, was shoot by the father of his would-be bride. Roger's body was dumped in the swamp on which the hotel now stands. He haunts Room 309 and the hallway. They also say that a gambler was shot and then died in his room - 309! Something shakes the bed in Room 309 in the middle of the night waking those sleeping there as well as openning the armoire door. The lights go off and on by themselves and objects move on their own power. Instead of the usual cold spots, Room 309 gets hot and can not be cooled by the air conditioning. Often the sound of someone playing cards can be heard in the locked and vacant room. Guests have even seen the indentation of a form on the bed. In addition, other polite and some what friendly ghosts haunt the hotel. A Madam Ida Bailey, who ran a brothel on the site before the present hotel was built, must have liked the new digs as she is said to still greed guests. A group of ghostly people dressed in formal 1880's clothing has been seen floating down the grand staircase.

Strange things happened at MacDonald's on Miramar Road in San Diego after the staff had closed and got things ready for the morning. Various items such as straws, napkins and tubs of packets of mustard, were found flung across the floor in the morning. A picture of the devil appeared in the wood grain on the door of a stall in one of the bathrooms and the door had to be replaced. Too many people were lining at that bathroom up just to see the devil.

Something or someone unknown may be hiding in the Taco bell washroom in Mission Valley, a valley that lies within San Diego's city limits. Staff there have heard whisperings coming from what was thought to be an unoccupied bathroom. On one occasion, an employee saw what he thought was another employee go into that bathroom. When no one came out after awhile, he checked and found that there no one was there. Oh, and don't forgot the trash doors swinging open one at a time. Scary? Enough to raise goose bumps on your neck and arms!

Ghosts appear to be active in the Montgomery High School football stadium. People wandering around in there at night have been spooked by disembodied screaming and balls of light which chased them out of the place. Strange voices have also been heard in the school's washrooms, which of course, were empty at that time.

Ever since a female student bumped her head during PT and died, people walking in the halls of Murlands Middle School have heard strange noises behind them but saw no one when they turned to look. This might be called an audio haunting.

In the late 1960's, the crew of a F-8 Crusader Jet died when their plane crashed at NAS Miramar in San Diego. Now their ghosts are said to hang around Hanger 1. Maybe they are hoping to fly again.

After an elderly customer died in the small Japanese grocery store, the Nijiya, in San Diego, Strange noises have been heard in the middle of the night while someone unseen would whisper the name of the person working alone. Products also kept falling off the shelves.

Many marines killed in World War II are buried at Point Loma Cemetery in San Diego. Legend has it that at night the spirits of the fallen marines would rise up out of their graves and walk to the nearby cliffs to look out over the Pacific Ocean to see if their country was safe and secured. When satisfied that it was, they would return quietly return to their resting places.

There is a different kind of ghost running around Presidio Park. A small white deer has been spotted but disappears right in front of the witness's eyes.

Students in the band room at Ramona High School have a hard time keeping their instruments in their place in their locked cases. Something or someone unknown and unseen seems to not like music as the instruments are ejected from the cases after the locked lids fly open. Maybe a spirit really likes music and is in a hurray to get the show started.

The Whaley House and Museum in the historical Old Town section of San Diego has been designated an official haunted site by the U. S. Department of Commence. It seems to be chocked full of ghosts. Here are a few to wet your morbid appetite. A man called Yankee Jim Robinson (no relation to me) was hung in 1852 for stealing a boat on the site where the Whaley house stands now. He is heard tramping around in his big boots up stairs and the spot where he was hung is now the archway between the music room and the parlor. People passing under the arch have reported feeling like someone or something was strangling them. Then there is the phantom of a little woman with a swarthy complexion wearing a calico or gingham full skirt with small print. You can see her dark hair and eyes under a cap and gold hoops in her ears. Mr. and Mrs Whaley still occupy their beloved home after all these years. A little red-hair girl in late 1800's clothing plays in the garden and also with toys in the playroom. A spirit in a frock coat and pantaloons will suddenly appear and then fade away. A spotted dog pads its ghostly way through the house. There are the usual cold spots, the sound of children laughing, a baby crying, disembodied music and whistling, smell of cigar smoke, fragrance of perfume and the smell of baking in the kitchen during the Christmas Season.

The noisy ghost of a man walks the halls and sometimes enters rooms at the U.S. Grant Hotel in San Diego. Is he a former guest or employee that liked the hotel so much that he decided to stay on instead of passing on?

Amanda, a tall blonde or red-haired young woman, is often seen in room 325 at the Vagabond Motel at Garnet and 5 Freeway. Guests have experienced feelings of sadness, dread and oppression in this room and the outside hallway. This may be due to the fact that Amanda was a former model and Beauty Queen who killed herself there. They say she wants you to pray for her. If you do and smell jasmine and feel a sense of peace and calm, you know she is thanking you.

The Villa Montezuma in San Diego was originally for an unusually talented musician named Jesse Shepard in 1887. Jesse channeled great musicians and became rich and famous but died destitute. His ghostl and that of a widow who owned the house at one time haunt the place. She is often seen looking out of a window in the tower. It is said that some beautiful stained glass showing famous artists, composers and writers display some unusual qualities. Beards on some of the men depicted look like they are growing and their hair is turning gray as if they are growing old in the portraits. Visitors have reported feeling that someone or something was looking through their eyes out a window and seeing scenes from the past. A strong presence is also felt. Piano music has been heard coming from a locked and empty room. The place is now a museum and open to the public.

The Star of India sailing ship is docked at the Maritime Museum of San Diego and has had a tragic history at sea. They say that some of the history stayed on the ship. Sometimes a loud party can be heard in progress on the ship but no one would be there when the ship was checked. The ghost of a fifteen year old stowaway, who died when he fell from the rigging back in the 1880's still hangs around the ship often setting off the alarms. A disembodied voice as well as ghostly footsteps have been reported. Investigators have communicated with the spectral image of a woman called Suzette who claimed she was murdered. A light floating through the air showed up on an infrared video. In one investigation, the researchers asked a spirit named Ben to let them know he was there by touching a pole. Ben complied apparently leaning out the darkness and touching the pole with his arm. Scary stuff! There are other tales told about the Star of India. Visit the ship and ask around.

The McConaughy House is located in Heritage Park in Old Town San Diego. The spirit of the original owner, John McConaughy, haunts the house today. Lawyers who work in the building have heard footsteps in an otherwise empty upstairs hallway. The sound of trees swishing against the outside walls, even thought there are no trees close enough to the house, is often heard. Some feel that John McConaughty is letting us know that he is watching over the house.

VALLEY CENTER

The spirits of dead Indians still chase buffalo complete with sound effects in the Valley Center area in San Diego County. Could this be because the spot was once an Indian burial ground?

San Francisco County

SAN FRANCISCO

San Francisco, the fourth most populous city in California and the twelfth most populous city in the United States, is both a city and a county at the same time and home to many ghosts.

The old St. James Presbyterian Church on Leland Avenue in San Francisco, San Francisco County is said to be haunted for a while. Disembodied footsteps can be heard trudging up the stairs while doors are shut by unseen hands. Occasionally, normally easy to open doors will not budge but will be found wide open later.

Alcatraz in San Francisco Harbor is famous as a federal Prison, museum and for its ghosts. Apparently, well before it became a prison, the local Indians avoided the island as they felt it was the abode of evil spirits! The ghostly sound of footsteps and cell doors clanging resound through the buildings. Disembodied voices and cold spots are common in the Dinning Hall. The most dangerous place they say is Cell 14 D. The appearance of a pair of evil, glowing eyes in the cell made the most harden criminal scream in terror. When one inmate started screaming, the guards did not respond. Later that inmate was found strangled to death in the locked cell. Other areas where the ghouls hang out are the hospital, cell block C, Warden's house and utility door. There are too many stories about Alcatraz to relate here. These few should get you on the road (sorry, boat) to Alcatraz!

Drivers on the lower deck of the Bay Bridge heading to Oakland late at night have been startled by the knocking on their windows and the vision of a headless man pacing their car. It is believed that he was killed in the 1989 earthquake. Be careful if you are driving on the bridge late at night and you heard a knocking at your window!

The basement of the Cameron House in Chinatown, San Francisco, was once used as a refuge for female Chinese immigrants fleeing from prostitution and slavery. Some people burned down the house to prevent the owners from helping the Chinese and a number of the women died in the flames. Today, the doors in the house, now a church, are sealed by red and gold charms to keep the spirits from getting out to disturb the living. I am not sure if the charms are working. White figures have shown up in the back ground of pictures taken in the building. The spirits of immigrant Chinese boys sexually abused in the basement when the house was a Presbyterian Mission in the 1950's, 60's and 70's are also said to haunt the Cameron House. They say that the cries of both the Chinese women and the boys can be heard coming from the basement on dark and lonely nights!

Urban legend tells of an elderly religious lady who was murdered when she was deliberately pushed down a steep stair case and her body hid in a dumpster at or near the CCS Elementary School in San Francisco. Now she can be heard praying "Hail Mary" by girls using the bathroom near the staircase.

A building that one of the Child Support Services has their offices in in San Francisco is haunted by the spirit of a woman who often is mistaken as one of the employees as she walks around moving things. She is known to bug the cleaners after hours by losing heir badges and keys and blocking their vacuum cleaners.

An interesting situation is apparently happening in the Golden Gate Park. Some drivers speeding have been pulled over by an officer and given a ticket. When they go to pay it or fight it in the courts, they find out the officer named on the ticket has been dead for ten years. Some think that under the circumstance, you should not pull over until you are out of the park as the officer will then disappear. I would not take the chance that it is a ghost. I would pullover. If the ticket is definitely from the ghost, maybe you could sell it on EBay!

The ghost of the late senator Broderick is said to have been seen pacing back and forth in the Haskell House in San Francisco. No other information is available at this time. You know something about this haunting, I would happy to hear from you.

An old apartment on Hugo Street in San Francisco did not have a good feeling to it. One resident experienced a lot of strange things there. Noises of love making have been heard coming from the otherwise empty room and a brown haired, unknown person has been spotted sleeping in the bed when the owner of the room was not there. When a fire was lit in the fireplace in the room, it flared up and out into the room instead of up the chimney. Strange shadows were seen around the room. Sometimes the bed would start shaking at night. The room's resident woke up one night to the feeling of some heavy sitting on his chest. He screamed and struggle trying to get up. His friends who lived there found him on the floor covered with scratches.

A dead girl named Elisabeth often walks up the stairs and hangs out in the 2nd floor girls bathroom at James Denman Middle School in San Francisco. She has been known to close the stall door and flush the toilet. She is also thought to rattle invisible chains on the third floor. Or, maybe that might be another ghost. Anyone know?

An old abandoned army hospital in Park Presidio now gone was brought by Lucas Films. Before the sale of the property, there were reports of phantom footsteps and flashes of light in the derelict building. Could it have been street people in there or real ghosts?

Claudia, the daughter of the original owner of the Mansions Hotel in San Francisco, has been seen and heard by guests and staff even though she passed away years ago. They say that Claudia likes to communicate with the living through toys.

Johnny was a bully who attended Martin Luther King Middle School and was disliked by all and sundry. One day he got permission to go to the bathroom on the second floor and never returned. When someone checked the bathroom, Johnny was nowhere to be found. He has not been found according to the story, unless you count the unexplained knocking coming from the inside of the bathroom door. Johnny is still apparently there and can not get out. Let that be a warning to all bullies!

The Neptune Society Columbarium at One Loraine Court, San Francisco, originally part of the Odd Fellows Cemetery. Guess what? That is right! Ghosts have been seen there! For instance, a visitor felt a hand on her back and turned around to see who it was. No one was there! Even more eerie was the white hand print on the back of her blouse. There are other stories still to be told about that place. As far as I know the place is open to the public and donations are accepted.

Flora Sommerton , a young lady from Nob Hill in San Francisco apparently was not too enthusiastic about her social debut in 1876. She disappeared the night before the big event but is known to have died some years later in Butte, Montana. Maybe she had some regrets about skipping out or maybe she just missed Nob Hill. She is thought to be the spirit of the happy, young girl all dressed up in a white Victorian gown that walks the area of Nob Hill between Jones and Powell.

An old tunnel lies next to the sunken building of the Ocean Beach Sutro Baths. Stories tell that the tunnel there was used for human sacrifice. And stories tell that if you place a lighted candle at night at the end of the tunnel, someone or something will throw the candle into some nearby water beyond some rocks. Hard to believe but, I for one, am not going into that tunnel to find out if the story is true or not.

The tale goes that a girl was raped and murdered in the warehouse that was there before the place became Orchard Supply Hardware. Her ghost now walks the area in high heels (many have heard the sound of the heels clicking). As well as screaming, laughing and moving boxes around, this ghostly young lady likes to blow in men's ears and tug at the long hair on girls.

The Queen Anne Hotel was once a school for girls in San Francisco. One of the dedicated teachers, Miss Mary Lakes, died but is apparently still looking out for her girls. They say she still occupies her Room 410 in ghostly form. There are the ubiquitous cold spots and Miss Mary is often sighted as a misty form. The lady is very helpful, unpacking hotel guests suitcases and tucks people in bed at night.

A Safeway store in the middle of San Francisco between 17th Avenue and Taraval is the playground of a young boy who died some time ago. No one seems to know who he is and why he haunts the place. He has been seen sitting behind some crates or at the end of a hallway facing the wall. His image is is blurry and hard to see.

The San Francisco Arts Institute was supposedly built on a cemetery in the early 1900's. As a result the place may be haunted by a few restless ghosts. They have been blamed for doors opening and closing by themselves, lights flickering, power tools turning on by themselves and for series of accidents to workmen renovating the building and the bell tower.

A madam who used to own the San Remo Hotel in San Francisco many years ago still occupies Room 33. Madam likes to knock on doors in the same hallway that her room is on. Of course she is not there when the people answer the door. The spirit of a little girl roams the hallways and seem to be unsuccessfully trying to get into Room 42. Maybe that is where the light everyone talks about is? There are the usual cold spots and a sense of someone unseen watching you but, all in all, there is reportedly a feeling of calmness.

At the former MacAteer High School, now the School of the Arts High School, there is a ghost that likes to sing in the empty 3rd floor bathroom. It may be the same ghost that knocks on 3rd floor lockers and on the inside doors of locked classrooms. This ghost never graduated to the Light! Maybe it is on permanent detention!

In the 1920s-30s, a pregnant woman successfully her condition from her family until she gave birth. After she got rid of the baby, she killed herself in Stove Lake in the Golden Gate Park. She had different feelings as a ghost as she walks Strawberry Hill at night near the lake in search of her Baby.

A gray form comes out of the men's bathroom at Trinity Episcopal Church In San Francisco and passes through the opposite wall in the hall. There's more. People have reported seeing an apparition in a white suit, the three directional shadow of an unseen person and felt mysterious drafts of cold air out of no where. I think the place maybe haunted.

They say that an exorcism was performed on the Pediatric 8th floor of the USCF Medical Center Intensive Care Nursery in San Francisco. Why? Apparently, women who died in child birth as well as those children who passed away still linger in the building.

A strange figure has been seen after hours standing by one of the stalls in the 3rd floor boys washroom at San Francisco's Washington High School. No one knows who it is or why it is there. When they try to ask, the mysterious figure vanishes before their startled eyes.

San Joaquin County
LATHROP

So far, the city of Lathrop in San Joaquin County has only one reported ghost story. In the 1970's, a young man ended his life by jumping off the Mossdale Bridge over the San Joaquin River at Lathrop. Now his ghost, dressed in blue jeans and red checkered flannel shirt, haunts the bridge at dusk.

MANTECA

The city of Manteca has at least three ghost stories and maybe more. The last theater in the hallway of Cinema 10 has two patrons who must love movies very much as they have not left even after having passed away. In the late 1950's, when the site was a drug store, a fire started and killed at least three people before it was extinguished. Now the spirits of a little boy and an old man haunt the place. They may be two of the three who died in the blaze and maybe not. Voice and tapping are now heard on the theater's upper level.

The Kelley Brothers Brewing Co. in Manteca was once the El Rey Theater before it burned down years ago. Interestingly, the movie "Towering Inferno" was playing the night of the fire. Hot spots occur often in the building, while the lost spirits of firefighters and movie patrons are still trying to find their way out. That all must make for an interesting dinning experience.

The ghost of a murdered girl has been spotted late at night in Manteca's Home Depot. Laughter and music has also been heard after the store is closed and is apparently not employees causing it as when they check the noise stops and no one else is found in the area the music and laughter was coming from.

STOCKTON

Stockton is the county seat of San Joaquin County and its County Courthouse is haunted. Late at night shouting can be heard coming from the empty holding cells underground. The sound of a holding cell door on the second floor slamming closed is often heard. Again there was no one in the area.

Disembodied voices and mysterious footsteps have been heard in Stockton's University of California Stanislaus College. Chairs seem to move under their own power and rooms are said to turn very cold extremely fast. There you go - some of the classic symptoms of a haunting.

 On Eight Mile Road on the east side of Highway 99 near Stockton, drivers at night are startled by the vision of women clothed all in white just standing beside the road. Be careful as these same women had suddenly appeared in the back seats of cars but they are only visible in the rearview mirror! During the day in the same area, an Indian maiden sporting jewelry often walks along the road before disappearing!

TRACY

Tracy is the 2nd largest city in San Joaquin County in the San Francisco Bay area. The former owner of the Banta Inn died in 1967 of a heart attack while on duty at the bar. He or she is still there in ghostly form having fun knocking things off the walls, stacking coins in the cash register drawers as well as opening and closing doors. Some say that they have heard the disembodied laughter of a woman when alone in the building late at night.

The hills around the Bethaney Reservoir at Tracy resound at night to the sounds of screaming. Local legend say that in 1962 a drunken father on a fishing trip with his kids went insane, staking his two daughters and three sons before killing them. Now the dead children have been spotted running and screaming for their lives through those hills.

The supposedly abandoned Bryon Inn in Tracy had some famous Hollywood actors and actresses stay there. People say that some of those famous Hollywood personalities are still there haunting the place. However no names are mentioned but don't you think those people having sought publicity in life would do so in dead? Well, maybe!

Someone unseen walks around Building 100 at the Defense Distribution Depot San Joaquin in Tracy during the evening hours and turns on the water in the men's room. People feel that it maybe one of three ex-employees who died by suicide or fatal illness.

San Luis Obispo County
ARROYO GRANDE

The Tower Room at the Rose Victorian Inn in Arroya Grande, a city in San Luis Obispo County, is haunted by Alice, a nine year old girl. She has been seen several times and guests have heard her laughter. She wears a long dress with a small apron and her hair is done up in pig tails. Oh, yes! She apparently likes cats as many have inexplicably been see sleeping near the tower. Usually cats hiss at ghosts but apparently theses like Alice's ghost. If you would like to read more about this ghosts and others check out "Ghosts of the Haunted Coast", by Richard L. Senate.

MORO BAY

Morro Bay is a waterfront city in San Luis Obispo County. There are usual reports of mysterious happenings indicative of a haunting at Morro Bay High School. Cold spots abound and lights turn off and on in both the old and the new gym. Of course, the strange occurrences are blamed on the ghost of young boy who died when he fell off the old gym bleachers. Well, that explains the phenomena in the old gym but what about the new gym. What is the connection?

The ghosts of two boys have been spotted late at night playing on the pirate ship at Morro Bay's Pirate Ship Playground. No other information is available. Who are these boys and why are they stuck there?

OCEANO

Black Lake at the community of Oceano in San Luis Obispo County is haunted by an Old Spanish lady in a black ruffled dress and a glowing light instead of a face who walks around the lake at night, startling passersby.

PASA ROBLES

Paso Robles' full name is El Paso de Robles '- The Pass of the Oaks' - and it is a city in San Luis Obispo County. Employees at the Paso Robles Hotel and 911 operators are always getting calls from the unoccupied Room 1007. When the room is checked, it is always empty. The ghost of a night clerk who died when the former building burnt down is thought to be to blame. The new building was rebuilt from the bricks of the burnt one. Goes to show that you should never use material from a building in which someone died. You may get a resident you did not ask for.

The Adelaide Cemetery is just outside Paso Robles. There are two ghost stories told about the place. Years ago, when the area was first settled, a woman's husband and all of her children past away leaving her alone. She missed them so much that when she died, she did not go into the Light but stayed in the cemetery searching for them. Every Friday night, she appears as a glowing figure who walks the cemetery crying out for her beloved children before disappearing. Now this second story may be a different version of the first but may also be about another ghost. Note the similarities and judge for yourself. Here goes! Every Friday night between 10:00 and 12:00 PM a figure like a bright light in human form appears near the cemetery gates and then approaches a grave with the name Charlotte on the stone and lays flowers there before disappearing. Well, what do you think?

There is supposed to be an old Indian Burial ground out near the airport in Paso Robles. Witnesses who ventured out there at night claim to have heard disembodied voices speaking in the natives' tongue and spotted unexplained lights in the area.

SAN MIGUEL
San Miguel is another small community in San Luis Obispo County. The San Miguel Mission was the scene of a massacre in 1848 when a band of pirates attacked the mission and killed thirteen people. The bodies were so cut up that they were buried in a mass grave. Now, the ghost of the thirteen lost souls are said to wander the grounds of the mission.

San Mateo County
BELMONT
The city of Belmont in San Mateo County is located half-way down the San Francisco Peninsula in the San Francisco Bay Area . A little boy walking alone unsupervised one day along the shores of Waterdog Lake in Belmont disappeared! Local legend claims that the Ghost of Waterdog Lake got him. Supposedly this ghost is the man who killed a 12 year old boy and dumped his body by the lake. He is still there in ghostly form looking for more victims. Local legend also warns disbelievers that if they try to go to the lake to disprove the story, they may not return! Well, maybe.

DALY CITY
If you are driving through the intersection of Skylin and Hickey Boulevards in Daly City, the largest city in San Mateo County, on a foggy day, check your rear view mirror. You just might see a ghostly woman in white appear in it. Do not bother to turn to see if she is in the big seat. Apparently she only appears in the rear view mirror.

FOSTER CITY
The Foster City Levee in Foster City, a city in San Mateo County, is haunted by a man who, after being chased by the police for killing a co-worker, killed himself by the levee.

Cold winds seem to blow there even in warm weather. Mysterious shadows and strange shapes roam the area at night and phantom gunshots reverberate in the darkness.

HALF MOON BAY

The coastal city of Half Moon Bay in San Mateo County has one ghost story that I know of. You may be in for a surprise if you drive Highway 92 near the Skyline Cemetery at about 300 AM. A cold hand just may clamp on your shoulder. Look in your rear view mirror. It looks like there is a woman sitting in your back seat! But she won't be there when you look back over your shoulder. The woman was apparently killed in a 1970's car accident and is now looking for a ride home.

MENLO PARK

The city of Menlo Park is located the San Francisco Bay area of San Mateo County. The Peninsula School is situated in the Coleman Mansion. Carmelita, the wife of the original owner of the mansion, was accidentally shot dead by her husband. She is still there hanging around the big building.

Then there is the young woman who died in 1906 when she threw herself down one of the steep stair cases. She also may haunt the place. Shimmering lights and mysterious footsteps have been reported. Many have seen the apparition of a thin shimmering woman dressed in green. She seems to like children and staff as she has not played any nasty tricks on them. Then there was Carmelita's father, R. Nuttail, who communicated through a medium that he had paid for the mansion and he had a right to be there. He, he said, often visited the school and loved the children. So, there!

MILLBRAE

Millbrae is a city in San Mateo County just west of San Francisco Bay. The trouble at Millbrae House apparently started when some friends used a Ouija board as a game. The room went suddenly cold. Crashing noise and loud footsteps resounded in the building. It may be that they stirred up something or someone better left alone. Often footsteps were heard overhead and people would see something flash by in the corner of their eyes. A disembodied female voice would cry out "Help me! Help me!" The door bell would ring, and no one would be there. There was so much activity that the place was visited by the psychic researcher, Hans Holzer and the medium, Sybil Leek. Sybil communicated with a male spirit called Wasserman, who was killed in the house because of an mistaken identity. Mr. Holzer convinced the lost spirit to leave as his killers were long gone. Things quieted down after this. Millbrae House is apparently no longer haunted. Well, maybe.

MOSS BEACH

Moss Beach is a community in San Mateo County. The phantom known as the Blue Lady resided in the Moss Beach Distillery. When the establishment was a speak-easy during prohibition, she was a woman who was murdered by her husband when he found out she was having an affair. Despite her brutal demise, they say that the Blue Lady is a friendly and mischievous spirit.

PACIFICA

The Seaview Twin Theaters used to be open in Pacifica, a city in Sam Mateo County. Now closed and probably demolished, it was thought to have been haunted. Staff heard phantom footsteps and saw things move around after the place was closed. Several people claimed that they were chased by something unseen. Of course, they did not stick around to find out what it was!

PACOIMA

Pacoima a district in the San Fernando Valley region of the city of Los Angeles. The girls locker room at Charles Maclay Middle School may be haunted. If you have been paying attention so far, you will recognize the following symptoms of a ghostly infestation. There are cold spots, of course, and many reported that they feel the presence of a little girl running around the locker room when they are alone there. Others have spotted the specter of an Aztec Indian in full dress occasionally wandering around the school. If so, don't you think that he is a little lost?

RAVENSWOOD

At night if you are driving down a street in Ravenswood, a community near Menlo Park and you see a woman wearing a trench coat and standing under an old fashioned street light as if waiting for a ride, you may be in for a surprise. Some drivers have looked back and she and the street light have disappeared. That's right! The street light was a ghost. And, oh yes, so was the woman!

REDWOOD CITY

Redwood City, the county seat of San Mateo County, is located on the San Francisco Peninsula in Northern California, about twenty-five miles south of San Francisco. Some strange things seem to be happening at Canada College. Around 1:15 PM people riding in the Learning Center elevator have been assaulted by the smell of a dead dog. No one has been able to explain it. Just as weird is the vision of a naked man doing the splits in the parking lot before disappearing in front of startled women and sundry other witnesses.

SAN BRUNO

Customers at Chuck E Cheese in the city of San Bruno in San Mateo County have experienced, apparently, some of the now familiar and classic symptoms of a haunting. There are inexplicable cold spots in the showroom. Many have had the weird feeling that someone was watching them but when they looked around, no one could be seen. The shadow of an nonexistent person has been spotted late at night in the facility. Looks like it maybe haunted, don't you think?

Santa Barbara County

LOMPAC

The city of Lompac, pronounced Lom-Poke, can be found in Santa Barbara Country. Many years ago a boy hung himself in a Lompac Burger King ladies restroom. Now they say, when staff check the place just before closing they often find a seat from the restaurant in the ladies' bathroom at the very spot he hung himself. It was always tipped over as if he was still trying to hang himself. A ghostly white figure has also stares at the workers as they close shop. As staff are leaving, they often hear loud banging coming from the inside of the restroom door. Of course, no one is there when they investigate. And do not forget the cold spot at the table behind the straw dispenser. Just another tall tale? Well, maybe.

The second floor of the Lompoc Furniture Store on H Street in Lompoc used to be the town morgue. There appears to be something or someone left over from those days. The specter of a woman has been spotted walking on the second floor landing and there are the usual cold spots in a backroom on the second floor.

The large chapel in Lompoc's Mission La Purisma has two ghosts. One is a priest while the other is a young girl who's happy and youthful playful presence can be really felt behind the baptismal font.

They say that the Tahitian Village Apartments in Lompoc was built over an Indian Burial ground. Well, maybe as some strange things happen there and may not necessarily connected to the burial ground. A faint sound of a man playing a guitar can be heard inside an apartment closet. People have also heard what they describe as two men stealing food from a pantry. Some tenants have awoken in the middle of the night and found scratches on their faces. Caused by ghosts? Well, maybe.

MISSION HILLS

The spirit of a lady in a white dress and a white scarf covering her head still prays in the front row of the chapel at San Fernando Mission in Mission Hills in Santa Barbara County. I wonder if anyone has explained to her that it is long pass the time for her to enter the light!

SANTA BARBARA

Do I need to say it? Ok! Santa Barbara is a city in the county of Santa Barbara. Are you happy? Over five thousand pioneers and Native Americans are buried in the old graveyard at the Santa Barbara Mission on Laguna Street. Some of there spirits are restless and have been seen walking around the cemetery.

In the 1950's, a student named Edwin died when a counterweight sandbag fell from the cat walk in the theater at Santa Barbara's La Cumbre Junior High School. Edwin is still there. He has been seen on the upper cat walk and in the theater.

SANTA MARIA

Santa Maria on the Central Coast of California is also a city in Santa Barbara County. One or more houses on Camon Lane might be haunted. Why? Well, spirits have been seen turning the lights off and on while the computers go off and on by themselves. A faulty electrical system? No colds spots reported. Judgement is reserved.

The Santa Maria Inn has a historical section where scents of women's perfumes are often smelled in a room at night. The door to that room often locks itself as if someone inside did not want company. Then there is the elevator that when it goes to a certain but unspecified floor, stops for fifteen minutes and then starts up again. This strange behavior occurs at the same time each day. Sorry, no specters, apparitions or cold spots.

SUMMERLAND

A ghostly lady is thought to haunt the Big Yellow House Restaurant in Summerland in Santa Barbara County. Looking lonely, she often stands around by herself but disappears when approached. Tips often disappears from the tables but this happens without ghostly connivance in other restaurants. Have you ever heard of a ghost with sticky fingers?

VANDENBERG AFB

They say that at Space Launch Complex 5 (SLICK 5) on Vandenberg AFB in Santa Barbara County the ghost of an unknown man will approach a security policeman's guard post and inquires about a fire. Then he ups and disappears! I know that there is not much to this story but maybe, just maybe someone has more details. What do you say, eh!

VANDENBERG VILLAGE

A number of ghosts like to linger around High School Theaters. Take the theater at Vandenberg Village's Cabrillo High School in Santa Barbara County. The restless spirit of an unknown girl appears in the spotlight room. Her voice, well a female voice, has been heard coming from behind locked doors. Sometimes she plays tricks on the drama students by locking them in their dressing rooms. Maybe she wants to take their place on stage. Speculation has it that she died when she fell from the indoor balcony.

Santa Clara County

CAMPBELL

The city of Campbell in the San Francisco Bay area is a suburb of San Francisco and part of the Silicon Valley in Santa Clara County. The building where Securitas Security is located may not be secured. Do not worry. The only intruders may just be ghosts. Staff alone at night get the feeling that they are not alone. Something can be seen out of the corner of the eye running down the hallway and disappearing a round a corner. A ghostly form is often seen in that same hallway. Doors on the first floor are often heard slamming when there was supposedly no one around to slam them!

GILROY

Gilroy is the southernmost city in Santa Clara County. At night a small carousel in the Claudia's Garden section of Bonfante Gardens turn on by itself. Its lights and music start up and the carousel begins to turn. No one of course is any where near it.

Highway 152 in Gilroy is also called Blood Alley. Why, I do not know but I have heard of the lady ghost seen searching for her lost child. There is also reports of the sound of snorting horses and a stagecoach passing by. Then there is the story of woman killed by a truck driver and now supposedly appears in trucks' passenger seat, starts screaming like a banshee and then disappears!

The ruins of a mansion and the surrounding area at Mount Madonna State Park near Gilroy are where Henry Miller, the former owner, and his daughter still hang around. The daughter, killed in a riding accident, still rides her horse in the open fields. She sometimes appears as a girl in a long white prom dress walking down a wooded road. I have not seen any reports of Mr. Miller wandering around but I suspect he is there somewhere keeping a spectral eye on his darling daughter.

They say that years ago when the old Gilroy Hotel was open a man raped and murdered a woman and a little girl there. Now the ghosts of his two victims haunt the place. The little girl is often seen in the hallway or gazing out a window while the woman appears at the top of the stairs. There are other signs of a haunting. The keys on the unplugged electric piano are struck by unseen hands and phantom footsteps can be heard. Doors rattle as if someone is on the other side trying to get out and the lights go off and on by themselves.

There is not much to the ghost story at Gliroy's South Valley Junior High School except that nightshift staff have heard disembodied footsteps inside the old ROP building. But then again, something or someone must be making those footsteps.

SUNNYVALE

Sunnyvale is a city in Santa Clara County and is one of the major cities in Silicon Valley. The ghost of Mr. Bishop, for whom Bishop Elementary School was named apparently keeps an eye on the school. He is said to walk in the auditorium and through the halls of the school.

LOS GATOS

The Billy Jones Wildcat Railroad and Bill Mason Carousel has been operating at the Oak Meadow Park and Vasona Park in Los Gatos, a town in Santa Clara County, since 1970. Mysterious noises have been heard coming from the carousal building mostly after dark. The sound of gates being opened and closed, doors being shut as well as lights turning off and on by themselves have been reported. When the staff checked the building, there was no one there.

The building in which the Green Valley Disposal Company is located is home to a ghost called Julius. Usually he only plays around at night rolling a chair across the wooden floor overhead. Note that the upstairs floor has carpet on it. Sometimes he fiddles with the electric calculator on a staff member's desk while that staff member is sitting there. An office on the first floor and a storage room both have the ubiquitous cold spots. In the cold storage room upstairs, the filing cabinets will suddenly slam open and then slam closed for a few minutes and then stop. Julius apparently disconnect any call put on hold even when a new phone system was installed.

A biker killed on Hicks Road at Los Gatos still haunts the roads. Wearing a trench coat he rides a bike with no wheels around midnight. He has no face and you can only see him in your mirrors.

A ghost was caught on camera at the Opera House in Downtown Los Gatos. Apparently he likes to pull instruments out of the hands of musicians playing for weddings in the banquet hall. What has he got against weddings? Maybe he was stood up once?

The ghost of a young woman 17 to 18 years old is often seen walking or sitting at the side of Old Santa Cruz Highway at the summit of the Santa Cruz Mountains near Los Gatos. No one seems to know who she is or why she is there. It is an unusual place to be looking for a ride, but then again, maybe not for a ghost.

MILPITAS
The city of Milpitas in Santa Clara County is a suburb of the major city of San Jose. The Ed Levin Park Cemetery, now closed, experienced paranormal activity, some occurring even in daylight. Cars parking at the cemetery experienced electrical problems. Disembodied moans were heard. Electronics in the vicinity of the place shut off and turned on by themselves. There were flashes of unexplained light and do not forget the cold spots. What is a good haunting without cold spots.

MOUNTAIN VIEW
Mountain View is a city in the San Francisco Bay Area in Santa Clara County. Several buildings on Moffett Field, the old naval base, were said to be haunted. The phantom of a little girl dressed in old style clothing was often spotted staring at people from within the old infirmary.

The Rengstorff House was moved from Stierlin Road to Shoreline Park where it was restored and opened as a museum. Many people lived in it over the years but most did not stay long due to the reported paranormal activity on the second floor. The ghost of a young lady who give off vibes of sorrow often looks out an upstairs bedroom window. Often the crying of a young lady whose heart was obviously broken could be heard. People staying in the place are woken up by bangs, thumps and other mysterious noises. Do not forget the cold spots. This was all before they moved the building. She does not seem to be in the place in its new location. Maybe she is still at the old site wondering where her audience went?

PALO ALTO
Palo Alto can be found in the San Francisco Bay area in the northwest corner of Santa Clara County. Years ago, a girl was killed by a train when her bike got stuck on tracks near JLS Middle School. A bench at the school was dedicated to her and she seems to have really appreciated it. Her apparition can be see sitting on it most nights. They say if you, yes you, sit on her bench at midnight, you can hear her crying and whispering in your ear. Look at the bike racks while you are there and you just may see her blue cruiser bike, totally wrecked, sitting there. Look quickly before it disappears before your eyes.

SAN JOSE
San Jose is the county seat of Santa Clara County and the third-largest city in California. If you are out and about on the East Quimby Road late at night, keep an eye out for the

Quimby Jogger. You should be able to recognize him as he is a ghost and only jogs at midnight.

The Mt. Hamilton View Restaurant in East San Jose over looks the entire Silicon Valley. The place has another attraction - a ghost! The specter of an unknown young girl has been spotted standing out on the lookout balcony. Lights are known to flicker off and on by themselves in the dinning area. When the place is closed and empty at night, passersby have seen the place all lit up. It is, of course, empty when people check the closed building to see who playing with the lights. Well not quite empty. There is the ghost!

A strong presence or maybe a poltergeist may be at work in San Jose's AMC Saratoga 14 Theater complex. A shadowy form has been seen by projector number 5 in the projection booth. Patrons and staff have heard disembodied whispers and laughter, lights flicker off and on and especially in Theater 5 the armrests on the seats are raise up by unseen hands. It is very distracting when you are trying to enjoy a good movie.

In the 1970"s, a boy was stabbed many times in the back at Arbuckle Elementary School in San Jose. People passing by the school at night have been startled by his apparition complete with a knife sticking out of his back.

A man named Henry died while building the gym at San Jose's Boys and Girls Club. It is said that he is still there often bouncing a ball. Why? No one seems to know.

Many years ago, a girl was running up a stairs in the girls locker room at Burnett Academy Middle School that went to a class room. She tripped, fell and died. Girls in the locker room after a basketball game have heard noise on that stairs as if someone was falling. Is the ghost of that poor girl doomed to fall down that stairs forever? Let that be a lesson to all and sundry. Do not run up stairs or down them for that matter!

A little girl is said to haunt the third floor of a Chuck-e-Cheese in San Jose. This is what I do not like about these types of stories. No meat to them, to use an old expression. Who was she? How did she die? Why is she haunting a Chuck-e-Cheese, of all places?

In 1942, a boy was murdered on the football field at Del Mar High School by his best friend. If you just happen to be on that football field at approximately 3:15 AM, they say that you will heard the ghost of the murdered boy screaming for help and if you are unlucky, see him running down the bleachers.

I do not know about this story but I will tell it here. Supposedly, a little girl got angry at her parents at a party at Dottie's Pond at Bernal Adobe in San Jose. How angry was she? She, a little girl, hung her parents in a barn there! Do not ask me how. It is what the story says. Then so that they all could be in Heaven together she drowned herself in the pond. Logical, eh? Well it seems that after the deed was done, she decided that she really did not want to die. Now you can supposedly hear her screaming for help late at night. Kind of late in the game for that!

A mysterious ghost named Michael T. haunts San Jose's Dove Hill Elementary School. He wears regular clothes and appears to be young but his face is missing. There are no eyes, nose or mouth - just flat skin. Michael T. wanders the basket ball courts late at night and has been blamed for the lights turning off and on in the classrooms at night. No one has apparently died at the school and many wonder what he is doing there.

In the early 1970's, a maintenance employee at El Rancho Verde Apartments in San Jose raped and murdered two female high school students in the building's main garbage room. Locals passing by late night claim that they feel spooked and can hear the tormented cries of the victims.

Some time ago, a young woman hung herself at Evergreen Valley College and now, night students getting out of class have said that they could see her. But was she hanging or just hanging around? That seems to be the question.

The Foxdale Apartments are said to have been built over an old graveyard and as a result is home to some ghosts. Then they also say that a young lady hung herself in one of the apartments when she was abandoned by her parents. Her ghost has also been reported to have been seen around the complex.

The apparition of a woman in a short red dress with a black belt and long black hair, murdered in the 1970's, haunts the creek behind the Baby Zoo at Happy Hollow Park. That so far is all that is known about her.

George is a presence that is felt in the theater at San Jose's Independence High School. While working on the catwalks in the theater, the living George supposedly fell off one to his death. He apparently appears in three different ghostly guises. One is that of a business man standing against the wall. The second one is that of a little boy who runs around back stage trying to catch his toy ball. The third is a very large man who sat in the aisle blocking it completely. In what ever ghostly attire, George has been around since the building was built and has been blamed for seats flipping up and down and the lights flickering off and on. The lightning booth started to shake all by itself one night. There was no earthquake to blame so George got the blame.

Staff and guests at the three story Ramada Limited Motor Inn by the San Jose Convention Center have experienced some paranormal activity. They have heard disembodied screaming, the rattling of locker doors and spied a mysterious green glowing light. A couple have been seen dancing in the ballroom just before they disappear in front of startled guests.

Julia is a specter that still hangs around the Hyatt Hotel St. Claire in downtown San Jose after she killed herself when her fiance took off from their wedding ceremony in the Palm Room in the 1930's. They say you can hear high heels clicking on the floor and the image of a wedding gown train above a bride's feet often appear in the background of pictures taken in the building. Supposedly strange things have happened on the second and sixth floor but no one, living or dead, are talking about them.

Years ago a distraught nun at Notre Dame High School hanged herself off the balcony when she found out she was pregnant. Her apparition is supposedly still seen there and supposedly the gym at the school was closed because it was too haunted. Well, maybe.

There are or were some old horse stables behind Yearba Buena High School in San Jose. Many young people go there at night in the hopes of having a good scare. The old owner of the stables is supposed to haunt the stables. Ghostly voices have been heard and the specter of a man has been seen. For a good free scare go to.......

A janitor who worked at Overfelt High School and passed away in the early 1980's still likes to do his job. Many have heard his cart being pushed unseen around the school at night.

When a young girl's parents died in a car crash while she was waiting for them to pick her up, the student in sorrow hung herself at Piedmony Hills High School in San Jose. Now the still mourning daughter haunts the school wandering the halls alone and opening and closing doors and possibly waiting for her parents to pick her up from school.

During WWII the old gym at San Jose State University was used as a collection point for Japanese internees. The bitterness and sorrow experienced by these internees may still linger, as it is said that the sound of their crying and their voices can still be heard in that old gym late at night.

Amy, a young ghost, haunts the theater of Silver Creek High School after she hung herself inside one of the bathrooms behind the stage. She is one of a number of female ghosts in California who have hung themselves in a school. Whose says school is not stressful?

They say that at San Jose's Solonaker Elementary School a child was accidentally run over and killed by his uncle. His ghost may be one of the spectral children playing outside while the living students are inside studying hard. I remember when I was in class, I often heard children playing outside while slaved over a desk. Or may that was just self pity.

The haunted Winchester House is famous. The original owner, Sarah Winchester, is one of the ghostly residents along with, they say, the dead who were killed by her husband's invention, the Winchester Rifle. There are the usual paranormal activities such as disembodied laughter, talking, cold spots, impression on beds like someone lying there, unseen hands pushing people and, of course, the ghosts themselves putting in an appearance.

SANTA CLARA

The city of Santa Clara is of course in Santa Clara County. Where else did you think it would be?

The Agnews Insane Asylum was rebuilt around 1918 after the original one burnt down in 1912. Then inn 2003, the Agnews developmental center was torn down and the SUN Microsystems Santa Clara Campus was erected in place of it. From 1912 to 2003, staff at the site experienced disembodied laughter, screams and cold spots. Freezer doors often flew open and the contents violently ejected. Ghosts of unknown people were also spotted wandering around. With the SUN Microsystems campus there, I wonder if the phenomena has continued? Guess what? I just found out that some phone technicians working at the SUN Campus one night in 2004 were so scared by the ghost of a little girl with her arms open that they fled the building and refused to return.

In an old Baptist church in the north valley in Santa Clara, they say that in the 1960's, a mass cult suicide including innocent children took place, Ghosts are said to haunt the place since that time. Pentagrams have appeared on the floor and blood has covered the walls. Visions of mangled bodies and the screams of the slaughter children wait to greet the morbidly curious! They even say that these poor victims will hit at you to get you to leave the appalling site of their ghastly deaths.

At Paramount's Great America site, the ghost of a ten year old boy who was killed on a now closed ride still plays in the aisles after the park is closed. He must have loved that place to still want to play there. A man haunts Paramount's big Arcade over by the Drop Zone and has been spotted on security cameras. When guards check the area, they see no one but the guard watching the cameras still saw the ghost stand just behind the living guards. In the Great America Paramount IMAX Theater the lights turn on and off by themselves and disembodied whispering is often heard. This place must be really haunted. A man has been seen walking across the stage before disappearing into thin air. The building has the usual cold spots and odd noises as well as someone unseen brushing ghostly fingers on the back of people's necks, tapping their shoulders and speaking their names in their ears. How do ghosts know the names of strangers? Years ago, a man wearing a blue shirt got locked in the freezer at Paramount's Great America Roast Beef Shop and froze to death. Now, it is claimed that every night between 10:00 PM and 12:00 Midnight, his screams for help can be heard coming from that freezer.

There is supposedly a cemetery next to the mission at Santa Clara University. People passing that cemetery have heard eerie moans and the locked doors at the O'Connor building start to open and shut. The ghosts of long passed away Jesuit priests are seen praying in the bell tower. Is it the over active imagination of studied out students? Maybe a trip some night to the campus will tell the truth of the tale.

SARATOGA

Bella Saratoga in the city of Saratoga in Santa Clara County has experienced some ghostly phenomena. Patrons and staff has seen to their amazement water taps turn on by themselves and the water start running. In addition there are the usual cold spots associated with hauntings. So far, no apparitions have been reported.

Ghosts on the lower floor at a small antique shop on Big Basin Way in Saratoga like to startle people by tapping them on the shoulder. So if you are shopping there and feel a tap on your shoulder it might be a staff member and it might not!

SUNNYVALE

Bishop Elementary School in the city of Sunnyvale in Santa Clara County was named after a certain Mr. Bishop. He must have liked it so much that now that he has passed away his ghost is said to walk in the auditorium and in the halls of the school. I wonder how the students react to the sight of him?

Another ghost apparently walks the second floor halls at Homestead High School. He has appeared to staff and students and likes to lock and open doors as well as tap unsuspecting people on the shoulder. What is this tapping by ghosts on the shoulder? Is a good old fashioned "BOO!" no longer politically correct?

A man, some time ago, died of a heart attack in one of the rooms at a Sunnyvale Quality Inn Suites and is still there making mysterious noises in an otherwise vacant room. At least one apparition maybe more has put in an appearance in front of startled guests.

A young boy or man, Jonny Jonson (pronounced Yonny Yonson), a farm worker is said to haunt Toys R Us in Sunnyvale. Why? We do not as yet know why. But he is blamed for bicycles been ridden around after hours, toys laying in the aisles and balls rolling around all by themselves. Someone apparently took a picture or two of the frolicking ghost but I have not seen them. Have you?

UVAS CANYON

Uvas Canyon County Park, a part of the Santa Clara County Park System, lies on Swanson Creek at the end of Croy Road. There are at least tow apparitions appearing there. One is a woman dressed all in white nun-like apparel while the other is a man in Vitorian stye clothing who hangs out in one of the houses.

SANTA CRUZ COUNTY
BOULDER CREEK

Brookdale Lodge is on Highway 9 near Boulder Creek in Santa Cruz County. They say that there are forty nine different ghosts at the lodge mostly from the prohibition days. One is a young lady in a formal attire who rushes across the lobby before disappearing into thin air. Disembodied voices and soft music can be heard in the otherwise empty Mermaid Room. A brook runs through the Book Room in the lodge and a little girl did drowned in it. Now she often returns roaming the grounds or sitting by the fireplace in the lounge. Then there are rumors that the lodge has hidden rooms and secret passages. I hear it is a wonderful place to eat and savor the supernatural.

CAPITOLA

The city of Capitola lies on the coast of Monterey Bay in Santa Cruz County. There was all kinds of racket and voices coming from the Capitola Theater. Sounded like it was packed full of theater goers. But the problem was that the theater was empty except for the ghosts! Did they pay for their tickets with phantom money or were they watching "Casper, The Friendly Ghost" or maybe "House on Haunted Hill"?

An old house on Soquel Drive in Capitola was said to be very haunted. Orbs of light flitted about and strange noises were heard coming from the place. Things moved from room to room inside while an old man stands on the third floor balcony like a guard as it was said that the only way to enter the house was to climb to the 3rd floor balcony and get past the ghost. I do not think I am up to trying that trick even if that old house was still there.

FREEDOM

In the 1950's, a man living on Hawthorne Lane in the community of Freedom in Santa Cruz County killed his wife and dumped her body in Pinto Lake. His house remained vacant until the 1970's, possibly because it was haunted. There were cold spots near the wife's closets and the piano played all by itself. Often a car door or truck could be heard slamming. When checked, there was only two rusting, weed grown wrecks.

LA SELVA BEACH

La Selva Beach is a community in Santa Cruz County. Tyler House, now a teenage recovery house, was the site of the Leonard House built during the gold rush in the mid 1800's. Residents at Tyler House have heard strange noises and seen objects moving under their power as well as windows opening and closing on their own. Do you think it might be haunted?

SANTA CRUZ

Santa Cruz is the county seat and largest city of Santa Cruz County. Graham Hill Road Cemetery is on the left hand side when going up Graham Hill road off of Highway 17 in Santa Cruz. Local legend has it that if you pull your car into the driveway near the end of the cemetery and leave your headlights on you will be rewarded with the sight of a ghostly white form approaching you. The legend also warns that as soon as you see it, get out of there. Apparently this ghost does not like to be disturbed! Orbs abound and can be seen with the naked eye. Dark shadows float above tombstones while faces peek out of the headstones. Mysterious noises were heard coming from the cemetery's east end. The ghost of an unknown lady all dressed in white wanders around the road near the woods in the back of Graham Road. Sometimes, if you listen carefully, you will heard the voice of an old woman coming out of nowhere.

The specter of an old Indian man walks along Highway 17, startling drivers or that is what some claim when they try to explain why they crashed their cars.

A woman killed by her boyfriend at the Red, White and Blue Beach is seen often there. Perhaps she is looking for her killer or maybe someone to take her place!

A man with glasses has been seen in the fireplace on the ground floor of the Rispin Mansion. Yes! In the fireplace not outside it. I hope no fire was burning in it at the time. Upstairs the spirit of a woman in a Victorian style black dress keeps looking for a book even though she might have a hard time reading it once she finds it. She is also known to open with ease nailed or bolted doors and windows. The basement was at one time was used by police to train search dogs. One must have failed the course as there are reports of a very angry ghost dog down there. Cries for help have also been heard coming from that basement. Maybe the ghost of the instructor who failed the ghost dog is being chased by his angry student. Now that would be a hunting I would love to see!

The University of California Santa Cruz Porter College's A Building is haunted by a student who killed himself. He walks the fifth floor still wearing the same clothes he died in. They say other ghosts reside in the building but I have no information about them. On Porter college's B Building first floor there are three rooms that have so much paranormal activity that there are called the Bermuda Triangle. There were reports of a very malicious presence in the place, objects flying across the room and disembodied voices and mysterious noises there. A ghost known as Lily hangs around the meadow at Porter College in the 1970's. She was apparently a transient and was dressed in rags or no clothes at all.

SCOTTS VALLEY
There maybe ghosts in Theater 2 at the Scotts Valley Cinemas in the small city of Scotts Valley in Santa Cruz County. Staff have felt that someone was watching them after hours but if it is a ghost it is not felt to be malevolent.

WATTSONVILLE
Redman House in the city of Wattsonville in Sanra Cruz County is boarded up or was and sits right off a freeway. At night spots on the roof light up blue and orbs are seen flitting around outside the old building. Doors slam open and close by themselves and the screams for help of a boy and some adults can be heard far away from the haunted derelict. Locals believe that a number of people were murdered in that sad old house.

Shasta County
ANDERSON
The Anderson City Hall, a dance hall during the 1800's, was the scene of the murder of an Indian woman and her child. Now staff have heard late at night the cries of the murdered child as well as Indian dance music.

BURNEY
The community of Burney in Shasta County has at least two ghosts stories told about the small town. A ghost of a little girl clothed all in white walks on Black Ranch Road in front of started drivers if they have been drinking. I wondered if that scare was enough to stop drivers from drinking and driving? Well, maybe.

The local fire department has had numerous calls that the Bartle House was on fire. There is no fire when they get there. People swear that they saw the roof glowing green at night and thought it was on fire. Maybe the house is haunted? Yes, that is it! The specter of Mr. Bartle, the original owner, has been seen wandering in the hallway. He apparently turns on the heater and opens cabinet doors.

Sierra County
DOWNIEVILLE

The community of Downieville is the county seat Sierra County. The Downieville River Inn Resort used to be a boarding house. Room 1 is possibly haunted by a former boarder who may have liked it so much he stayed there instead of passing over. Visitors feel that someone is climbing in bed with them or laying down on top of them but there is no one there. Water taps turn off and on by themselves. What do you think?

Siskiyou County
WEED

The Wayside Inn that used to be off I-5 in the city of Weed in Siskiyou County is thought to be haunt. There is some dispute to whether it is or not haunted. Strange noises have been heard coming from unoccupied rooms. Guests have heard knocks at their room door but found no one there when they checked. Once or twice might have been someone having fun but for it to persist all night bespeaks of paranormal activity. Some of the backrooms overlook a cemetery and spirits from the graveyard may just be having a little fun. But then again, some guest have complained of glowing red eyes peeping at them through bathrooms windows that also overlooked the cemetery.

Solano County
BENICIA

The city of Bernica is a waterside community in Solando County. Bernica's old Town Theater/Portuguese Hall sounds like a great place to be, paranormal wise. A ball of fire soars around the place while disembodied footsteps can be heard on the back stairs. There are the usual cold spots and lights flash off and on. The specter of an old woman is known to put in appearance often.

Not much really happens at Captain Blythers, a restaurant that was once upon a time a home. The owner of the home did have a slight problem with alarms going off for no reason and pictures jumping off the walls. Not a ghost? Well, maybe. But do not count on it.

In the 1800's a young woman distraught over a failed romance hung herself in a room in the Union Hotel in the historical town of Benicia. Her ghost stands in a window facing Main Street but sometimes wanders the hallways and several other bedrooms. Often you can hear her crying. In addition the lights in the hotel go off and on by themselves. A young man also haunts the place. Many feel he is somehow part of her tragic story. His spirit hangs around the bar and the dinning room always looking towards the stairs or pacing back and forth as if he was expecting someone, maybe the young lady.

VALLEJO

Vallejo is the largest city in Solano County. There is a place out on Lake Herman Road that the notorious Zodiac killer killed two of his victims. Psychic investigators have recorded what sounds like a woman's heavy breathing. They also had the feeling of not being alone. Do the two Zodiac victims still hang out there waiting for justice?

At the Vallejo Naval Training Station, the ghost of a WWII sailor often climbs down a ladder into the engine room of one of the ships, walks to a cubbyhole with only a desk and chair in it and then disappears. Someone should tell him the war is well over and order him to stand down.

In 1897, the Royals of England took a train ride through the Napa Valley. The train derailed at or near Vallejo and two royal princesses and many of their servants died. Their ghosst are said to still haunt the area.

Years ago, a man was accidentally shot on Rancho in Vallejo and apparently killed. If he was only wounded then this may be a case of a haunting before the fact. Either way, the man was none too happy about it as every monday night gunshots are heard as well as his screaming for help. Occasionally blood is found on driveways but no one knows how it got there!

The present Vallejo Museum was once the site of the Vallejo Canteen, a popular spot in the early 1900's. In 1922, a famous singer named Rose Borgia, the wife of the King of Portugal, was somehow left behind when visiting her nephew and was sold by her translator to the Marche-Maher family and locked up in the attic of the family home. Sounds almost preposterous but they say it happened. After two years of imprisonment she died apparently of suffocation. Her ghost now haunts the upstairs of the museum practicing her singing with the help of another ghost. She and her friend disappear after a window in the room opens and then closes. You can apparently smell the scent of her favorite flower, Gardenia, which she wore in her hair.

The ghost of Little Boy Blue, aka Prince Louis Bonaparte Delacroix Montenegro Hollanzder of France, killed in 1879 on his way to see his girlfriend near Richardson Drive Old Marche-Maher Ranch Area, now known as the Borges Ranch every night since his murder kisses any woman in the houses along these streets and goes house to house watching over them. Sorry, it was bit long winded but does give you some idea about this haunting. Little Blue Blue is easily recognized. He has short dark hair combed back, blue eyes and wears a blue army/military suit with a white collar.

Sonoma County
BODEGA BAY

The town of Bodega Bay in Sonoma County is supposed to have a Vortex. What is a vortex? Well it is an area where energy seems to concentrate producing phenomena such as antigravity, twisting of plants and weird feelings in humans. They are also thought to be gateways or portal to other realms of existence. Some people say that strange unexplainable things happen in Bodega Bay. Maybe that is why there are no ghosts there. Maybe they all got sucked into the vortex!

GEYSERVILLE

The Warm Springs Fish Hatchery in Geyserville, a community in Sonoma County, has possibly four ghosts on site. An elderly Indian couple like to walk the grounds while a woman in the main building likes to change the radio station and insult employees. The specter of a child likes to climb in bed with people staying in one of the four houses on site. In another house someone unseen likes to turn the shower on at any time of the day or night.

GLEN ELLEN

Jack London's house - Wolf House in Glenn Ellen in the Sonoma Valley in Sonoma County - can be a bit eerie. Visitor have experienced feelings of dread and have had visions of the house burning. Other have heard disembodied cries for help.

A railway crossing at Glenn Ellen is said to be haunted by some kids who apparently died there on the tracks in a car-train accident. As the story goes, you park your car on the tracks and leave it in neutral. Of course, make sure a train is not coming. The ghosts of these kids will push you off the tracks out of danger and leave hand prints on your trunk. This is another haunted gravity hill.

GUERNVILLE

Guerneville is a small town in Sonoma County. A woman walking on Mays Canyon Road at night has startled drivers when they drove right through her while trying to stop. This female spirit has even talked to passersby asking them if they knew any boys who took walks down the road. Is she looking for a ghostly date?

HEALDSBURG

The city of Healdsburg can be found in Sonoma County. The Victorian era Madrona Manor on Westside Road has several ghostly guests. Workers and guests have felt that someone unseen was watching them. Guests belongings seem to move around by themselves and one guest awoke in the middle of the night in Room 101 to the sight of a thirty to forty year old woman in a long black dress standing near her before it went and sat in a chair. When the guest asked what she wanted, the woman disappeared. The spirit of a small, gray-haired lady, in 19th century clothes appeared in the dinning room and spoke to a living person telling her that she was glad that someone could see her. She also commented that she liked what had been done to her house. Other paranormal things happened but the ghosts seem to be happy with the living souls being in the house.

PETALUMA

The Phoenix Theater in the city of Petaluma in Sonoma County burnt down when it was a movie theater and was rebuilt as an Opera House. The Opera House burnt down and some people died in the blaze. A white figure or a really dark shadow has been spotted in the balcony and mysterious sounds are heard coming from the bathrooms. The paranormal activity is even worse in the basement.

SANTA ROSA

Santa Rosa is the county seat for the county of Sonoma. People in the businesses in the area of Roseland Airfield reported seeing unexplained shadows appear out of nowhere on the walls of buildings at the airfield. It is rumored that the shadows are from the people who died at the airfield in the 1940's.

Ushers have been poked in the back by unseen presences in the theaters in the new wing of the Airport Cinemas in Santa Rosa. Staff have heard noises coming from closed and supposedly empty theaters but the noises stopped as soon as they checked inside and whoever was making the commotion had disappeared into thin air.

SONOMA

Sonoma is a community in Sonoma Valley, Sonoma County. Mountain Cemetery is a small area outside in the woods that still has some broken down stones. Many venturing into that area have experienced strange foul smells, strange lights and a strange feeling of over powering fear. And we must not forget the usual cold spots, a sure sign of ghosts, they say.

The old Sebastianni Theater in Sonoma has a permanent customer. The apparition of a young girl ten to twenty years old and wearing a yellow dress that looks like something out of the 1930's appears often in the mirrors in the women's washroom. She is not there when you turn around. Her name is Trixie. When you hear her laughter, expect the lights to go off and on seemingly by themselves. But I suspect it is Trixie playing tricks.

Sonoma State Hospital grounds may be haunted. People have said that screams of former mental patients can be heard coming from the main building late at night. A mysterious woman in white tries to hitch a ride on the road out front and demonic creatures roam the fields nearby. Shadows cast by invisible people can be seen walking around outside. Institutions of this type always seem to be a magnet for people's morbid imagination. Well, maybe.

Stanislaus County
KEYES

The Blue Lady, a female ghost with a blue glow, chases people off the Single T Canal banks in the city of Keyes in Stanislaus County. Rumor has it that she died trying to save her child who had fell in the canal and was caught in one of the irrigation pipes. I do not know why she is chasing people away. Maybe she is trying to get their help to save hie child. But people being people, when facing the unknown, get scared and vamoose!

MODESTO

Modesto is the county seat of Stanislaus County. Very mournful cries and scream are heard at any time of the day in the very old Acacia Cemetery and is acccompanied with a horrible feeling of foreboding. Of course, cemeteries are very scary for many people.

Modesto's Ambulance Station on Granger was supposedly the scene of a terrible murder back in the 1960's when it was a private home. Two parents killed their three children. In the early 1990's, an old Indian man passed away while praying alone to the Indian spirits. The room where he died is said to be filled with cold and feeling of dread. Windows and doors in the building are said to open and close by themselves. Things move around by themselves as well as the showers turn off and on. Disembodied voices and the sound of children playing have been heard as well as footsteps caused by unseen people. One voice even yelled at an employee to get out!

The apparition of an Indian man has been seen by joggers running near the creek at Modesto's Dry Creek Running Trail. There are two different opinions as to what this ghost is up to. Some say he is watching over the joggers while others feel he is trying to protect scared Indian land on which the park is built. Regardless, he does not seem to be a treat. Maybe he is just jogging? There is another spirit that has been seen in the park. A young man who jumped off a bridge in the park into shallow water and died is said to haunt that bridge. In the early morning or late at night, passersby hear a yell and then a splash near that bridge but find nothing when they check.

Fuddrucker's Restaurant in Modesto was previously a Blockbuster, a Beno's department store and a skate park. In the 1980's, a young boy skateboarder at the park fell and died from a broken neck. Employees at the old Blockbuster apparently had to deal with his ghost. He opened and closed doors, turned on battery activated toys, turned lights off and on, stocked things in a neat pile on the floor and even spoke to the employees through the sound system saying that they had been bad! It is not known if the ghost of the little boy has bugged anyone at Fuddruckers.

No one seems to know why but the ghost of a young man paces Modesto High School auditorium balcony. He just does! Supposedly, some old tunnels run under the school and strange knocking has been heard coming from under the hall floor where they think some of the tunnels are. Is someone or something under there is trying to get out of the tunnels?

The Red Lion Hotel in Modesto used to be the Holiday Inn and has experienced some paranormal problems, they say. Disembodied voices and the sound of plates and trays have been heard in what should have been an empty kitchen. Empty, except maybe for a ghost or two! The story is that a woman was murdered in the kitchen by an enraged boyfriend. When security patrols the parking lot at night, they often hear the sound of glass breaking but find nothing when they check the cars and the area out. Three rooms, 152, 206 and 420, seem to have activity also. In Room 152, all the electrical equipment seem to be the target as the apparatus keeps turning off and on by it self.

Local legend has it that four girls were raped and then killed in or near Modesto's Vintage Fair Mall. Their murderer had better not hang out at the mall as their ghosts are said to haunt a store in the mall and they may subject him or her to some good old fashioned ghostly justice.

TURLOCK

The Salvation Army building in the city of Turlock in Stanislaus County is also thought to be haunted. In the 1930's when the place was vacant, a lawyer was murdered on the 2nd floor. Now people claim to see shadows moving around and hear disembodied voices and footsteps upstairs.

Sutter County

YUBA CITY

Yuba City is the county seat of Sutter County and there appears to be only one ghost story in the city and the whole county. A number of students from the Yuba City High School were killed in bus accident back in the 1970s. Their ghosts often appear on stage at the school's theater and by the costume closets and light cage. There are cold spots in the tool room and there has been trouble with the lights during plays.

CHAPTER T, U
Tehama County

I could not find any ghost stories for this County. If you know of any, please, email me at jamesfosterrobinson@live.com or jimrobinson@hotmail.com

Trinity County

I could not find any ghost stories for this County. If you know of any, please, email me at jamesfosterrobinson@live.com or jimrobinson@hotmail.com

Tulare County
DINUBA

Like many schools, Dinuba High School in the city of Dinuba in Tulare County is haunted. Staff and students have reported feeling that they are being watched by someone unseen when they walk down the halls. Doors are heard opening and closing and lights turn on and off by themselves. Some people have even felt like they were being forced down stairs. All the paranormal activity is blamed on the ghost of a janitor who was electrocuted some years ago. Then there is the ghost of a girl who was murdered by her boyfriend after she broke up with him. He hid her body behind some black plastic at the back of the football field bleachers where it was not found for a week. Her ghost now runs across the football field at night.

PORTERVILLE

Porterville is a city in the San Joaquin Valley in Tulare County. Urban legend has it that some black men, tired of the antics of the KKK, hung a white man from a tree on Ed Trays Hill. They apparently cut off his head and buried it beneath him. Of course, now you can supposedly hear disembodied laughter, footsteps and rocks being kicked if you venture to that spot on the hill.

SPRINGVILLE

Scicon, the School of Conservation in the community of Springville in Tulare County, has its share of unexplained phenomena. A rotten smell is often reported in the building and the lights flicker. Floating lights are seen at night. In one building a ghost has been seen running into nowhere and disembodied footsteps are heard. Outside the phantom of a man walks nonchalantly up a nearby hill. Sounds like an interesting place to stay overnight.

There at at least three apparitions that are said to appear at the Springville Inn. Years ago, a young logger and local ladies man was shot for flirting with a man's wife. He died in the Inn and still haunts it. An old man also haunts the inn but little is known about him. The third ghost is that of a little girl and little is known about her also other than she sometimes grabs with her cold hands the hands of women going to the ladies room. Some patrons have felt a cold invisible hand on their shoulders or backs. When patrons head to the bathroom in the bar area, they feel that someone unseen is watching them. One ghost supposedly even made a phone call to an employee from the empty manager's office. It was not reported what the ghost said.

VISALIA

The city of Visalia is situated in the heart of California's agricultural San Joaquin Valley in Tulare County. The ghosts of three different kids hang out in the lobby of Cinema 1-2-3, bothering and following theater goers. They are apparently transparent but solid enough that an usher's flashlight beam will not shine through them. Then there is unexplained banging and scream in the old theater while many people have said that they have seen the ghostly replay of a young boy being thrown off theater roof by a shadowy figure. Some locals insist that close to three hundred ghosts hang out in the theater. Better watch where you sit. It just might be in a ghost's lap!

The old Santa Fe Tracks where Avenue 271 turns into 272 are said to be haunted. Supposedly a ghost train comes roaring down the tracks around 3.00 AM some nights. Local legend claims that if you stop your car on the tracks and turn off the engine, you will see ghostly people walking towards you and hear a train coming. Time to start the car again. Oop's! I forgot to tell you that you may have trouble starting your car again. Maybe you should get out and run for it in case it is a real train. Maybe you should not have stopped your car on the tracks in the first place. I hope that you read these paragraph all the way through before even thinking of trying this stupid stunt!

The specter of a little girl has been seen walking along the top of the railing on the second floor of the Golden West High School Library in Visalia. Check where there is dust on the floor and you might see ghostly footprints appear in it in front of your eyes. If you are alone and listen carefully, you may hear her and other ghostly children singing.

The phantom of a chubby man has been spotted following employees at MWI Veterinary Supplies in Visalia. The sound of trays being dropped have been heard by people working alone. No one seems to know who the chubby man is and why he apparently drops trays.

Joggers on the the trail along St. Johns River often see the apparition of a male Native American walking his horse on the side of the trail. That is all! He just walks his horse.

Tuolumne County
COLUMBIA

When the original Fallon House Theater and Hotel in Columbia in the county of Tuolumne burnt down years ago, it was rebuilt exactly like it was before the fire. Now the place appears to be haunted, if it was not already haunted. Disembodied voices have been heard as well as mysterious noises. There appears to be sometimes an overwhelming smell of smoke but, apparently, no fire. Strangely there is also the whiff of whiskey in the air in one room. A female spirit is often seen in Rooms 9 and 13. Shadows of what looks like people are seen in the theater where the lights go off and on by themselves.

GROVELAND

The Groveland Hotel, a Bed and Breakfast on Main Street, has a permanent resident, an old miner called Lyle. He died in his sleep in Room 9 and still wanders the hotel. He is said to be friendly but does not like women's make up on his old dresser. He will toss it over onto the sink. He often takes a shower but you can not see him in the running water.

JAMESTOWN

An old gold mine under the Willow Steak House at Jamestown, a village in Tuolumne County caved in and killed twenty three miners in the 1800's. Now the dead miners haunt the hotel. No further information is available at this time.

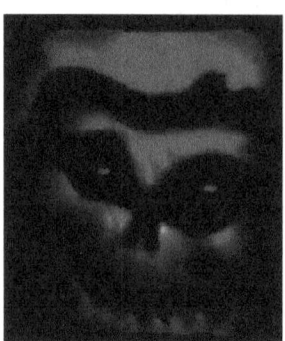

CHAPTER V, W
Ventura County
CAMARILLO

Channel University in the city of Camarillo in Ventura County was once the Camarillo State Hospital. It became the University in the 1990s. Of course there are ghosts there. Disembodied children's voice are heard at the Childrens Center. The apparition of an old woman appears at the Bell Tower and asks passersby for directions. She also may be the old woman in white that wanders the halls. Someone unseen asks for people to be quiet in the restrooms. If you walk in the parking lot, you may see what looks like a man spinning. Keep watching and he will disappear near a lamp post. Students and staff have complained of unexplained nausea, headaches, extreme tiredness and feelings being threaten and unsafe as well as of being watched. There are a number of apparitions wandering around the grounds from a phantom by the bus stop, a nervous ghost hiding in the the Bell Tower, some one women's restroom chattering and making a strange rustling noise to a beautiful woman in white who likes to wander the Bell Tower halls at any time of the day.

FILLMORE

A woman in white, said to have been killed during the Mexican- American War, floats among cars on an unnamed road in the city of Filmore. Look for a sycamore tree beside the road and that is where you may find her. Unless of course, someone cut down the tree. Unless of course the tree is also a ghost. Unless ... enough!

MOORPARK

Moorpark, a city in Ventura County has a haunted Gravity Hill of its own. If you drive down near the north end of Walnut Canyon Road stop after it dips over a small hill. At the bottom of the hill put the gears in neutral. Your car should back slowly up the hill. Local legend says that children killed years ago in a wagon accident are trying to push the car to safely back up the hill.

NEWBERRY PARK

Newberry Park is a community in the Western part of Thousand Oaks and Casa Conejo in the county of Ventura. The Stage Coach Inn was an original stage coach stop. A ghost named Pierre haunted the original building for years after he was killed there. After the inn was rebuilt in its present location, Pierre moved into his new digs, the copy of his old room, at the new Stage Coach Inn. That new room like his old one is always colder then the rest of the rooms. Pierre likes to roll up the upstairs rug runners and stack the books in a pile in the upstairs library. Footsteps have been heard coming from the upstairs when staff know it to be empty. The figure of a man has been spotted looking out an upstairs window when no one was known to be up there. Several people have said that they have talked to a older, strangely dressed man who would vanished when they turned away for a moment and turned back to talk more with him. Sounds like Pierre.

OJAI

Ojai is a small town in Ventura County near the shores of the Pacific Ocean. Four ghosts are said to haunt Creek Road at Ojai. One is the phantom of a man who was burned to death and seeks revenge on his killers. He often appears on the bridge on that road startling drivers. They call him the Chairman supposedly because he looks burned to a crisp. But that does not make sense. Crispy Critter would be a better name. The apparition of a woman rides her horse recklessly down the road on the night of the anniversary of her passing. When she comes to a certain curve, the horse rears up and throws the woman to her death. Another female spirit is that of of a woman in a blood soaked wedding dress who tries to hitch a ride on the road. The last known ghost is that of a headless motorcyclist careening recklessly down that winding road. If you travel the haunted road, keeps your wits and your eyes open.

This next story is like something out of a horror movie. In the 1980's, a strange, reclusive man from Europe purchased a farm near Creek Road. Then the strangeness started. First cattle were found drained of blood. Then humans were found in the same condition. To add to the weirdness, the new neighbor out on Creek Road was never seen during the day. Of course the rumor started and quickly became the truth in many minds. Armed with crosses and holy water, a bunch of locals decided to pay the stranger a visit in the day light of course. They found a stone sarcophagus under a tree on his property. Guess what they found in the stone sarcophagus? That is right! The stranger asleep! Suddenly a big black dog appeared and tried to drive them off. But the locals using liberal doses of holy water drove the dog off. They then pounded a wooden stake into the stranger's heart. When they sprinkled holy water on his body and the casket, both body and casket disappeared, apparently never to be seen again. Oh I forgot to mention that the stranger was a vampire. What? You already knew that?

OXNARD

Oxnard is the largest city in Ventura County. Tennants at the Los Arbolitos Apartments may have a ghost or two to deal with. Residents would turn off lamps only to find them turned on again. Once a glass was pushed slowly by an unseen hand into an apartment sink where it shattered. Often residents would catch a whiff of lavender. Rumor has it that the apartments were built on the site of an old cemetery. Even though it was relocated down the street, apparently some bodies still remained.

Spirits of the dead are said to stare down at people from the top windows in the old St Johns Hospital in Oxnard. Strange noises have been heard coming from the suposedly closed building.

They say that if you walk through the Oxnard draining ditch tunnel, you might experience some strange activity. There may be mysterious tapping on the tunnel walls and then strange footsteps all around you. Watch it! A weird shape may block the light at the end of the tunnel!

The Oxnard Performing Arts Center may also be haunted. There has been reports of someone talking in the Green Room when there was no one there. A coldness is often experienced in the dressings rooms. The doors to the dressing, even though closed at night, are often found open in the morning. Lights turned off are often found turned back on apparently by unseen hands.

Many years ago a woman was walking down Rose Avenue near Central Avenue when she was run down and killed by a drunken driver. She is now known for trying to hitch a ride and if you do not stop for her, she will suddenly appear in your back seat.

The toy department at Walmart in the Rose Shopping Center in Oxnard is thought to be haunted by a preteen Mexican American girl. You can not miss her. She wears two pig tail braids, a blue dress 1950's or 60's style and appears sometimes in solid form and sometimes in a misty form with only half her body showing. She often smiles and giggles at night shift workers whom have also seen balls bouncing all by themselves. Speculation has it that she was killed in some sort of accident on the site before the store was built there.

Santa Clara Cemetery in Oxnard is said to be scarier than most cemeteries. A strange mist sometimes covers the ground and there is often a chill in the air even when it is warm. Visitors have reported seeing what looked like a man trying to hid behind the tombstones. When they approach to check him out, he disappears.

Nuns should to live in Santa Clara High School in Oxnard. The building is thought to be haunted. Why? Well, maybe the apparition of a hooded figure floating down the hall or the disembodied chanting and voices coming the closed and empty chapel might explain it. Then there is Joey, a student at the school, who was killed in a car accident while going to a basketball game at the school. Now unseen he bounces a basketball in the gym and slams locker doors late at night after the school is closed.

PORT HUENEME
Port Hueneme is a small beach city in Ventura County, boarded by the city of Oxnard and the Pacific Ocean. The Bard Mansion, which resides inside the Port Hueneme Navy Base is rumored to be haunted by Mrs. Bard, wife of the late senator Bard. Her ghost is often seen, they say, walking the grounds as if checking to see if everything was in order.

SANTA PAULA
Rooms 23, 103 and 305 in the Glenn Tavern Inn in Santa Paula are said to be haunted. A ghost has been seen looking out of a window in Room 23. The ghost in Room 103 knocks over things or stares in the window at the person staying in the room. The one from Room 305 likes to walk the halls on the third floor passing through the closed doors of the various rooms and sometimes hangs out in the lobby. A young boy who died in the building is often seen playing in the lobby and on the second floor. Someone unseen plays the piano in the lobby. It sounds like an interesting place to stay in.

Staff at the Santa Paula's Wallace Theatres / Santa Paula 7 theaters are a little wary of working in Theater 6, or so it is said. Apparently when the lights are turned off, that theater is darker then the others. A man has been seen sitting in one of the seats after closing. When approached, he vanishes. Apparitions have also been seen hanging around the projection booth. Some times the sweet smell of perfume can be detected in the theater. I have worked as an Assistant Manager in a movie theater complex but the only scary thing I have encountered were customers.

SIMI VALLEY

Simi Valley is a city located in a valley of the same name in the southeast corner of Ventura County. A young boy skateboarding down Maricopa Hill in the Indian Hills area fell tearing up his face, hands and knees so bad that he apparently died. His ghost still skates down the hill and when approached skates away at an impossible speed disappearing into the night.

The apparition of a man wearing a white shirt, black tie and black pants has been seen in Jons Market on Tapo Canyon. One object at a time have fallen off the shelf as if someone knocked it off. Is it the specter of the man in the white shirt and black pants?

Some years ago, a janitor at the Simi Elementary School hung himself in the cleaning closet. His ghost is often see running around the soccer field or standing in the goal area and other spots. If you go near that closet, they say you can see light flickering around the edges of the door.

A boy shot and killed his mother and sister in an old barn now demolished on the site of the present of the Simi Hills Golf course before sitting on a chair and killing himself. They say that you used to be able to see the dead boy with his gun sitting on the chair. Balls of light used to be sighted in and around the old barn but now that it is gone, there does not seem to be any ghostly activity.

Something strange is going on in Sycamore Park in Simi Valley. A furry white creature that runs on all fours is some times seen in this park running very fast like a sudden flash of light. Apparitions float from tree to tree in the blink of an eye. Glowing spots appear in the grass and, they say, that if you walk into them, you disappear from the sight of others. A strange man sits on the rocks staring at people and then stands up. It is not reported what happens then. Haunted? Well, maybe. Tall tales? Well, maybe.

THOUSAND OAKS

Thousand Oaks also known as T.O., is a city in southeastern Ventura County. Mount Clef Dormitory at California Lutheran University is haunted by several ghosts. One of the more well known entities is that of a little boy who was murdered when the site was a hotel. He wanders the upstairs hall on the 300 side, unlocking doors, leaving mud in beds which shortly disappear, and yanks pillows out from under the heads of sleeping students and flinging them across the room. Shortly after, disembodied whispers and cries are heard. Sure sounds like the place is haunted at least by one ghost.

The United Artists Theaters in Thousand Oaks has a permanent customer, they say, in

Theater 5. He was supposedly killed in a freak accident during the theater's construction during the 1970's. He has been there even since watching every movie played in Theater 5 since. Disembodied laughter, phantom footsteps, banging on the exit doors and walls, cold spots and flickering lights have been experience in the theater itself and in the projection booth.

VENTURA

Originally known as San Buenaventura until 1891, Ventura is the county seat of Ventura County. The old Bard Hospital, now an office building, is home to an unknown spirit that likes to move things around and turn lights off. They say that if you want the lights turned back on, all you have to say is that you are not finished yet and the lights will pop back on!

Some years ago a "lady of the night" killed herself in Room 17 of the Bella Maggiore Hotel and is still hanging out there. A mist is seen occasionally near a window while there is a strong odor of roses in the hall as well as in the room. She is often heard singing to herself. What song is not known.

A depressed teenager and outcast hung himself from a tree in Ventura's Cemetery Park. He still hangs there staring wide eyed, they say, into the distance. Passersby have claimed to feel a strong malevolent feeling there as well as a cold chill.

There is a strong friendly feeling at Santa Buena Ventura Mission not exactly ghostly but definitely a strong friendly presence. In addition, they say that you can hear children talking, soft chanting and cries in the early morning hours.

No one knows who she is or why she is haunting the Olivas Adobe but her ghost is often seen in a window upstairs.

The Santa Clara House, now a restaurant, was once a Victorian home. Years ago, a young girl got pregnant by a salesman and killed herself. Now her ghost stand in a window also looking for her lover to return to her. She is going to have a very long wait.

Toby, a teenage boy who hung himself from a catwalk when his advances towards a girl he loved were refused, still haunts the small, old auditorium at Ventura High School. A broken heart just will not go away. His body can still be seen hanging from that catwalk.

The Victorian Rose Bed and Breakfast used to be a church and is thought to be very haunted. What is known as the Emperor's Bedroom and considered the most haunted used to be a choir loft and was the scene of the death of a female member of the choir who fell from the loft to her death. You can hear her singing in that room. A long passed away minister likes to tuck in bed guests staying in the Timeless Treasures Room. The Fleur-De-Lis Room has a ghost that likes to give foot rubs. Hmmm, that sounds like a room I would like to stay in. Last but not least, disembodied footsteps have been heard in the central lobby. This B&B get a four G rating. Psss! G stand stands for "ghost".

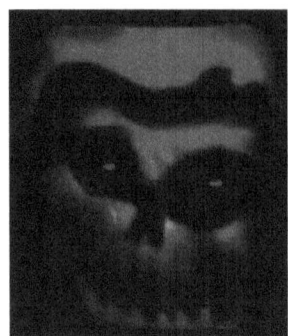

CHAPTER X, Y, Z
Yolo County
DAVIS

The old city hall and police station in Davis, a city in Yolo County, was vacated for a new station. After the move, the apparition of a wild hair, redheaded woman was seen running towards the second stall in the women's rest room and then disappearing. No one, apparently, found out who she was and why she appeared there in ghostly form.

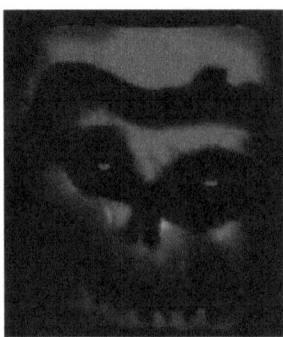

INDEX by Community

CALEXICO - Imperial County
CALICO - San Bernadino County
CALISTOGA - Napa County
CAMARILLO - Ventura County
CAMERON PARK - El Dorado County
CAMPBELL - Santa Clara County
CAMPO - San Diego County
CAMP PENDLETON - San Diego County
CANOGA PARK- Los Angeles County
CAPITOLA - Santa Cruz County
CARLSBAD - San Diego County
CARSON- Los Angeles County
CASTRO VALLEY - Alameda County
CATHEDRAL CITY - Riverside County
CENTERVILLE - Fresno County
CERRITOS- Los Angeles County
CERRO GORDO - Inyo County
CHEROKEE - Butte County
CHICO - Butte County
CHINO - San Bernadino County
CHOWCHILLA - Madera County
CHUALAR - Monterey County
CHULA VISTA - San Diego County
CITY OF INDUSTRY- Los Angeles County
CLAREMONT- Los Angeles County
CLAYTON - Contra Costa County
CLEAR LAKE- Lake County
COLOMA - El Dorado County
COLTON - San Bernadino County
COLUMBIA - Tuolumne County
COMMERCE- Los Angeles County
CONCORD Contra Costa County
CORONA - Riverside County
CORONADA- San Diego County
COSTA MESA - Orange County
COVINA- Los Angeles County
CRESCENT CITY - Del Norte County
CROCKETT Contra Costa County
CYPRESS - Orange County

"D"
DALY CITY - San Mateo County
DAVIS Yolo County
DEATH VALLEY JUNCTION - Inyo County
DELANO - Kern County
DEL RAY - Fresno County
DE LUZ - San Diego County
DEVOURE - San Bernadino County
DIAMOND BAR- Los Angeles County
DINUBA - Tulare County
DORRINGTON - Calaveras County
DOWNEY- Los Angeles County
DOWNIEVILLE - Sierra County
DUATE- Los Angeles County

DUBLIN - Alameda County
DUNLAP - Fresno County

"E"
EAST HIGHLAND - San Bernadino County
EAST LOS ANGELES- Los Angeles County
EL CAJON - San Diego County
EL CENTRO - Imperial County
EL DORADO - El Dorado County
ELFIN FOREST - San Diego County
ELK GROVE - Sacramento County
EL MONTE- Los Angeles County
ENCINO- Los Angeles County
EUREKA - Humboldt County

"F"
FAIRFAX - Marin County
FAIR OAKS - Sacramento County
FALLBROOK - San Diego County
FERNDALE - Humboldt County
FILLMORE - Ventura County
FOLSOM - Sacramento County
FONTANA - San Bernadino County
FOREST FALLS - San Bernadino County
FORT BRAGG - Mendocino County
FOSTER CITY - San Mateo County
FOUNTAIN VALLEY - Orange County
FREEDOM - Santa Cruz County
FREMONT - Alameda County
FRESNO - Fresno County
FULLERTON - Orange County

"G"
GARDEN GROVE - Orange County
GEORGETOWN - El Dorado County
GEYSERVILLE - Sonoma County
GILROY - Santa Clara County
GLENDORA- Los Angeles County
GLEN ELLEN - Sonoma County
GORMAN- Los Angeles County
GRANADA HILLS- Los Angeles County
GRASS VALLEY - Nevada County
GROVELAND - Tuolumne County
GUERNVILLE - Sonoma County

"H"
HALF MOON BAY - San Mateo County
HANFORD - Kings County
HARBOR CITY- Los Angeles County
HAWTHORNE- Los Angeles County
HAYWARD - Alameda County
HEALDSBURG - Sonoma County
HEBER - Imperial County
HEMET - Riverside County

HERMOSA BEACH- Los Angeles County
HERNDON - Fresno County
HIGHLAND PARK- Los Angeles County
HIGHWAY 94 - San Diego County
HOLLYWOOD- Los Angeles County
HUNTINGTON BEACH - Orange County
HUNTINGTON PARK- Los Angeles County

"I"
IDYLLWILD - Riverside County
IMPERIAL - Imperial County
IMPERIAL VALLEY - Imperial County
INDIO - Riverside County
INGLEWOOD- Los Angeles County
IRVINE - Orange County

"J"
JAMESTOWN - Tuolumne County
JOLON - Monterey County
JOSHUA TREE - San Bernadino County
JULIAN - San Diego County

"K"
KEDDIE - Plumas County
KEENE - Kern County
KELSO - San Bernadino County
KERMAN - Fresno County
KEYES - Stanislaus County
KINGSBURG - Fresno County

"L"
LAFAYETTE - Contra Costa County
LAGUNA HILLS - Orange County
LAGUNA WOODS - Orange County
LA HABRA - Orange County
LA HABRA HEIGHTS- Los Angeles County
LA JOLLA - San Diego County
LAKE BALBOA- Los Angeles County
LAKE ELSINORE - Riverside County
LAKE FOREST - Orange County
LAKE HUGHES- Los Angeles County
LAKESIDE - San Diego County
LAKE TAHOE- Los Angeles County
LAKEWOOD- Los Angeles County
LA MIRADA- Los Angeles County
LANCASTER- Los Angeles County
LA PUENTE- Los Angeles County
LA QUINTA - Riverside County
LA SELVA BEACH - Santa Cruz County
LATHROP - San Joaquin County
LA VERNE- Los Angeles County
LEMONGROVE - San Diego County
LEMOORE - Kings County
LENNOX- Los Angeles County

LINCOLN- Los Angeles County
LINCOLN - Placer County
LIVERMORE - Alameda County
LOMA LINDA - San Bernadino County
LOMPAC - Santa Barbara County
LONG BEACH- Los Angeles County
LOS GATOS - Santa Clara County
LOS ANGELES- Los Angeles County
LYNWOOD- Los Angeles County

"M"
MAGALIA - Butte County
MALIBU- Los Angeles County
MANTECA - San Joaquin County
MARINA DEL RAY- Los Angeles County
MCFARLAND - Kern County
MECRED- Mecred County
MENLO PARK - San Mateo County
MENTRYVILLE- Los Angeles County
MILLBRAE - San Mateo County
MILPITAS - Santa Clara County
MISSION HILLS - Santa Barbara County
MODESTO - Stanislaus County
MOKELUMNE HILL - Calaveras County
MONROVIA- Los Angeles County
MONTEBELLO- Los Angeles County
MONTEREY - Monterey County
MOORPARK - Ventura County
MORENO VALLEY - Riverside County
MORO BAY - San Luis Obispo County
MOSS BEACH - San Mateo County
MOUNT SAN ANTONIO- Los Angeles County
MOUNTAIN VIEW - Santa Clara County
MURPHYS - Calaveras County
MURRIETA - Riverside County

"N"
NAPA - Napa County
NEVADA CITY - Nevada County
NEWARK - Alameda County
NEWBERRY PARK - Ventura County
NEWBERRY SPRINGS - San Bernadino County
NEWPORT - Orange County
NORTH HILLS- Los Angeles County
NORWALK- Los Angeles County

"O"
OAKLAND - Alameda County
OCEANO - San Luis Obispo County
OCEANSIDE - San Diego County
OJAI - Ventura County
ONTARIO - San Bernadino County
ORANGE - Orange County
OXNARD - Ventura County

"P", "Q"
PACHEO PASS- Mecred County
PACIFICA - San Mateo County
PACOIMA - San Mateo County
PALMDALE- Los Angeles County
PALM DESERT - Riverside County
PALO ALTO - Santa Clara County
PALOS VERDES- Los Angeles County
PANORAMA CITY- Los Angeles County
PARAMOUNT- Los Angeles County
PARKER DAM - San Bernadino County
PASADENA- Los Angeles County
PASA ROBLES - San Luis Obispo County
PETALUMA - Sonoma County
PICO RIVERA- Los Angeles County
PITTSBURG - Contra Costa County
PLACERVILLE - El Dorado County
PLACENTIA - Orange County
PLEASANTON - Alameda County
POLLOCK PINES - El Dorado County
POMONA- Los Angeles County
PORTERVILLE - Tulare County
PORT HUENEME - Ventura County
PRUNDALE - Monterey County

"R"
RANCHO CUCAMONGA - San Bernadino County
RANCHO PALOS VERDES- Los Angeles County
RAVENSDALE- Lassen County
RAVENSWOOD - San Mateo County
RAYMON - Madera County
REDLANDS - San Bernadino County
REDONDO BEACH- Los Angeles County
REEDLEY - Fresno County
REDWOOD CITY - San Mateo County
RIALTO - San Bernadino County
RICHMOND - Contra Costa County
RIDGECREST - Kern County
RIVERSIDE - Riverside County
ROCKLIN - Placer County
ROSEVILLE - Placer County
ROSEMEAD- Los Angeles County
ROWLAND HEIGHTS- Los Angeles County
RUBIDOUX - Riverside County

"S"
SACRAMENTO - Sacramento County
SALINAS - Monterey County
SAN BERNARDINO - San Bernadino County
SAN BRUNO - San Mateo County
SAN CLEMENTE - Orange County
SAN DIEGO - San Diego County

SAN DIMAS- Los Angeles County
SAN FRANCISCO - San Francisco County
SAN GABRIEL- Los Angeles County
SANGER - Fresno County
SAN JACINTO - Riverside County
SAN JOSE - Santa Clara County
SAN JUAN CAPRISTRANO - Orange County
SAN LORENZO - Alameda County
SAN MIGUEL - San Luis Obispo County
SAN RAFAEL - Marin County
SANTA ANA - Orange County
SANTA BARBARA - Santa Barbara County
SANTA CATALINA ISLAND- Los Angeles County
SANTA CLARA - Santa Clara County
SANTA CLARITA- Los Angeles County
SANTA CRUZ - Santa Cruz County
SANTA FE SPRINGS- Los Angeles County
SANTA MARIA - Santa Barbara County
SANTA PAULA - Ventura County
SANTA ROSA - Sonoma County
SARATOGA - Santa Clara County
SCOTIA - Humboldt County
SCOTTS VALLEY - Santa Cruz County
SEASIDE - Monterey County
SELMA - Fresno County
SHINGLE SPRINGS - El Dorado County
SIMI VALLEY - Ventura County
SOLEDAD - Monterey County
SONOMA - Sonoma County
SOUTH EL MONTE- Los Angeles County
SOUTH GATE- Los Angeles County
SOUTH PASADENA- Los Angeles County
SPRECKELS - Monterey County
SPRINGVILLE - Tulare County
STANTON - Orange County
STOCKTON - San Joaquin County
STRATFORD - Kings County
SUMMERLAND - Santa Barbara County
SUNNYVALE - Santa Clara County
SUN VALLEY- Los Angeles County
SUTTER CREEK - Amador County
SYLMAR- Los Angeles County

"T"
TEHACHAPI - Kern County
TEMECULA - Riverside County
THOUSAND OAKS - Ventura County
TORRANCE- Los Angeles County
TRACY - San Joaquin County
TRUCKEE - Nevada County
TURLOCK - Stanislaus County
TUSTIN - Orange County

"U"
UVAS CANYON - Santa Clara County

"V"
VALENCIA- Los Angeles County
VALLEJO - Solano County
VALLEY CENTER - San Diego County
VANDENBERG AFB - Santa Barbara County
VANDENBERG VILLAGE - Santa Barbara County
VAN NUYS- Los Angeles County
VASCO ROAD - Alameda County
VENICE- Los Angeles County
VENTURA - Ventura County
VICTORVILLE - San Bernadino County
VISALIA - Tulare County

"W"
WALNUT- Los Angeles County
WATTSONVILLE - Santa Cruz County
WEED - Siskiyou County
WEST COVINA- Los Angeles County
WEST HILLS- Los Angeles County
WEST HOLLYWOOD- Los Angeles County
WEST LOS ANGELES- Los Angeles County
WESTMINSTER - Orange County
WEST VALLEY RESERVOIR - Modoc County
WESTWOOD- Lassen County
WHITTIER- Los Angeles County
WIDOMAR - Riverside County
WILLOWS - Glenn County
WILMINGTON - Los Angeles County
WOODLAND HILLS- Los Angeles County

"X", "Y", "Z"
YUBA CITY - Sutter County
YUCAIPA - San Bernadino County

REFERENCES

Websites

abnormalssanctuaryblog.blogspot.com/

alt.folklore.ghost-stories

angelfire.com/indie/anna_jones1/vortexes.htmlartsfusion.com/millsghosts/main.html

asksprice.com/infos/ro954025432o/page_8291350232

bayareanewsgroup.com/

cellardining.com

charlespeden.wordpress.com/2009/10/27/ghost-hunting-at-the-faculty-club-at-uc-berkeley-with-a-journalist-for-a-radio-story/

cinema-suicide.com/

csgr.us/CaseHI021503

EzineArticles.com/?expert=Abhishek_Agarwal

EzineArticles.com/?Alcatraz-Haunting"Exposing-the-Ghosts-of-a-Haunted-Prison&ampid=3259

ghost-mysteries.com/forum/index.php?showtopic=3858

ghosts.org

ghost-sighting.co.uk/GoThere.com/sandiego

goldcountrymedia.com/

hoteldel.com/ Travel article about the hotel and its ghost Investigation by Eeeek-Net

inetours.com

kfrc.radio.com/2010/10/25/bay-areas-most-haunted-places/

lang.dailybulletin.com/projects/cooperwatch/news/042305_joshua_statement.aspocweekly.com/news/

libnet.ucsd.edu

letsgoseeit.com

mtdemocrat.com/special-sections/mysterious-cary-house-hotel-remains-close-to-the-action/

nbcsandiego.com/news/local-beat/A-Ghost-Hunt-Below-Deck--106376319.html

o2.aolcdn.com/dims-shared/dims3

rsconst.com

sandiegohistory.org

scvhistory.com/scvhistory/sg042603.htm

scvhistory.com/scvhistory/pico.htm

sebar.com/haunted

sluggosghoststories.blogspot.com/2011/04/meux-home-fresno-ca.html

The_Claremont_Resort_Haunted-Berkeley_California.html

TheShadowlands.net

thesycamoreinn.com

tradingmarkets.com/news/stock-alert/tvch_real-life-ghostbusters-on-travel-channel-1410511.html

tripadvisor.com/ShowTopic-g32066-i664-k1428576

unexplainable.net/

urbanchillers.com
weirdfresno.com/
weirdus.com/
wikipedia.org/wiki/Barque

BOOKS
_____, An Abridged Guide to the Winchester Mystery House, the World's Strangest Monument to a Woman's Fears (Tour Booklet)
_____, Hotel Del Coronado The History of a Legend (tourist photo album), 1995 Hotel Del Coronado

Austin, Joanne, Wierd Hauntings/ True Tales of Ghostly Places, Sterling Publishing Co., INC. 2006
Belanger, Jeff, Encyclopedia of Haunted Places, Carrer Press Inc., 2005
Carrico, Richard L., San Diego's Spirits Ghosts and Hauntings in America's Southwest Corner, 1991 Recuerdos Press, San Diego
Dwyer, Jeff,Ghost Hunter's Guide to California Gold Rush Country
Hauk, William Dennis, The National Directory of Haunted Places, 1996, Penguin Books
Hauk, William Dennis, The National Directory of Haunted Places, 2002, Penguin Books
Kyle, Douglas E., Historic Spots in California by 1990 Stanford University Press
May, Alan, The Legend of Kate Morgan The Search for the Ghost of the Hotel del Coronado. 1990
May, Antoinette, Haunted Houses of California, 1993 Worldwide Publishing/Tetra
Mead, Robin, Haunted Hotels, 1995 Rutledge Hill Press
Senate, Richard, The Haunted Southland, 1994, Charon Press
White, Gail, Haunted San Diego A Historic Guide to San Diego's Favorite Haunts, 1992 Tecolote Publications, San Diego

OTHER
Branson-Trent Gregory, Ghost Hunter's Blog
Darnell , Brandon, The Ghosts of Sacramento's Past, October 22, 2010, Sacramento Press
Honeycutt, Mimi Daily, The Ghostly City of Angels, Trojan Posted October 13,
Sherwood, Lyn, The Ghosts of San Juan Capistrano, OC Now, March 23, 1998
Winchester Mystery House (Tourist Guide)

ABOUT THE AUTHOR

James Foster Robinson was born in Ogdensburg, New York, USA but grew up in Prescott, Ontario, Canada. He has lived and worked in Ontario, Manitoba, Alberta and . In 2005, he moved to West Virginia and married his present wife, Betty. Jim has two books published by Mika Publishing, Belleville, Ontario Amazing Tales from Eastern Ontario, 1987; Strange But True Tales From Eastern Ontario, 1989. He has also published numerous articles in national magazines, daily and weekly newspapers. While living in Vancouver, BC, Jim was a Feature Writer on Suite101.com for topics - The Art of Storytelling, Storyteller's Korner, Sleep Disorders, Professional Security, and Liechtenstein. In addition, he was a Storyteller both in Kingston, Ontario and in Vancouver, BC, Canada. James has also published "A Ghostly Guide to West Virginia", "An Encyclopedia of Lake and River Monsters", "Riotous Times, An Unauthorized History of Riots and Violent Protests in British Columbia, Canada", "A Ghostly Guide to Kentucky", "West Virginia Weird and Wonderful" and a children book "Tales To Tell My Children" on Amazon.com. He is presently working on Ghostly Guides to the remaining 49 states and the 10 provinces of Canada as well as several novels.